ALAN CRIBB spent his first eight years in the bush of western Queensland where he developed a keen interest in natural history.

In the early 1950s he worked as a research officer with the CSIRO studying the giant alga, *Macrocystis pyrifera*, in Tasmania. Then in 1952 he began lecturing in the Department of Botany at the University of Queensland. He gained his Ph.D. from the University in 1958 and has been head of the department since 1978.

JOAN CRIBB's early interest in natural history was fostered by her parents, both of whom were botanists. She gained her Master of Science from the University of Queensland and has been a tutor at the University. She has also been a lecturer and tutor at the Queensland Institute of Technology.

Dr and Mrs Cribb's interest in the many and varied uses of Australian native plants has resulted in their writing two other highly successful books—WILD FOOD IN AUSTRALIA (1975) and WILD MEDICINE IN AUSTRALIA (1981).

Useful
Wild Plants

IN AUSTRALIA

A. B. & J. W. Cribb

Fontana/Collins

© A. B. and J. W. Cribb 1982
First published 1981 by William Collins Pty Ltd, Sydney
First issued in Fontana Books 1982
Typeset by Jacobson Typesetters Ltd, Auckland, New Zealand
Printed in Hong Kong by South China Printing Co.

National Library of Australia
Cataloguing-in-Publication Data:

Cribb, A. B. (Alan Bridson).
Useful wild plants in Australia.
First published: Sydney: Collins, 1981.
Includes index.
ISBN 0 00 636397 0
1. Botany, Economic – Australia. I. Cribb, J. W.
(Joan Winifred). II. Title.
581.6′1′0994

By the same authors
WILD FOOD IN AUSTRALIA
WILD MEDICINE IN AUSTRALIA

Contents

PREFACE

Apart from timbers and plants used for feeding animals, not more than about a dozen of our native plant species are now commercially exploited in Australia. Yet many hundreds have been used either by Aborigines or white men in the business of living, and it is these that are the subject of this book. Although we have attempted to be reasonably comprehensive, and have included more than 450 entries, it would be neither possible nor interesting to list every species which has been used by somebody at some time.

We have not personally tried out each of the plants described here, although we have tested as many as practicable. We have not, for example, used the fish poisons; such a procedure would be both illegal and highly undesirable from a conservationist point of view. Although we have used some home dyes and tans, it has not been possible to test them all.

Available information on Aboriginal uses of plants is patchy and was dependent on the presence of a capable observer who could make records. Thus we have detailed accounts of the Aborigines of northern Queensland thanks to the copious writings of Dr W. E. Roth, who was Protector of Aborigines around the turn of the century, and a keen anthropologist; on the other hand we have very little information on the Tasmanians, as those unfortunate people were wiped out before much intelligent interest was taken in their activities. The first comprehensive work on the subject, published in 1889, was *Useful Native Plants of Australia* by J. H. Maiden, then curator of the Technological Museum of New South Wales; this contained records of most then-known economically useful plants including those used for food. Unfortunately, many of the botanical names used then have since been changed, and of course much additional information has become available.

There are in addition excellent books available on the useful plants of Malaysia and India, and these give much information on the unused potential of our flora. A list of some of the more important reference works, on both traditional and modern uses, is provided for those who require further background information or detailed instructions such as in the use of dyes.

A number of plants have several uses; where a species is listed in more than one chapter, it is described in detail once only; reference to the index will show such multiple entries. An asterisk before the name of a species in the text indicates that it is an introduced plant.

One major use of plants has been as medicine, and we had intended to include Australian medicinal plants in this book. However, as there are 500 or more which have been used in various ways we have decided to deal with them in a later work which will be published towards the end of 1981.

We should like to thank our son Robert for reading much of the manuscript, and Miss Lyndell Danaher for typing it.

A. B. CRIBB
J. W. CRIBB

INTRODUCTION

Before the Industrial Revolution, and to a considerable extent up until the last few decades, man was almost entirely dependent on natural products for his food, shelter, clothing, medicines, lighting and any luxuries he wished to enjoy. He was able to adapt some of these materials through selection, but basically he used what was available in his environment, and built his culture around it.

Especially in the last thirty years or so, there has been a tremendous explosion in production of man-made fibres and plastics for almost every purpose. On the whole these are very convenient, relatively cheap to produce, and often have some desirable qualities not present in the natural product they replace. With the great increase in world population, and in the desired standard of living, it is necessary that such products should be used, as it would be impossible for naturally-occurring or cultivated plant materials to keep up with the demand.

Many people however, while accepting the inevitability of a largely synthetic environment, are deeply interested in the natural alternatives. There is satisfaction to be derived from using a wooden bowl for a salad, rather than a plastic one; from wearing a woollen scarf dyed with eucalypt leaves or wattle blossom; from having a necklace of native wistaria seeds, each seed a little different from the next one; even from using a gum leaf as a bookmark; we know a young man who is the envy of his friends because he has a hat made from the skins of rats which he caught himself and tanned with wattle bark, although admittedly this would not be everyone's idea of perfection in headgear.

For the Aborigines, use of natural products was not a matter of choice. Everything they needed had to be found or prepared by simple means. Limited by their stone tools, they used all ways open to them to survive in an environment which was harsh enough to cause the death of many white people. As a result, an impressive list of plants was used as fibre sources or fish poisons, both important to the indigenous people in food gathering.

When white men first settled in Australia they had an immediate interest in the natural environment, although it was not an interest that would be shared by many modern conservationists. The settlement was about nine months by sea from England, and supplies of materials for building and life in general were meagre. There were two reasons for examining closely the local flora; the first, more urgent, was for their own survival and comfort, to satisfy the need for food and shelter; the second, more long-term, was to find natural products that could be exploited for export. At first these latter investigations were mainly towards finding useful fibre plants or dyes, both relatively unsuccessful searches; in time it was realized that the grasslands provided the answer with the development of the pastoral industry.

By the time European settlement came to Australia, the pattern of life and culture in overseas countries was well set. Unless native plants were found to yield products similar but superior to those already known, they would not be of much interest outside this country. Some of course were used as substitutes when the preferred European product was unavailable, such as bark used as a roofing material. There were early success stories in the essential oil industry and tannin production, but both are considerably reduced now because of competition from other countries using Australian species with low-cost labour. The most successful of the Australian native plant industries is that of timber, where *Eucalyptus* in particular is pre-eminent, being the most important hardwood source in the world.

There are about 20,000 native plant species in Australia. From the point of view of man's direct utilization, many of these have no significance at all, although of course they make up our environment and contribute to our well-being through their interactions in the ecosystem. Taking the broader view, our life depends entirely on green plants which not only supply us directly or indirectly with all our food and nearly all our fuel, but even make available to us the oxygen we need to stay alive. However, in this book we are concerned only with the species that we can use for particular purposes, rather than with the value of the plant kingdom as a whole.

Not all of us would be prepared to surrender the comforts of civilization such as electric power, synthetic fabrics or even plastic bags, to survive with only natural plant products. In any case, the pressure that would be put on the native flora if the majority of the population decided to use it in this way would make it impossible for many species to survive. Laws differ in the different States but in general collecting of plant material is restricted in the interests of conservation and those with a respect for the natural environment would not want to despoil it, even if permitted.

However, there are in the community today a significant number of people who prefer the simple lifestyle, depending on natural products, and who find a joy in this living with the land. There are many others who, while not abandoning modern amenities, take an interest and delight in knowledge of the native flora, this knowledge extending to using plants and plant products to add variety and personality to a sometimes monotonous and impersonal world.

1

The Good Oils

ESSENTIAL OILS

'John Brown's baby's got a cold upon his chest,
So we rubbed it with camphorated oil.
Everybody shouted Euca,
Euca-lyptus that's the dinkum oil.'

Children's song

THE WORDS are perhaps lacking a little in poetic quality, but the popularity as a children's chant of some years ago is at least an indication of the widespread medicinal use of eucalyptus oil. No home medicine cupboard was without it; we can well remember inhaling eucalyptus fumes from a steaming basin, with a towel over the head, to relieve a head cold, or going to school with a few drops of the oil on a corner of a handkerchief to sniff at convenient intervals. Now, like so many of the older treatments, the use of eucalyptus oil in medicine is greatly reduced in favour of more recently developed compounds with, at least in the case of the common cold, little more likelihood of a cure.

Volatile or essential oils are regarded as 'essences' in the way we think of vanilla essence or lemon essence, not as something necessary to the life of the plant or of man. Essences are obtained usually by distillation of the plant material. The oils may be present in any part of the plant — many occur in fruits and seeds — but the greater number are to be found in leaves. It is the essential oil which, if present, gives the characteristic scent when a leaf is crushed. In flowers the oils evaporate so readily and are often so freely produced that one can smell the perfume without crushing the flower. Oils in leaves are often to be found in glands which show as clear spots if the leaf is held up against the light; small glandular dots may need use of a hand lens to see them. A remarkably high proportion of the native flora is rich in essential oils — the eucalypts, the tea-trees, the boronias, the mints — yet comparatively few species are used commercially for the production of oils.

There are reasons why so few of our sources of essential oils are commercially exploited. As has happened with native food plants, there has been no cultivation or selection of desirable varieties. The indigenous population had no use for distilled oils, and Europeans had already developed habits of use and cultivation based on Old World oils. Although essential oils are used in a wide variety of products — soap, perfumery, pharmaceuticals, drinks both soft and hard, and foods — it is not easy to introduce a new oil to the market. It may be difficult to find an immediate use for the unknown essence, and experimentation may produce disappointing results. Only one of our indigenous flowers, the brown boronia of Western Australia, *Boronia megastigma*, with its outstandingly beautiful fragrance, is used commercially.

In the main, the native oils which were first exploited in Australia were those which had characteristics similar to already known essences. The first oil to receive attention, and indeed one of the first products to be exported from the infant colony of New South Wales, was oil of the Sydney peppermint, *Eucalyptus piperita*. In the appendix to *Journal of a Voyage to New South Wales* by John White, Esq., Surgeon-General to the Settlement, published in London in 1790, it is stated, 'The name of "Peppermint Tree" has been given to this plant by Mr. White on account of the very great resemblance between the essential oil drawn from its leaves and that obtained from the "Peppermint" (*Mentha piperita*) which grows in England. This oil was found by Mr. White to be much more efficacious in removing all cholicky complaints than that of the English "Peppermint", which he attributes to its being less pungent and more aromatic. A quart of the oil has been sent by him to Mr. *Wilson*.'

And so Australia's essential oil exports began.

Backhousia citriodora   LEMON IRONWOOD

An attractive medium-sized tree, *Backhousia citriodora* is one of the the natives which is becoming popular as an ornamental. Flat-topped clusters of small white flowers are produced in summer, in great profusion if the plant is kept pruned to shrub size. The strongly lemon-scented leaves are the best source known of high quality citral, the essential oil consisting 95% of that ingredient. In nature the plants are not common, occurring only in some areas of southern Queensland rainforests; exploitation has been somewhat irregular and only small quantities have been produced. The tree has not been successfully grown in plantations.

Dried leaves of this species can be used to make sachets, similar to those described for *Eucalyptus citriodora*, to give a pleasant perfume to the linen cupboard.

Like some of the eucalypts discussed below, *B. citriodora* occurs in two distinct varieties; these are indistinguishable in form but contain different chemicals in their oils. The less common variety contains citronellal instead of citral; both are lemon scented, but as citronellal can be readily converted into a rose-scented chemical, it would be of use in perfumery if obtainable in commercial quantity.

There are several other species of *Backhousia* that produce interesting, but not profitable, oils. The crushed leaves of *B. myrtifolia*, the ironwood or carrol, which occurs on creek banks and rainforest margins from the Sydney district to Fraser Island, have a delightful spicy odour, due to the presence of up to 80% elemicin, the distinctive constituent of nutmeg; it has been suggested as a commercial source. *B. anisata*, a large tree with a restricted distribution in New South Wales, owes its common name of aniseed tree, and its scientific name, to the pleasant scent produced on crushing the leaves and shoots.

Distribution: *B. citriodora:* Qld
                 B. myrtifolia: Qld, N.S.W.
                 B. anisata: N.S.W.

Cinnamomum oliveri   OLIVER'S SASSAFRAS, CAMPHORWOOD

This large tree of New South Wales and Queensland rainforests is closely related to the well-known camphor laurel, *Cinnamomum camphora*. The shiny leaves contain camphor identical with that of the camphor laurel, and on crushing give the same odour; in appearance they differ from those of the cultivated species, being opposite and comparatively long and narrow. Large rough pustular bumps on the brown trunk are of help in recognizing the tree. The bark is very fragrant, containing camphor, safrol and other chemicals which combine to give a pleasant long-lasting 'sarsaparilla' odour similar to that of the American sassafras. During the nineteenth century it was hoped that the species could be commercially exploited for sassafras oil but this did not eventuate as the percentage yield was too low. Nevertheless the bark was used by some medical men as a convenient astringent for diarrhoea, and would have been more pleasant to take than some other prescriptions.

Distribution: Qld, N.S.W.

Cyperus rotundus   NUT GRASS

This very persistent and unpopular weed has a string of underground 'nuts' or tubers which make it difficult to eradicate. The tubers are very aromatic, and can be steam distilled to give a balsamic essential oil. In India the dry tubers are sold in bazaars for use in medicine and perfumery; they are used in native medicine for digestive disorders. The essential oil is used in perfumery and soaps, for scenting clothes, and as an insect repellent.

Distribution: All mainland States

Dacrydium franklinii   HUON PINE

No longer available because of the short supply of the timber, a valuable oil was formerly obtained from sawdust and waste material of this Tasmanian conifer. The oil, forming 3-5% by weight of the wood, was produced by steam distillation. Heavy and pale yellow, it was used both as a preservative in casein preparations and in medicine for treatment of wounds and tinea.

Distribution: Tas.

Darwinia fascicularis   CLUSTERED SCENT-MYRTLE

This shrub of the sandy soils in the Sydney region resembles the heaths in its crowded cylindrical leaves and twiggy growth, but belongs to the same family as *Eucalyptus* and *Melaleuca*. It has clustered, small, white or pink-and-white tubular flowers with the petals closed over at the top except where the style extends up to a centimetre beyond the tube.

On experimental distillation, the leaves yielded about 0.3% of

oil of approximately the same composition as that of *Eucalyptus macarthurii*, being very rich in geranyl acetate, and thus a useful oil for perfumery purposes. However to obtain it in commercial quantities the plant would have to be cultivated and this is not economically feasible. This plant and *Callitris tasmanica* were used for a time during World War I, when overseas supplies of perfumery ingredients were scarce.
Distribution: N.S.W.

Eremophila mitchellii　　　　　BUDDA, BASTARD SANDALWOOD

Just as the wood of this eastern Australian species is used as a substitute for sandalwood (p. 121) it has been suggested that the oil may be of value in place of sandalwood oil. Although not the same in constitution as the latter, the product has a pleasant sweet odour which lasts well. The wood contains 3% of a dark viscid oil which can be extracted in the same way as that of sandalwood.
Distribution: Qld, N.S.W., S.A.

Eucalyptus　　　　　　　　　　GUM TREE

There are more than 500 species of *Eucalyptus* in Australia, all of them bearing oil in their leaves. However, for various reasons, only a few species are exploited. Eucalyptus oil is not a constant product from one species to another — there are about forty known constituents, any number of which may be present in a particular species, so the oil may smell strongly of peppermint or lemon, rather than the expected 'eucalyptus' scent. The oils of some species strongly resemble oil of turpentine.

Wide variation exists in the actual amount of oil produced by different species of *Eucalyptus*. The most prolific yield 3-4% by weight of oil from foliage, whereas some may have a yield as low as .02%; obviously the latter have no value for extraction. Much work has been done on eucalyptus oils, particularly in earlier days by Baker and Smith. These workers showed that, in general, species which are closely related according to structural characters also show a relationship in their chemical makeup and in their oil constituents. For example, the bloodwoods, which can be recognized by their flaky bark and by the almost transverse parallel veins in the leaves, are rich in pinene; these pinene-rich oils which resemble oil of turpentine but are impractical for exploitation as such a product is so much more easily and cheaply obtained elsewhere.

The substance which most of us regard as the 'dinkum oil' was given the name eucalyptol. It has been found to occur in a wide range of plants in most of which it would be quite undetected by the layman's nose; it occurs in lavender, sage, mint and many others where, in small concentrations, it makes a contribution but does not dominate the mixture. In fact eucalyptol was found to be an already known oil, cineole, so named from *Artemisia cina*, the Levant wormseed, from which it was first isolated. It is cineole (or eucalyptol) which is the desirable oil for medicinal use; it occurs in much greater amounts in certain species of eucalypts than in any other plants, and those which have 70% or more cineole content in their oil are the ones in demand. Oils of this type are used in inhalants, cough lozenges and sprays, also as antiseptics. Many people use the oil as a spot remover, particularly for tar and grease.

Other eucalyptus oils can be used for various industrial processes as described under the separate species. The largest use was formerly in the mining industry where orders for supply of 50 or 100 tons of the cheaper oils were placed for use at mining centres such as Broken Hill, the oil being used in the flotation process for separating metallic sulphides.

It has been suggested in the past that eucalyptus oil could be substituted for kerosene for lighting purposes, but we fear that the opportunity for that is past, and it will not catch on today.

Eucalyptus oil production in Australia has traditionally been based on extraction of the oil in fairly small stills in areas where the source trees are in plentiful supply. The crude oil is then sent to major centres, particularly Sydney and Melbourne, where it can be refined.

There is considerable variation in the type of still used, but a simple and commonly used one is made from a ship's tank, fired by the wood of branches whose leaves have been distilled. Leaves and branchlets of the eucalypt are placed on a grid in the tank, suspended over water which, in boiling, produces the steam that distils the oil from the leaves. Steam and oil vapour are carried through a pipe which is watercooled to condense them; water-cooling is most conveniently done by a creek or river which often determines the placement of the still. The condensed water and oil are received in a vessel from which the oil may be removed as it floats on the surface. There are, of course, many elaborations of this method. For those interested in home production, perhaps from their backyard or neighbourhood trees, such a still requires a licence from the Customs Department if it has an output of more than five litres per hour.

The majority may feel that operating a backyard still is either too much trouble, or too likely to cause unwelcome speculation by the neighbours, but there are other ways in which the scent of the eucalyptus oil can be enjoyed without first removing it from the leaves. One of the joys of camping in the bush is the smell of the campfire with a few gum tree leaves to start it. A few leafy twigs taken home to burn in the home barbecue or fireplace will bring with them the scent of the bush, while simply crushing and sniffing the leaves is a pleasurable experience in itself.

For a eucalypt to be commercially exploited for its oil, not only must the oil be of high quality but it must be present in a high percentage yield in the leaves, and trees must be both accessible and abundant. Virtually the whole of the Australian industry is based on naturally growing trees, not on plantations. It is interesting that almost all the useful species occur in south-eastern Australia; the industry is largely confined to New South Wales and Victoria where a number of high-yielding species with good quality oils, particularly those of the mallees, are exploited. Smaller amounts were formerly obtained in South Australia and Queensland. The eucalypts described in the following pages include a few of the principal commercial sources as well as some of interest because of the unusual oils they contain. The latter species, although not used in this country on a commercial scale, can make an interesting addition to a garden for the pleasant and unexpected scent they give on crushing the leaves.

Eucalyptus citriodora   LEMON-SCENTED GUM

A tall handsome tree, the lemon-scented gum is cultivated in many parts of Australia as an ornamental. Very similar in appearance to the more widespread spotted gum, *E. maculata*, it has a smooth dimpled bark, blotched in grey, cream and pink; it can be distinguished from spotted gum by the strong citronella scent of its crushed leaves. The species occurs in the drier coastal areas of Queensland from about Maryborough to Mackay, and in a further area on the Atherton Tableland.

Although it is naturally a tall straight timber-producing tree with sparse foliage this gum can, with suitable pruning, be kept shorter and more leafy. The leaf oil contains 65-85% of citronellal, the richest source of that chemical in the world. Citronellal is in demand for production of menthol and the rose-scented citronellol used in perfumery. However, Australian-produced oil cannot compete on the world market with that produced from the same species in Brazilian plantations, where ten million trees are cultivated to produce about 140 tonnes of oil per annum. Guatemala, too, is a successful producer of oil from *E. citriodora*. The oil must also compete with a similar product from the citronella grasses cultivated in Taiwan, Indonesia and Sri Lanka.

The pleasant lemon scent of the leaves makes this species a suitable one for perfuming the linen cupboard; for that purpose leaves should be dried and enclosed in a small cloth sachet. During the last century they were regarded as a good repellent for cockroaches and silverfish which were much greater nuisances then than now. Probably it will be found necessary to rub the leaves together in the sachet from time to time to release the scent. Distribution: Qld

Eucalyptus dives   BROAD-LEAVED PEPPERMINT

From investigations early in this century into the oils of different eucalypts, it was realized that the oil composition was fairly constant in any one species; it seemed to be such an important character that prime importance in separating species was given to this chemical constitution. However in 1927 researchers found that in a small group of broad-leaved peppermints growing together, there were two distinct oil varieties, one rich in cineole, the other in piperitone; the trees were otherwise indistinguishable. Further variants have since been found in this species and others, and they are distinguished only as chemical varieties of the same species. *Eucalyptus dives* is perhaps the most interesting of of these, two of the four forms being of importance for different products.

E. dives is a small tree with a freely branched large crown; the fibrous, typical 'peppermint' bark is absent from the smaller branches, but persistent on trunk and larger branches. It is widespread in south-eastern New South Wales and in much of eastern Victoria particularly on slopes and foothills of the Great Dividing Range. There is an oil content of 3-4% in the leaves of *E. dives* 'Type', which is the first-described form of the species; the oil is about 50% piperitone, and is the chief source of that product, having replaced *E. piperita*. The oil was formerly used in the mining industry for the separation of metallic sulphides in a flotation process, and later as raw material for industrial conversion to menthol and thymol; menthol is familiar to many of us as a flavouring in confectionery and in preparations such as cough syrups, nasal inhalants and toothpastes, while thymol is used industrially as a fungicide and preservative.

E. dives var. 'C', although indistinguishable in form from the 'Type', produces an oil which, with 70% cineole, is one of the finest for medicinal use, and as the leaves yield 3-4% oil by weight, it is one of the most used species. Large trees are inconvenient for harvesting: *E. dives* has the advantage that it coppices well; trees can be cut continuously for years and will continue to produce suckers.

This species is under cultivation in eastern Transvaal. Like many other Australian trees it has taken well to cultivation in southern Africa, and production from there has considerably reduced the less sophisticated production from New South Wales. Distribution: N.S.W., Vic.

Eucalyptus globulus   TASMANIAN BLUE GUM

Tasmania's floral emblem is her blue gum, a large handsome tree with smooth, pale grey bark and long glossy leaves; the four-angled buds, large creamy white flowers, and four-ribbed gum-nut fruits make it a distinctive species. Specimens were first collected by the famous French naturalist Labillardière from Tasmania in 1793, before that island was colonized by the British. Labillardière was travelling in the ship *Recherche* on the journey in search of the lost explorer Comte de la Pérouse; the ship anchored for about a month in Adventure Bay on Bruny Island south of where Hobart now stands. There are fascinating accounts of the Frenchman's meetings with the now vanished Tasmanians, including a story of the great naturalist's demonstration to a native girl of how to don a pair of woollen pantaloons. Labillardière made invaluable observations on the natives and their simple life style, and also collected animal and plant specimens. *Eucalyptus globulus* was described by him in his journal of the voyage.

The species is not naturally widespread; its main area of occurrence is south of Hobart, but it extends further north, and some specimens are found in the southern parts of Victoria. However it has achieved wide distribution through man's efforts, having been introduced into many overseas countries, and being extensively cultivated in some. Large-scale plantations have been developed in Spain where the production of oil from the leaves of this and other species is an important industry; most of the annual 300 tonnes of the oil is exported mainly to Europe and U.S.A. and competes with the Australian product. In Portugal the plantations have a twofold purpose; the timber is used for paper pulp and firewood, the leaves for essential oil production. In the Nilgiri Hills in India, *E. globulus* is the most commonly cultivated species of eucalypt being mainly grown as a fuel supply, but there is essential oil production at a cottage industry level. In the U.S.S.R., the species is one of those cultivated for oil production on the Black Sea Coast region of the Caucasus. In Brazil also there is a considerable *E. globulus* oil production. This oil was in great demand during the last century as it is of high cineole content and therefore valuable for medicinal use. It also compared very favourably in quality with oils from some other species which gave a higher oil yield but lower percentage of cineole. However this tree is not exploited at all in Australia because of its low percentage yield, less than 1% of leaf weight, and it is only in countries with relatively low labour costs that it has been found an economic proposition.

The history of the Tasmanian blue gum in California is interesting. Several species of *Eucalyptus* were introduced to that State around the middle of the nineteenth century, and soon after this plantations of about 8000 hectares were established, especially of *E. globulus*. It was intended to use these trees for production of both timber and essential oils. However the demand did not materialize; with relatively high labour costs it was not worth-while processing the leaves for oil, and the industry languished. The species is used now principally as a windbreak for citrus orchards, and is otherwise well represented as an ornamental tree. Keen watchers of old cowboy films will have noticed how frequently the characters gallop past *Eucalyptus* trees; these are usually *E. globulus*.

Distribution: Vic., Tas.

Eucalyptus macarthurii   CAMDEN WOOLLYBUTT,
                                                PADDY'S RIVER BOX

Appropriately named for its area of occurrence, Camden woolly-butt is found naturally in a relatively small area of New South Wales in the Central Tablelands and Blue Mountains to the west of Sydney. The specific name honours the collector Sir William Macarthur, son of the famous merino sheep pioneer. These trees are quick growing and attractive to look at; although large and spreading in the wild, they respond well to pruning and can be kept low with branches to the ground, making them ideal specimens for windbreaks. As implied by the common name, the bark is persistent on the trunk, becoming rough and woolly at the base, with all but the larger branches smooth.

The easiest way to recognize this tree is by the scent present in both bark and leaves. There is no cineole, and the typical euca-lypt smell is absent, the oil instead being sweetly scented, rather flower-like. With a content of up to 70% geranyl acetate, the oil is useful for perfumery. However, although a very small plantation was established at Emerald in Victoria in 1911, it has been found, as with the other species, uneconomic to produce in Australia. Limited amounts have been produced commercially in the Black Sea Coast region of U.S.S.R., where the tree's frost-resistant qualities were found to be a great advantage.

Distribution: N.S.W.

Eucalyptus piperita   SYDNEY PEPPERMINT

In considering oil production, *E. piperita* is of interest only in a historical sense, as it was the first species whose oil was exported from Australia in 1790. It is not now exploited commercially, as

E. dives, the broad-leaved peppermint, is a much more useful source of the peppermint essence, piperitone. As the common name suggests, the species is restricted to coastal New South Wales. It is most common on sandstone between Gosford and Nowra, but extends somewhat further both north and south.

Trees may be recognized by the typical peppermint bark, which is grey and fibrous, persisting on the trunk and large branches, and by the strong peppermint odour of the crushed leaves.

Distribution: N.S.W.

Eucalyptus polybractea (E. fruticetorum)   BLUE MALLEE, SILVER-LEAF MALLEE

A typical mallee, *E. polybractea* is abundant in the low rainfall areas of Victoria and southern New South Wales. The mallee type of growth, with several slender stems arising from a large rootstock, is a convenient form for harvesting, and as this species produces oil of excellent medicinal quality with high cineole content, it is much in demand. Natural stands of the trees are crushed by a heavy roller, after which treatment there is a burst of young coppice growth which is ready for harvesting in twelve or eighteen months. There is less of the species now than formerly, as large areas of the Mallee district have been cleared for wheat-growing, but a considerable amount remains, and this is one of the principal commercial species, providing about one-third of the total medicinal oil.

Other mallees, which occur generally in similar areas, may be exploited with *E. polybractea*. These include the acorn mallee, *E. oleosa*, the dumosa mallee, *E. dumosa*, and the green mallee, *E. viridis*. Another small mallee, *E. cneorifolia*, which is restricted to Kangaroo Island off the South Australian coast, was used for many years, but now extraction there is carried on by one small distiller only.

Distribution: N.S.W., Vic.

Eucalyptus radiata   NARROW-LEAVED PEPPERMINT

Although oil of *Eucalyptus piperita* was sent to Britain from the infant New South Wales in 1790, the essential oil industry did not really begin until the middle of the nineteenth century, when, at the urging of the great botanist Baron von Müller, oil production was commenced in Victoria. At Dandenong Creek a crude still was set up by Joseph Bosisto, a Victorian pharmacist who founded a firm of pharmacists and oil distillers, and who was a leading figure in that State. The species he used was *E. radiata*, a member of the peppermint group of eucalypts very common in the area, and widespread through the ranges of Victoria and New South Wales. Several different names have been used for this eucalypt, which is somewhat variable; it has the peppermint characteristics of short-fibred bark persisting on the trunk and large branches, and leaves with copious oil dots; the leaves tend to be narrower than in *E. dives*. Specimens grow fast, and respond to cutting by producing good coppice growth.

Like *E. dives*, *E. radiata* has a number of chemical varieties, two of which are of commercial value. Oil of the 'Type' variety is high yielding, and is a fine medicinal quality, cineole-rich product in good demand; this variety is sometimes known as *E. australiana*. Another variety, *E. radiata* var. 'B', known as *E. phellandra*, produces up to 4.5% of an oil used in disinfectants and deodorants. Distribution: N.S.W., Vic.

Eucalyptus sideroxylon   RED IRONBARK, MUGGA

Naturally widespread on the drier slopes of the Dividing Range in south-eastern Australia, this handsome tree has been planted frequently as an ornamental, particularly in parks and as a street tree. The black, deeply furrowed bark contrasts well with the greyish foliage and pink to red flowers. Leaves of *E. sideroxylon* contain high-quality medicinal oil with at least 70% cineole content, and the species is used commercially. Distribution: Qld, N.S.W., Vic.

Eucalyptus smithii   GULLY GUM, GULLY PEPPERMINT

Deeply-furrowed compact bark below and smooth, white gum bark above help to distinguish this species which occurs naturally in a restricted area of southern coastal New South Wales extending to a small extent into Victoria.

The oil produced from the gully gum has a high cineole content but also some objectionable ingredients which can be removed by refining. Use in Australia has been only spasmodic, but there are successful plantations in some overseas countries where timber and oil are obtained from the crop.

Distribution: N.S.W., Vic.

Eucalyptus staigeriana   LEMON-SCENTED IRONBARK

In its natural occurrence confined to the Palmer River district of far north Queensland, *E. staigeriana* seems an unlikely species to be commercially successful. It is a slow growing, small, irregular tree with the typical dark furrowed bark of an ironbark, but with a strongly lemon-scented oil of high quality. The oil has a close resemblance to lemon oil and could be used as a substitute for it. Although it can be grown in southern parts of its native State, it is not frost-resistant, which restricts its usefulness.

Production of oil from this species is not economic in Australia, but it is being grown to some extent in several overseas tropical countries such as Brazil and Guatemala.

Distribution: Qld

Several other species of *Eucalyptus* are exploited for their high cineole content. These include the bundy or long-leaved box, *E. goniocalyx*, of the Dividing Range areas of New South Wales and Victoria, extending into some of the South Australian Ranges; the yellow gum, *E. leucoxylon*, of western Victoria and southern ranges of South Australia; and the red box, *E. polyanthemos*, which is widespread in Victoria and southern inland New South Wales.

Leptospermum   TEA-TREE

Nowadays the leptospermums are appreciated for their beauty as flowering shrubs and small trees of the bushland, and are being grown very commonly as garden ornamentals. Their form varies widely: they may be gracefully arching or stiff, with the bark papery, furrowed or smooth; the flowers are usually white, occasionally pink, and five-petalled with copious nectar in the cup-like base of the freshly opened blossom. The early settlers' name of tea-tree was given from their use as a beverage; the flavour of the 'tea' varied with the species used and even within the species, as some have a number of varieties, and it is the different essential oil of the leaves which determines the taste of the brew. The name 'tea-tree' is now used equally widely for the melaleucas (p. 140).

The amount of oil in the leaves of the various leptospermums is less than in many species of *Eucalyptus*, usually less than 1%. As with the latter genus it is the combination of a number of chemical ingredients, sometimes with a particular one dominating, that gives the characteristic odour. Oil can be distilled from the leaves in the same way as from the eucalypts, but many people will prefer the less bothersome method of enjoying the essence by adding a leafy sprig to the teapot when making a 'cuppa'. One is impressed by the strong flavour produced by the small amount of essential oil in just a few leaves.

Leptospermum petersonii (L. citratum) LEMON-SCENTED TEA-TREE

Although not widely distributed in nature, being found in scattered areas of the eastern Australian ranges, the lemon-scented tea-tree has become well known as a garden plant; the narrow leaves, 3-4 cm long, give a strong lemon scent on crushing and provide an infallible identification. The tree is popular both for its scent and for its attractive form; it grows rapidly and can be pruned repeatedly to be kept as a shrub if required, making it ideal for hedges and windbreaks. These same characteristics suit it for commercial oil extraction, but limited quantities only have been produced in Australia.

The lemon scent is due to the 90% content in the oil of two chemicals, citral and citronellal. Citral, in particular, is in demand for use in perfumes of the lemon and verbena types and for scenting soap; some is used for flavouring soft drinks; it can also be employed for synthesis of Vitamin A and ionone, the scent of violets.

As with so many Australian native plants, the commercial exploitation of the lemon-scented tea-tree is undertaken largely beyond Australia's shores, in this case in plantations in Kenya and Guatemala. It is ironic that much of the oil of this species used in Australia is imported from Kenya.

Distribution: Qld, N.S.W.

Leptospermum liversidgei   SWAMP MAY

Another tea-tree with a lemon scent, this species can easily be distinguished from *L. petersonii* by the small leaves only 5 mm long. It is a swamp-dwelling species with pink flowers, and may grow to small tree size. There seem to be several chemical varieties of *L. liversidgei*, one with a large amount of citral in the oil, another with a very high proportion of citronellal; both, of course, are lemon-scented and both would be good sources for oil. The plant is common in some areas of the Northern Rivers district of New South Wales.

Tests carried out at the University of Adelaide to determine antibacterial activity of the essential oils of some Australian native plants showed, in general, that they were not strongly active. The few species which gave comparatively good results included *Leptospermum liversidgei*, *L. petersonii* and *Backhousia citriodora*. Distribution: Qld, N.S.W.

Melaleuca   TEA-TREE

Although *Eucalyptus* is the outstanding producer of essential oils, there are other Australian natives of importance or interest as well. Many of them belong, as does *Eucalyptus*, to the family Myrtaceae which is of great prominence in the Australian flora. Members of this family have glandular dots in the leaves which when crushed release essential oils of varying constituents which varying yields.

Melaleuca is a large genus of the Myrtaceae which includes a number of the paperbarked tea-trees. The flowers in many are of the bottlebrush type and may be distinguished from the similar *Callistemon* by the long stamens united at their bases to form five distinct bundles. Several of the species are of interest because of their essential oils, but only one or two are of commercial importance in Australia. The oils are generally similar to those of eucalypts in constituents and variety, but as a rule the yield is rather low.

Melaleuca alternifolia   NARROW-LEAVED PAPERBARK TEA-TREE

Commercial tea-tree oil is extracted from the leaves of one of the paperbarks, *M. alternifolia*, a swamp species with narrow leaves occurring in coastal areas of northern New South Wales and southern Queensland. The oil is a pleasant-smelling mixture of a number of ingredients including less than 10% cineole; it is of use in dentistry and medicine, being germicidal but of low toxicity to the patient. A commercial preparation of this oil is available in Australian pharmacies.

This species is one of the ugly ducklings of the Australian flora. Formerly it was regarded as a pest by Northern Rivers dairy farmers as it was very difficult to eradicate and grew very quickly again after cutting; since it has been found to be of commercial use these characteristics have become appreciated rather than cursed, particularly as the trees thrive in the swampy areas less suitable for dairying.

Distribution: Qld, N.S.W.

Melaleuca bracteata   BLACK TEA-TREE

Black tea-trees are locally common along the banks of some creeks and rivers, particularly in Queensland. They are large trees with finely furrowed bark and sharply pointed narrow leaves about 2 cm long; the small cream bottlebrushes are produced often in great profusion early in summer and, like the other melaleucas, are attractive to nectar-seeking birds.

Leaf oil of this species is very unlike that of the other species of *Melaleuca* or of the eucalypts. The 1% yield consists very largely of methyl eugenol, a chemical which can be used in insecticides such as pyrethrum sprays to increase greatly their potency. However, the small quantities used in Australia are not produced here, but imported from Kenya.

An interesting early suggestion was that this oil could be used for the synthesis of vanilla, but the idea has not come to commercial fruition.

Unlike many other of the essential oils, this one is heavier than water, which necessitates some alteration to the distilling process.

Distribution: Qld, N.S.W.

Melaleuca cajuputi   CAJUPUT TREE

Another of the paperbarks, this tea-tree is widespread and very common in South-east Asian countries where it sometimes forms large swamp forests. It occurs from India to Australia, and in this country is to be found only in the far north, being best represented in the Northern Territory. The species has long been cultivated overseas for its cajuput oil, distilled from the leaves and twigs. Stills used in the Moluccas and described by early writers function in the same way as our models, but have interesting local features such as bamboo water pipes and coconut-shell funnels.

Cajuput oil is a mixture of ingredients, dominated by cineole. It is used medicinally in ointments and liniments, and in some places is used as an effective insect repellent.

There has been considerable confusion in the names of various melaleucas, and it is not possible to rely on accounts in some of the earlier literature. Thus there are references to cajuput trees in New South Wales but this is the result of a mistaken identification.

Distribution: Qld, N.T.

Melaleuca quinquenervia   BROAD-LEAVED PAPERBARK,
                                             BELLBOWRIE

This is the common paperbark of swampy ground and hillsides along the whole east coast of Australia north of Sydney, often growing in pure stands. Its natural occurrence extends to New Caledonia where it is common, and where it is exploited commercially for its essential oil, exported as *niaouli*; the oil is similar to cajuput oil. Its extraction is not commercially viable in Australia.

M. quinquenervia exists in several chemical varieties, and in fairly recent years it has been found that two of these varieties are worth exploiting for their nerolidol and linalool, two naturally occurring alcohols whose pleasant scents are of value in the perfumery industry. These varieties have been distilled commercially in the Northern Rivers district of New South Wales, although competition from synthetics and from Brazilian oils has been strong.

Bellbowrie is a common name used for this tree in parts of New South Wales, and has been adopted as the name of a new suburb in Brisbane.

Distribution: Qld, N.S.W.

Melaleuca thymifolia   FEATHER HONEY-MYRTLE

A popular garden ornamental, this native shrub is distinctive for its attractive mauve flowers with their five feathery bundles of stamens. It occurs naturally in east coast districts, and is also found in a handsome inland form.

Although unlikely to be used as a commercial source, this species produces a good yield of oil from the numerous glands in the leaves. The high quality oil is rich in cineole and comparable with the better eucalyptus oils.

Distribution: Qld, N.S.W.

Microsorium scolopendria (Polypodium phymatodes)

This is an easily recognized fern found mainly in rainforest margins and light rainforests in tropical Australia. It has a broad green stem up to 8 mm wide covered with brownish scales and is generally found creeping on boulders and bases of tree trunks. The fronds are deeply lobed with several coarse lobes on each side. Coumarin, the substance responsible for the attractive scent of new-mown hay, occurs in the creeping stems, and in Malaysia these stems were placed among clothes to impart a fragrance. They were also used for scenting coconut oil.

Distribution: Qld, W.A.

Native Pines

The pine trees of the northern hemisphere do not occur naturally in Australia, although they are planted on a large scale for forestry purposes. There are, however, a number of native trees of the same cone-bearing group, some of them being of great importance as timber trees (ch. 6). One tends to think of plants of this type as being rich in oils and it comes as something of a surprise to learn that none of the natives has sufficient yield to be worth exploiting. *Callitris*, the Australian cypress pine, is one which has been studied; the leaf oils consist of a mixture of ingredients constant for the species, but usually of low yield; the oil of *C. tasmanica*, for example, is rich in geraniol and its derivative, but yield is only 0.14%. In the case of *Araucaria cunninghamii*, the hoop pine, the leaves contain only .005% oil — hardly worth sniffing, let alone distilling.

Santalum spicatum (Eucarya spicata) AUSTRALIAN SANDALWOOD,
SANDALWOOD

This small tree of the Western Australian and South Australian desert regions is of use mainly for its scented timber (p. 146). However there is also a market for the wood oil, which is of excellent quality and has been claimed to be better in some respects than oil from *Santalum album*, the true sandalwood; although the oils are not identical, the principal ingredients of both appear to be the same. As the wood is valuable, it is mainly the roots and butts which are used for oil production; the material is pulverized, then extracted with a solvent and lastly vacuum distilled.

In 1880 the first shipment of sandalwood oil from Australia was made, when the Western Australian Distillery Company shipped the first instalment of twenty cases of oil prepared at its plant near Albany. The oil at that time was in demand for medicinal purposes, but now is used chiefly for perfumery. At the present time processing is carried out in Perth from wood collected over widely scattered areas of the State.

Distribution: S.A., W.A., N.T.

*Tagetes minuta STINKING ROGER

Critics of this introduced weed, which is described by courteous people as highly aromatic, may be surprised to learn that the essential oil distilled from the leaves is in demand for perfumery purposes. There are distilleries producing the oil in France and in America, and it is described as 'highly valued' for the perfume trade.

Stinking Roger is a tall annual plant native to South America; it has opposite compound leaves around the margins of which on the under surface can clearly be seen the small brownish oil glands. A member of the daisy family, it produces numerous flowers in small elongate heads at the apex of the plant.

The oil, which is steam distilled, is a blend of about a dozen different aromatic compounds. Although many people find the odour of the crushed leaves somewhat overpowering, if diluted it becomes much more pleasant, and has been likened to passion-fruit or apples. The perfume is similar to that of the hardy summer garden annuals known as French marigold and African marigold; both are species of *Tagetes*, native to Mexico in spite of their common names.

Tagetes oil is used commercially to a limited extent in some American countries as flavouring for confectionery and desserts. Distribution: Qld, N.S.W., Vic.

FLOWER PERFUMES

Extraction of flower perfumes is usually a very different process from extraction of aromatic leaf oils. Frequently the flower oils are more unstable and may be destroyed by steam distillation, so the perfumes are generally extracted either with volatile solvents such as petroleum ether, or with non-volatile solvents, i.e. fats.

A hundred years or so ago there was a much wider interest than now in our flower perfumes. The pharmacist J. Bosisto extracted the essence from a wide variety of native plants including a number of the acacias; there was at that time a considerable demand for these in European markets. Exploitation at present in Australia seems to be confined to brown boronia, whose perfume is produced by a Western Australian firm.

Acacia farnesiana   PRICKLY MOSES, MIMOSA

One of the wattles, *Acacia farnesiana* is important as a perfume source known as 'cassie' in France, Algeria, northern India and the Philippines, and in Mexico as 'huisache'. Although widely distributed in the warmer parts of all the continents including the Americas and Australia, its exploitation has been limited to a few countries.

Prickly Moses is a large, straggly, uncomfortable shrub armed with long spines which, in inland Australia at least, help to make it a safe nesting site for finches. The fluffy, round, yellow flower-heads are sweetly and strongly scented, and have for a long time been used in overseas countries in perfumery. In France the plants are cultivated from seed on a large scale.

The essence may be extracted from the flowers in the same way as from *Boronia megastigma*. An alternative process is maceration and extraction with hot fat. The flowers are crushed and placed in purified melted fat, which may be beef fat, lard or olive oil, for several hours; the spent flowers are removed and replaced by fresh ones, the procedure being repeated eight to ten times. The fat is then strained and cooled and the oil may be extracted from it with alcohol. Used fat can be made into soap. Those who like to try such pioneering skills as making soap from rendered dripping may wish to improve the product with a native flower perfume in this way.

Distribution: Qld, N.S.W., S.A., W.A., N.T.

Boronia megastigma   BROWN BORONIA

This West Australian native is a graceful shrub of fine foliage, reaching about 2 metres in height. Although the nodding flowers are not showy, they are attractive in appearance with the four petals a rich dark brown on the outside, yellow on the inside. A botanist in the Victorian era suggested this species would be suitable for graveyard planting, because of its dark flowers. The blossoms are very heavily scented with a delightful fragrance reminiscent of violets. Always a popular perfume, this is the only native plant commercially exploited in this country for the purpose; some of the perfume is used in Australia, some exported to France.

Brown boronia perfume is extracted with petroleum ether. On gathering, the blooms can be placed directly in the drums of ether which acts as both a preservative and solvent for the volatile oil. In further processing the solution is concentrated and the solvent removed to leave a greenish mass, the 'concrete', which contains the volatile oil and from which the 'absolute' can be produced for perfumery.

Although *B. megastigma* is the only species of *Boronia* whose flower perfume is exploited, there are others with interesting aromatic oils in the leaves, and it is always worth crushing a leaf to check on the scent. One species, for example, has a high percentage of safrol giving it the scent of sarsaparilla, while another smells of both lemons and roses.

Distribution: W.A.

Cananga odorata   YLANG-YLANG, TOY-WOOD

Ylang-ylang is one of the best known perfumes of the Orient. It is obtained from the mature flowers of *Cananga odorata*, a large rainforest tree occurring throughout South-east Asia and extending to tropical Australia. It has been widely cultivated for the essential oil but no use seems to have been made of it in Australia. The trees have slightly drooping branches, pointed leaves to 20 cm long, and pendulous greenish flowers with six petals turning yellow at maturity.

The perfume is strongest at night and flowers must be gathered in the dark or at dawn to conserve the fragrance. Essential oil is extracted either with solvents or by steam distillation; the first fraction is the ylang-ylang perfume which is used in high-class perfumery and face powder, and is frequently mixed with other essences for better effect. The second fraction, known as cananga oil, is a lower grade product used for cheaper perfumes and soaps; blended with coconut oil, it is one of the components of Macassar oil which used to be so widely used as a hairdressing that our grandmothers had to protect their chairs from it with antimacassars.

Formerly the main production of the perfume was in the Philippines, plants being kept to shrub size for convenience of harvesting. A number of other countries have set up distilleries and a considerable industry has developed in some of the French colonies.

Distribution: Qld

OTHER PLANTS YIELDING ESSENTIAL OILS

A great deal of chemical investigation of the native oil-bearing plants has been carried out, often with results of great interest, at least to the chemists. While few of these oils have shown commercial application for reasons already given, there are some medicinal plants where the essential oil is the significant ingredient.

Some other scented oil-bearing plants of interest are:

Elionuris citreus (lemon-scented grass): lemon scent when crushed

Homoranthus flavescens: crushed leaves with scent of bananas

Lantana camara (lantana): oil distilled from leaves with odour similar to sage

Melaleuca linariifolia (a paperbark tea-tree): one variety with scent of nutmeg when fresh leaves are crushed

Guettardia speciosa: strong flower perfume extracted in India

SEED OILS

While essential oils in plants are regarded as secondary products, and have no immediately obvious function in the life of the plant producing them, there is another group of oils of great importance to the plant and to man who exploits them. These are the fixed oils, present in many seeds and in some fruits such as the olive; seed oils provide stored food which is used by the developing plant during germination. Such oils do not evaporate readily so are not normally extracted by distillation; they can be removed by pressing — the seeds are crushed, and the oil, sometimes present as 50% or more of the seed, runs out of the broken material. Domestically the oil is usually obtained by crushing the seeds, boiling with water, and skimming off the oil.

Seed oils can be extracted by either cold or hot pressing. The former process produces a higher grade product and is generally used for edible oils; the latter method gives a greater yield but the oil is usually darker and often with a characteristic odour. Pure oils are virtually tasteless and odourless; any taste or smell is due to small quantities of other materials present in the oil.

Oils that are solid at ordinary temperatures are known as fats — this is the only difference between the two, their food function being the same. Extraction of the relatively few solid or semi-solid plant fats is often carried out using solvents as the pressing process is inefficient.

Widely varying figures are given for the oil content of different seeds; this may be accounted for by variation in the samples tested, sometimes due to different conditions of growth. Often the discrepancy arises because some writers quote total oil content, while others quote the yield with a standard extraction method. In the case of a solid fat, percentage figures for extraction by pressing would be very much lower than if solvents were used.

Some of the seed oils are edible, and have been used particularly as cooking oils. Others, which are made inedible by traces of toxic or unpleasant substances, are used in various industrial processes; non-drying oils are generally useful as lubricants, while drying oils are often used in paints and varnishes. Virtually any oil can be used as an illuminant, being burnt in a lamp with a wick usually made of cotton.

The Australian flora, which is so rich in essential oil plants, is remarkably poor in seed oils. None has been exploited commercially in this country, although some, mainly found here as introduced weeds, are used overseas. In general it is thought more economic to import the oil, and in the case of the macadamia nut, the seeds are too valuable to be used for oil extraction.

Aleurites moluccana   CANDLE-NUT

This handsome tree of the tropical rainforests has found popularity in cultivation as an ornamental; the large, often lobed, leaves are covered when young with a white powdery substance which gives the tree a silvered appearance. Small white flowers are followed by rounded green fruits 3-4 cm in diameter. When the leathery wall of the fruit rots and flakes off or is removed, the woody shelled nut is seen to be wrinkled and slightly flattened, something like a walnut in appearance.

Kernels of the candle-nut contain about 60% of oil; this has been exploited in a number of countries, especially the Philippines and China. The oil is extracted by cold or hot pressing, the former giving a higher quality product. In the Philippines it is known as lumbang oil; a considerable industry has built up in that country, the oil being a good drying oil similar to linseed and tung oils. It can be used in making paints and varnishes, for illumination, for soap-making and as a wood preservative for boats; it was claimed, however, that when it was used in New Caledonia for the lamps in a lighthouse, it corroded the metal jets, even those made of platinum.

With the candle-nut the main difficulty is extracting the kernel from the shell. The shell is extremely hard, and the kernel firmly attached to it, so the nuts usually shatter on cracking. They can be split without shattering by heating on a fire or in an oven, or even in the hot sun for four or five days then cooling rapidly, usually with cold water. Unfortunately these processes usually brown the kernels and lower the quality of the oil. The only other methods are to extract from the crushed nuts without shelling, which gives a lower yield and a darker product, or to pick out the pieces of kernel from the broken nuts. Candle-nut oilcake is poisonous so unsuitable for fodder, but as it is high in nitrogenous content it makes a useful fertilizer for agricultural purposes.

Although the hardness of the shell is a disadvantage for oil extraction, it has been exploited in a Malaysian and Indonesian game, in which players attempt to break one another's nut with their own — a South-east Asian version of the English conkers. There is a specially hard-fruited race of candle-nut used for this game.

The nuts have such a high proportion of oil that they burn, although with a rather sooty flame. In some Pacific islands they were said to be used, strung together on a reed, in the form of a rough candle, giving rise to the common name. In Java they were ground to a paste with cotton and copra, and moulded around a bamboo splint to form a candle. This second method is fairly easy to copy: the nuts are ground with a pestle and mortar, mixed with about one-quarter their volume of cotton wool, and the wad pressed around a bamboo skewer such as those sold for preparation of satay. A candle about 1.5 cm diameter which we made from three candle-nuts burned for nearly twenty minutes.

In some parts of Indonesia the soot from the burnt oil is used cosmetically, as a substitute for kohl, for blackening the eyelids. The oil itself has been used as a hairdressing, while a mixture of the soot and oil was used by South Pacific islanders to make black patterns on mats.

Distribution: Qld

Argemone mexicana   MEXICAN POPPY

A warm-country weed of American origin, the Mexican poppy has been cultivated in some places for its attractive flowers. It has, however, become a widespread naturalized pest, especially in drier or well-drained positions such as riverside gravel banks. Its yellow poppy-like flowers are more attractive than the leaves which are so prickly that they found a use among the Chinese in stopping up ratholes.

In some countries where growth of the weed is prolific, it has been found worthwhile harvesting the seeds to extract the oil, which make up 30-40% of their dry weight. The oil is bitter and toxic, and is thought to have caused poisoning in parts of India when it was a contaminant of the widely used mustard oil. However it is suitable for use as a lamp oil, a lubricant and, if mixed with linseed oil, for paints. It has some reputation for protecting wood from white ants and borers.

The oil cake is poisonous, but useful as a fertilizer.

Distribution: All mainland States

Calophyllum inophyllum   ALEXANDRIAN LAUREL

The rounded green fruits of this handsome northern tree are about the size of a walnut; each contains a single thin-shelled seed. High yields of a green oil are obtained from the seeds, estimates varying from 50% to 75%. The oil is toxic and so unsuitable for eating or cooking, but is said to be excellent for soap-making. It has also been widely used for illumination.

Oil from this tree has various names in different areas — domba, poonseed, laurel nut, dilo and pinnay. It has been cultivated in plantations in the Philippines for oil production.

Distribution: Qld

*Carthamus lanatus   SAFFRON THISTLE

Safflower oil is a familiar product in many kitchens. It is obtained from the cultivated *Carthamus tinctorius*, a plant found occasionally as an escape from cultivation. Much more common is *C. lanatus*, a closely related species which is a widespread weed in Australia. The plant is similar to the Scotch thistle, with strong spines on the leaves but with yellowish green flower-heads.

Seeds of the saffron thistle yield a pale yellow oil similar to safflower oil. However the yield is only about 16%, which is about half that of safflower. It has been used in India, where it was found that the seeds should be harvested unripe as the oil content is reduced on ripening.

Distribution: All States

Cerbera manghas   DOG BANE

A tree of tropical shores, *Cerbera* has possibly been seen by more Australians in Singapore than in their native country, as it is a common flowering tree in that city. It is of moderate size with glossy leaves and clusters of white, somewhat twisted flowers; the tissues contain a milky latex.

The egg-shaped green fruits each contain two flattened seeds which are toxic and have been used to poison dogs. In Malaysia and Burma, oil is extracted by pressing the sun-dried seeds. This oil is poisonous as some of the toxin dissolves in it during extraction so it is not used in cooking, but can be used as a lamp oil; one writer, however, claims that the smoke is intolerable. In Burma the oil has been used as a hairdressing and insecticide, often both at the same time.
Distribution: Qld, N.T.

Cocos nucifera   COCONUT

Not known in Australia before the arrival of Europeans, the coconut is now well established and naturalized along our northern shores, and regarded as an essential ingredient of any tropical paradise. The nuts are sometimes eaten fresh in Australia, and occasionally the milk of green nuts is drunk, but compared with their use in neighbouring countries, they are largely neglected here.

Oil is extracted from copra, the dried flesh of the coconut, of which it may comprise up to 75%. Extraction is done on a commercial scale by expellers, which are continually rotating screw-presses in barrels with openings to allow release of oil. Domestically, the oil may be extracted from fresh coconuts by grating them finely, crushing in water and draining off the fluid which is then boiled; this causes the oil to float on the water layer and it can be skimmed off.

Coconut oil is solid at cooler temperatures, i.e. below 20°C, but in the tropics remains as a thick liquid. It has numerous uses; as an edible oil it may be separated into two fractions, one of which, a solid known as coconut butter, is used in confectionery. To some extent coconut oil is used in making margarine. The main industrial use is in the making of soaps and shampoos, but some is used as a base for ointments and hair-oils. So-called saltwater soap is usually based on coconut oil.
Distribution: Qld, N.T.

Ganophyllum falcatum

Although common in the coastal rainforests of the north, *Ganophyllum* is not a well-known tree, as it has no features to make it stand out in the huge diversity of species in that area. Trees are moderately sized with pinnate leaves 30-60 cm long, the individual leaflets being unequal sided. Small yellowish flowers are borne in usually large branched clusters in the axils of the leaves, the flowers being of separate sexes. The numerous fruits are rounded at the base, pointed at the tip, about 1.5 cm long, and contain a single seed.

Seeds of *Ganophyllum* yield a solid fat, rather than a liquid. This fat may be extracted by crushing the seeds and boiling them in water, when the oil rises to the surface. The product is not a commercial one, but is a traditional lamp fuel in some parts of the Philippines. It has also been used in making hard soap.
Distribution: Qld

Macadamia integrifolia, M. tetraphylla   QUEENSLAND NUT, MACADAMIA NUT

Macadamia nuts have the twin reputation of being the best nuts in the world for eating and the hardest nuts in the world to crack. The two species are subtropical rainforest trees restricted to Australia in their natural occurrence, but now cultivated overseas as well as in this country. *Macadamia integrifolia* has leaves in whorls of three and smooth-shelled nuts, while in *M. tetraphylla* the leaves are in fours and the nuts are rough. The kernels are similar.

Analyses have shown that the kernels contain up to 72% of oil of a high grade, equal to best quality olive oil. If ignited with a match, the nut burns for a couple of minutes with a strong flame. A candle made from a paste of the nuts as described for *Aleurites moluccana* will burn well enough; our experimental three-nut candle lasted for seventeen minutes with a strong clear flame. There is however, unlikely to be any commercial application for the oil as the nuts themselves are so valuable.
Distribution: *M. integrifolia*: Qld
                     M. tetraphylla: Qld, N.S.W.

Mallotus philippensis   KAMALA TREE

This small coastal rainforest tree is well known in India for production of kamala, used as a medicine and a dye (p. 72). The seeds also are of use as a source of oil, yielding 20-24% of a yellow-brown thick oil or semi-solid fat. Because of its high viscosity the oil is not easily extracted by pressing, and solvents must be used.

Kamala oil extracted with petroleum ether has been found in India to be a good substitute for tung oil in quick-drying varnishes and paints. A mixture of kamala oil and linseed oil in a 1:4 proportion is more rapid drying than double-boiled linseed oil, and produces an excellent gloss. The oil cake can be used as a manure, and has been combined with sawdust in manufacture of insulating boards and cork substitutes.

Distribution: Qld, N.S.W.

Pongamia pinnata   INDIAN BEECH

A gracefully arching tree of northern coastal rainforests, Indian beech is sometimes found as a street tree or garden specimen further south. Its white-and-purple sprays of smallish pea flowers are followed by short-beaked, flattened, woody pods each containing usually a single seed.

The seed oil is of value especially in India, where the tree is native and also widely cultivated. A yield varying from 27 to 40% of pongam oil is obtained on extraction; its chief use is in leather dressing but the oil can also be used as an illuminant, for soap-making, machinery lubrication and medicine. It has a bitter taste and is of no use for cooking purposes. The oil cake also is bitter and unsuitable for fodder, but having a high nitrogen content is useful as a manure.

Distribution: Qld

Ricinus communis   CASTOR OIL PLANT, CASTOR BEAN

The castor oil plant is a familiar weed in the warmer parts of Australia, and throughout the tropics. A large, branched shrub, almost a small tree, it has large, long-stalked, lobed, toothed, often reddish, leaves. There are separate male and female flowers on the same plant, the males showing a mass of stamens, and the females developing into a three-lobed spiny fruit. The seeds are smooth and mottled; their resemblance to a tick is responsible for the name *Ricinus*, this being a tick of sheep.

Ricinus is an important oil-seed crop in overseas countries, especially Brazil and India, but has not been exploited in

Australia. For cropping, selected varieties are used which give a good yield of oil and which are less inclined to 'pop' their fruit, casting the seed wildly in all directions; this habit is efficient for distribution of the species and occurs in the wild forms, but has obvious disadvantages in agriculture.

Oil can be produced domestically by crushing the seed, then boiling the meal with water and separating the oil layer. Commercially it is extracted by various means, usually at first by cold-pressing which gives the higher grade required for medicines, then a second, stronger cold-pressing, finally a hot pressing used for industrial purposes.

Apart from its medicinal use which takes a small proportion of the production, castor oil is used in over 200 products, including linoleum, patent leather, fly-paper, printing ink, polishes, hair-oil and cosmetics; it is a very good oil for leather dressing. A large amount is used in making Turkey red oil used in the textile and tanning industries. One of its important uses is as a lubricant for heavy machinery as it is a non-drying oil; it is used for aircraft engine lubrication as it does not solidify at temperatures well below the freezing point of water, yet remains viscous at high temperatures.

Castor oil is an excellent lamp oil and was extracted for this purpose by the ancient Egyptians, and by the Indians for many centuries; its replacement by kerosene has been relatively recent.

Seeds of castor oil are extremely poisonous, so the oil cake cannot be used for fodder; it makes a good agricultural manure. Sometimes the cake with some residual oil is used for fuel.
Distribution: All mainland States

Santalum acuminatum QUANDONG, SWEET QUANDONG

A small tree of inland areas, the quandong has pairs of grey-green leaves and small greenish flowers. The striking feature of the tree is its round, edible, shiny red fruit 2-3 cm diameter. Each fruit has a single deeply pitted stone.

Kernels of the seeds are very rich in oil. Maiden reports that they can be speared on a stick or reed to make a candle with a clear flame, in much the same way as *Aleurites moluccana*.
Distribution: All mainland States

SOME OTHER SEED-OIL PLANTS

Barringtonia asiatica, B. racemosa: seeds of both said to yield oil of use for illumination

Carallia brachiata (carallia wood): Seed oil used as cooking oil in parts of India

Entada phaseoloides (matchbox bean): fatty oil reported used in Sunda Islands for illumination

Hernandia ovigera: seed kernels containing about 34% of reddish brown oil, said to be used in the Philippines as hair restorer and for lamps

H. bivalvis (cudgerie, grease nut): kernels reported to contain 64% of oil

*Lactuca serriola (prickly lettuce): grown in Sudan for seed oil used in the same way as sesame oil

Terminalia catappa (Indian almond, sea almond): kernels containing 50% of edible oil, which does not keep well. Suggested as substitute for almond oil

Urtica (stinging nettle): oil expressed from seeds said to be used as an illuminant in Egypt

Ximenia americana (tallownut): solid fat extracted from seeds used as a substitute for ghee in parts of India

2

Plants for Tanning

'Tan me hide when I'm dead, Fred.'

Rolf Harris

ANIMAL HIDES provide man with a valuable and readily available material for shelter, clothing, vessels, harness, shields, armour and many other purposes. However, unless tanned to make leather, this material is subject to rapid decay and is relatively inflexible when dry. Communities in most parts of the world have discovered independently or learnt from others the use of various materials in the process of tanning which greatly increases the durability, water resistance and flexibility of skins. The discovery of tanning was probably one of the early developments in man's progress towards civilization. There is archaeological evidence of tanning in Europe as early as 10,000 B.C., and leather goods have been found in Egyptian tombs of 5000 B.C. Origins of the use of tannins are lost in antiquity and will never be known for certain, but it has been plausibly suggested that perhaps water leaking from the bark roof of a shelter on to animal skins below improved their quality, and indicated to an observant owner the possibility of deliberate improvement. Or, perhaps, changes in a skin accidentally lying in a small pool with certain leaves and twigs led to primitive experimentation and the eventual development of the tanning process. There seem to be only two references to the tanning of skins by the Australian Aborigines (pp. 54-5).

Tanning is often taken to include the use of materials other than tannins in the preservation of skins. Commercial tanning today uses not only tannins of vegetable origin but also various synthetic agents as well as chromium and aluminium salts. These mineral salts are, in the main, much faster tanning agents than tannin, the process taking a matter of hours or days rather than weeks or months with tannin. Even in earlier times there was some tanning by smoking, treating with oil, or rubbing with alum-containing rocks. However, until recent times, most tanning processes have used tannins of vegetable origin.

Tannin is not a single chemical. Rather, the term covers a complex group of substances which precipitate gelatin and produce insoluble material with gelatin-producing substances, thus converting them to leather. In heavy leather, the weight of tannin combining with the protein may be about half the weight of the dry skin.

With some iron salts tannins produce a blue-black or green-black colour, and such stains appearing on the blade of an axe are generally a good indication that the material being chopped has a high tannin content. The stains developing beside mild steel nails in new wood also are evidence of the presence of tannins. This reaction with iron salts is used in one of the simplest tests for the presence of tannins; boil some of the plant material in water, filter and add a few drops of 5% ferric chloride solution; in the presence of tannins a blue-black or green-black colour is produced. However, pigments of the flavone group may also produce a green colour; the presence of tannins can be confirmed by the precipitation of a 10% solution of gelatin dripped into the plant extract. The formation of coloured compounds with iron salts is the basis of the one-time inclusion of tannins in some inks, a use which has now almost entirely disappeared.

Tannins are very widely distributed in flowering plants and conifers although absent from some groups. A few families such as Leguminosae (containing the wattles), Rhizophoraceae (containing some mangroves) and Myrtaceae (containing gum trees) are particularly notable for species rich in tannins.

The function of tannin in the life of a plant is a matter of some uncertainty. One suggestion is that tannin is simply a waste product of the plant's metabolism. Another is that it may be involved with the formation of cork and in the development of anthocyanin (red and blue) pigments. Growth of some fungi is inhibited by fairly low concentrations of tannin and this has led to the suggestion that the presence of tannins may give the plant some protection against fungal attack. It has recently been found that if the bark of the Monterey pine (*Pinus radiata*) is mixed with the soil, the tannin inhibits infection of roots by *Phytophthora cinnamomi*, the soil fungus which has caused serious destruction of both native and introduced tree species in Australia.

Although tannins may occur in any part of the plant, often the greatest quantities are found in bark and in insect galls, and it is mostly from these parts that tannin has been extracted. In the tea plant, which is a species of *Camellia*, a high tannin content in the leaf contributes to the quality of the beverage prepared from the partly fermented and dried leaves. Unripe fruits commonly contain tannin which is astringent and is responsible for the 'fur' which is felt on the tongue after eating, for example, unripe bananas or persimmons. As fruits ripen, the tannin content is often reduced, in some cases by combination with something else to produce an insoluble substance, in others by being surrounded by some insoluble material so that it is not detected when eaten.

In prehistoric times when small groups tended to be largely self-sufficient, each family group probably did its own tanning. Likewise, in the early days of Australian settlement, when there was a great deal of enforced self-sufficiency, many of the pioneers tanned the skins of their domestic animals or of native animals which they had shot or trapped. Kangaroo skin makes particularly good leather. Fortunately for the early settlers, Australia is particularly well endowed with tannin-producing species, and there must have been few parts of the continent where some suitable source of tannin could not be found. Australia eventually became an exporter of tanbark, but today most of the tanning material used here is imported.

Although the main use of tannins has been and still is in tanning of skins, some is used in the drilling of oil wells to control the viscosity of the drill mud. Some was formerly used in the preservation of fishing nets, and a small amount went into the pharmaceutical industry; at one time tannin was widely used in the treatment of burns but has been discarded for this purpose.

Tannin is a soluble material and is fairly readily extracted by soaking the plant material in the water. It is usually the practice to break up the bark or other material into small chips to facilitate this process. The bark may be sold to tanneries in the chip form. However, particularly where transport costs are an important consideration, the tannin may be extracted near the source of collection by heating chipped or pulverized material in copper vessels and then evaporating the solution to a dark solid containing 50% or more of tannin.

For home tanning, innumerable recipes have been devised, many of them using mineral salts such as alum and common salt rather than tanbark since, in the main, these materials are more readily available, the mixtures can be prepared more precisely, and the tanned product is produced more quickly. Preparation of heavy leather using tannins may require several months but light skins may be tanned within a few days, and some people may be interested to try the process. The practice, on a home basis, is very much a matter of trial and error since tanbarks from different species vary so much in their tannin content, ease of extraction and type of leather produced.

As a rough guide only, the following could be tried as a basis which may need modification depending on the source of bark and the nature of the skin. Dry and break up the bark as finely as practicable, certainly into pieces no broader than 2 cm. Place the fragmented bark in a plastic, earthenware or copper container and just cover with water. After twenty-four hours pour off and keep the liquor and again cover with water, removing the second liquor after a further twenty-four hours. Place the thoroughly washed fresh or soaked skin in the second liquor for two days, then in the first or stronger liquor for three days or longer, in each case agitating the liquor whenever convenient to aid even penetration of tannin into the skin. Small pieces can be cut from the edge of the skin to determine whether the tannin has penetrated to the mid layers and thus whether the process is complete. The skin is then washed and, as with all tanning processes, must be dried slowly and worked at frequent intervals, by pulling it, flesh side down, back and forth over a smooth pole or towel rail so that the finished product will be soft and supple.

In addition to those noted below there are numerous species recorded as having been used occasionally, particularly during the nineteenth century. Most of these are of little or no commercial interest, and were used simply because they were locally available.

Acacia

With over seven hundred species in this country, the genus *Acacia* is better represented in Australia than in any other continent. Although mimosa is a common name for the group in some countries, the accepted name in Australia is wattle. This common name has an interesting origin. In the early days of settlement at Port Jackson some of the buildings were of wattle and daub construction in which a rough lattice or framework was covered with plaster. A tree commonly used for this purpose was *Callicoma serratifolia* and this consequently was given the name of wattle. Its fluffy, globular heads of flowers bore a superficial resemblance to those of many of the acacias and gradually the name wattle came to be transferred to this group.

Wattle bark is one of the most important tannin sources in the world and, particularly in earlier times, the local product was extensively used in Australian tanneries. Barks of most wattles, probably all, have some tannin, and numerous species were used in the earlier days of settlement. However there are only a few which are available in sufficient quantity and have a high enough tannin content to make them a commercially practicable source of tannin.

At one time up to 20,000 tonnes of wattle bark were exported annually from Australia. However, since about 1905 there has been, in general, a decline in production here. There has been widespread destruction of wild trees by stripping, and loss of large areas by clearing for grazing or agriculture; although some plantations have been established in New South Wales, Victoria and South Australia they have not met with great commercial success. These factors, together with the high labour costs of stripping the bark, have resulted in a decline in the tanbark industry in Australia and an increase in imports, mainly from South Africa.

Several Australian wattles have been introduced into South Africa, and one in particular, *Acacia mearnsii (A. mollissima)*, is grown there in extensive plantations totalling about 400,000 hectares. As far as is known, this species was first introduced from Australia to Natal by John Vanderplank, a retired schooner master. He used the plants as shade trees rather than as a source of tanbark; their attractive appearance and rapid growth ensured that the species became widespread in South Africa.

Particularly in Natal, *A. mearnsii* finds climatic conditions favourable. It grows rapidly in the absence of some of its natural enemies which were left behind in Australia, although some of the pests of acacias native to Africa have not been slow to colonize the immigrant. These favourable circumstances, coupled with the availability of cheap labour, have given it a great advantage as a source of tannin over the same species grown in its homeland, and made South Africa a major tannin producer. Since about 1916 the main export has been the extract, as this is more economical for shipping and provides a more satisfactory uniform product. In the plantations, trees can be cropped from six years, but delaying stripping for a couple of years enables more use to be made of the timber. It is desirable, both in terms of labour saving and quality of product, to treat the bark green, i.e. within forty-eight hours of stripping. Stripping may be done at any time except during dry weather when the bark is difficult to remove.

Although South Africa is the main producer of wattle bark from Australian species, *A. mearnsii* is widely grown and exploited to varying extents in other countries including Kenya, Tanzania, Zimbabwe, Indonesia, the Philippines, Sri Lanka and Brazil.

Several species of *Acacia* have been used as tanbark sources in Australia but *A. mearnsii* and *A. pycnantha* are the most important. Distribution: Some species in all States

A. mearnsii (A. mollissima)   BLACK WATTLE

For many years this widespread and important species was known as *A. mollissima*, a name well suited to it because of its softly hairy leaves. *A. mearnsii* is one of the species with bipinnate or 'ferny' foliage and fragrant flowers in globular yellow heads. Under good conditions it grows rapidly and a growth rate of approximately 8 m in four years has been recorded.

This is the species in widespread cultivation in South Africa. Distribution: Qld, N.S.W., Vic., Tas.

A. pycnantha   GOLDEN WATTLE

A. pycnantha is a small tree bearing leathery, sickle-shaped phyllodes with a distinct midrib, and flowers in golden balls.

The tannin content of its bark is high, in some cases exceeding 40%. It is widespread in South Australia where, in the past, it has been an important source of tanbark, the annual yield from natural stands reaching over 5000 tonnes. A small amount of extract was made from the tops and leaves. Now, however, the industry there has practically disappeared.

The species has been grown in plantations, and in Victoria more than 2000 hectares were at one time established.

Distribution: N.S.W., Vic., S.A.

Bruguiera RED MANGROVE

This mangrove bears some resemblance to the more common *Rhizophora* but lacks the prop roots of that plant. Its roots loop up above the mud at intervals to form the so-called knee roots which gradually thicken into excrescences a good deal more knobbly than the roughest of human knees. The bark has a satisfactory tannin content and in various tropical countries has been exploited along with *Rhizophora*. It seems to have been little used in Australia except at one time by fishermen for tanning their nets. As with *Rhizophora* bark, the leather produced with this species has an undesirable red colour.

There are four species of *Bruguiera* along the tropical and subtropical coasts, *B. gymnorhiza* being the commonest.

Distribution: Qld, N.S.W., W.A. N.T.

Callitris AUSTRALIAN CYPRESS PINE

In general appearance the Australian cypress pines closely resemble the northern hemisphere cypress (*Cupressus*) with a neat conical form and small, closely appressed leaves. However, the two are easily distinguished on leaf arrangement, the leaves of *Cupressus* being opposite in pairs on the twigs, those of *Callitris* being in whorls of three.

All but one of the fourteen species in this genus are restricted to Australia. Most have been shown to have appreciable quantities of tannin in the bark. The most notable tannin-bearing species is the black cypress, *C. endlicheri* (*C. calcarata*), which is widely distributed in eastern States. Its tannin content varies considerably between different localities, figures between 10% and 36% dry weight of bark having been recorded.

The tannin is less readily extracted from *Callitris* bark than from wattle bark, and fine grinding is needed for successful extraction. Unfortunately, *Callitris* tannin produces a fairly strongly coloured red leather. For sole leather this is no great drawback, but for some other purposes the strong colour is a disadvantage which can be partly overcome by mixing the *Callitris* bark with that from some other species.

White cypress, *C. columellaris* (*C. glauca*), is found in all mainland States with representatives from coastal sand dunes having usually deep green foliage, while inland specimens often are of a distinctly greyish appearance. Tannin content is lower than in *C. endlicheri*, varying from 11% to 23%.

Distribution: *C. endlicheri*: Qld, N.S.W., Vic.
            C. columellaris: All mainland States

Casuarina   SHE-OAK

Species of *Casuarina* occur in all States of Australia, most going under the common name of she-oak or some variant of it. The trees are always easily recognized by the slender jointed branchlets with leaves reduced to a whorl of minute scales at each joint.

Although none is likely to be of any commercial interest, the bark of several species contains sufficient tannin to be useful to amateur tanners. *C. equisetifolia* has been used for tanning in India and Ceylon. The coastal she-oak common on coastal sand dunes in eastern tropical and subtropical Australia is a variety of this species.

Distribution: Some species in all States

Eremophila longifolia   WEEPING EMU BUSH, BERRIGAN

In a report in 1888, J. H. Maiden, Government Botanist of New South Wales, stated, 'The aboriginals in the interior used the bruised leaves of this and some other species of *Eremophila* for tanning the skins of the male wallaby in order to make water bottles.' Unfortunately, no details are given of the method used.

The only other reference to Aboriginal uses of tanning materials is by W. E. Roth who notes the preparation of skin bags for carrying water by Aborigines of western Queensland. These bags were made from tanned skins of kangaroo, pademelon or possum, or occasionally of dingo. In one account Roth mentions 'bloodwood gum' as being used for the tanning. This may have been the long-fruited bloodwood, *Eucalyptus polycarpa*. However, in another very similar account he notes coolibah gum moistened with water as the tanning agent. It is not clear whether both these eucalypts were used or whether one report is the result of misidentification.

Distribution: All mainland States

Eremophila oppositifolia EMU-BUSH

Emu-bush is a shrub of dry country. Its slender, hairy leaves are hooked at the tips and are usually borne in pairs on the stem. The flowers are cream with pink tinges and have the form of a slightly curved bell.

It has been reported that the Aborigines used the bruised leaves of this plant for tanning wallaby and other skins for carrying water, but we have been unable to locate further information on this practice.

Distribution: N.S.W., Vic., S.A.

Eucalyptus GUM TREE

There are over five hundred species of *Eucalyptus* in Australia, many of them with appreciable quantities of tannin in bark or wood. However, for various reasons such as unavailability of supplies, difficulty of extraction, and high colour of the leather produced, most are not practical sources of tannin on a large scale.

The species noted below are those which have been commercially exploited and some of those which seem to have potential.

Eucalyptus alba WHITE GUM

This is an ornamental species notable for its beautiful smooth trunk, often white but sometimes marked with salmon or grey patches, and covered with a powdery bloom. It is widespread along the east coast north of Rockhampton, and also in the Northern Territory and the north-eastern part of Western Australia. *E. alba* can be distinguished from the ghost gum(*E. papuana*) which occupies much the same range and has a white trunk, by its relatively broad leaves, usually not more than three times as long as broad, those of *E. papuana* being usually more than three times as long as broad.

The bark of this species seems to have been little used for tanning but certainly has possibilities for this purpose. Although analyses of bark collected in Queensland showed only about 7% tannin, material from the Kimberleys yielded approximately 30%. The tannin was easily extracted with water and produced a good quality, light-coloured leather.

Distribution: Qld, W.A., N.T.

Eucalyptus astringens   BROWN MALLET

Although the timber of the brown mallet, which resembles that of American hickory, has been used for tool handles, the common name has no connection with that use. It is, rather, a corruption of the Aboriginal name 'maalok'.

Three mallets, the brown, *E. astringens*, blue, *E. gardneri*, and white, *E. falcata*, have been used commercially as sources of tanbark. All are smooth-barked small trees confined to semi-arid regions of south-west Western Australia. It is the brown mallet which has been the main source among these three, the other two species contributing relatively small quantities of bark which have been sold indiscriminately with that of brown mallet. This latter species has a remarkably high tannin content, in fact one of the highest of all commercial tannin sources; moreover, the tannin is readily leached out of the bark. Based on a moisture content of 10% in the bark, average figures for tannin content are in the vicinity of 45%, while exceptionally a yield of about 56% has been found. The bark is usually removed during winter or spring when it strips easily.

Leather produced with mallet bark has an acceptable light colour but, unfortunately, becomes reddish on exposure to sunlight. This disadvantage can be largely overcome by blending with other tanning materials.

The mallet bark industry began near the beginning of the present century and quickly boomed so that more than 20,000 tonnes of bark were produced in 1905, much of it being exported to Germany. However, the exploitation was widespread and de-destructive, with little consideration for the future. So thoughtless was the destruction that finally even saplings of a girth of 10 cm were being stripped. Still more trees were lost when forests were cleared for agriculture, others through fire to which the plants are

fairly susceptible, and after the peak year production fell away rapidly. It is not surprising that few mature trees remain. Regulations now prevent the stripping on Crown land of trees less than 38 cm girth, and some thousands of hectares of artificially regenerated forest have been established.
Distribution: W.A.

Eucalyptus calophylla MARRI, RED GUM

Marri is restricted to the south-western corner of Western Australia. The glossy green leaves which are responsible for the *calophylla* in its name make it an attractive tree. Although most specimens have cream flowers there is a pink form which has been planted extensively as an ornamental subject. Marri is one of the bloodwoods and has the bark characteristic of many species of this group: persistent, more or less fibrous and flaking off in small pieces. As is common among bloodwoods there is an abundant production of kino in the wood. This kino is a solution of numerous substances which exudes into and over the bark following injury and there evaporates to form a dark red shiny solid. The material contains considerable quantities of tannin. Although the bark was used by the early settlers for tanning it was largely discarded when the brown mallet was found to produce a superior result.

Nevertheless the tannin from marri has been investigated, and there were even experiments to determine whether or not the trees could be tapped for their kino much as rubber trees are tapped for their latex. Unfortunately, the results of these studies were not encouraging. Marri bark has the disadvantages that much of the tannin in the kino is not readily released in water, and that leather tanned with this material has a deep red colour. The first disadvantage can be overcome by heating the kino with 3-6% sodium metabisulphite, and the second partly overcome by blending with lighter coloured tanning materials.
Distribution: W.A.

Eucalyptus diversicolor KARRI

The Karri of the far south-west of Australia is best known as the tallest tree in Western Australia and as a source of very high quality hardwood which is second only to jarrah in importance.

Karri bark also is potentially valuable since it contains up to 22% tannin which can produce a leather of good quality and colour. Since the tree is of such importance in the timber industry, relatively large quantities of bark are available as a by-product.

Distribution: W.A.

Eucalyptus gomphocephala   TUART

Tuart is a rough-barked species occurring in a very narrow strip inland of the coastal sand dunes from roughly Busselton to a little north of Perth. The bark is poor in tannin but the wood contains 8-10% and is a potential source of the material. Tuart timber is heavy, strong and durable and too valuable to be cut for its tannin but faulty logs, branches and sawdust could be used.

Distribution: W.A.

Eucalyptus wandoo   WANDOO

The wandoo is distinguishable from most other smooth-barked eucalypts by lacking a sock of rough bark at the base of the trunk. It occurs mainly in a band inland of the jarrah forests of Western Australia. The bark contains 13-21% and the wood 8-13% tannin, and both are used for extraction. Trunks, larger branches and bark are mechanically rasped to a pulp, and the tannin leached out by a pressure-cooking method. The tannin solution is then evaporated to a solid containing 60-63% tannin. This material has been sold and exported under names such as myrtan and wandoo. Up to four factories in Western Australia have processed the wandoo and produced up to 8500 tonnes annually. Wandoo tannin is usually blended with other tannins and is particularly suited to the preparation of sole leather.

Distribution: W.A.

Rhizophora stylosa   SPIDER MANGROVE

Rhizophora is one of the most distinctive of the mangroves, being immediately recognized by its stilt or prop roots which emerge from the trunk like flying buttresses.

Bark and bark extract from several species in various parts of the world are widely used, and are important tanning materials.

Tannin content of the bark varies considerably but is usually in the range 20-40%. It has good 'weight-giving' properties and is particularly suitable for the preparation of heavy leather. However, it has the disadvantage of producing a highly coloured red leather which is rather hard and thick grained. It is not usually a practical proposition to bleach mangrove tannin but if mixed with other tanning materials the colour can be reduced to acceptable levels for many purposes.

The bark has been exploited in most tropical areas in which this mangrove grows, and appreciable export trades have developed in eastern Africa and the Malaysian region. At one time the bark itself was exported but today's trade is mainly in the extract. The early method of extraction was to boil the bark in vats and then to concentrate the solution by boiling to a syrupy consistency, when it was run into moulds to set into a hard solid. The modern method of extraction is to soak the bark in water heated by steam pipes and to evaporate the solution under vacuum; this method produces a better extract of a lighter colour.

Cutch is a name which has been widely used for the mangrove extract. This term was originally used for a similar material prepared from the wood of *Acacia catechu* in India and Burma; gradually, as the *Acacia* product came to be replaced by the mangrove material, the name was transferred to the latter and is mostly used in this sense today.

Large areas of *Rhizophora* occur with other mangroves on sheltered shores of tropical and subtropical Australia. Analyses of bark from Queensland have shown a tannin content of up to 34%. Although some concessions have been granted for the collection of mangrove bark in Queensland the material seems to have been little exploited and no export trade has been developed. The main use of the bark in Queensland seems to have been by fishermen who, before the advent of nylon, used *Rhizophora* and other mangrove bark for tanning their fishing nets.

In some countries even the leaves have been used locally in tanning but it is doubtful whether they have ever been used in Australia.

The minor nature of the exploitation of mangrove bark in Australia is something for which we can probably be thankful today. It is now realized that mangroves play an important part in coastal marine food chains and in sheltering marine animals at various stages of their development, and that the economic value of the forests in this role would far outweigh the value of the bark which could be harvested.

Distribution: Qld, N.S.W., W.A., N.T.

3

Vegetable Dyes

'Strike me pink!'

Australian expression

THE FIRST DYES that man used were of plant origin. For thousands of years he obtained blue, yellow or red colours from plants such as woad, safflower and henna. Some of the earlier products of dyeing have survived until the present day in coloured cloths from Egyptian tombs and similarly preserved remains.

When European settlement began in Australia, amongst the other investigations into natural resources there was a search for dye plants which could be used in this country and even exported to Britain. The Aborigines had no use for such materials, and on the whole the investigations and experiments of the settlers were disappointing. In 1856 the first synthetic dye went into manufacture in England, and before long synthetics had largely replaced the traditional vegetable dyes. There was no longer much point in looking for local dyes.

In recent years there has been a revival of interest in natural dyes from plant sources; this is associated especially with the renewed activity in crafts such as spinning and weaving. Many people find satisfaction in completing the processing of wool from fleece to garment, and this of course includes dyeing the wool, which can be done either in the fleece or in the yarn. Natural dyes complement the home industry perhaps better than do the synthetic dyes.

Very many of our native plants have been used successfully for dyeing on a craft or domestic basis. Almost any plants are worth trying; an extract of the leaves or other desired material is prepared by boiling it gently in water, then straining out the pieces. The wool to be dyed is first prepared by scouring, which is virtually a thorough washing and rinsing; it is then placed in a mordant, frequently a solution of alum in the proportions of 100 g alum with 30 g cream of tartar to 20 litres of water, and boiled gently for about an hour. A mordant enables the colour of the dye to be fixed in the fibres. The damp wool is then simmered in the dyebath for about half an hour. Detailed procedures and quantities for dyeing are available in several handbooks on dyeing. By varying the mordants, different colours may result from the same dyestuff; mordants used include various salts of chrome, tin, copper and iron as well as alum, and sometimes combinations of these. Hundreds of our native plants, especially *Eucalyptus* and *Acacia* species, have been used in this way. There is little point in listing all of these in this chapter; the species discussed are those of particular interest or historic use, including some of those traditionally used in Asia.

Acacia   WATTLE

As wattles are such a handsome feature of the Australian flora, and more than 700 species are known throughout the continent, it is not surprising that a number of them have been used in dyeing. Species ranging from the inland mulga, *Acacia aneura*, to the widely cultivated Cootamundra wattle, *A. baileyana*, have been used with a variety of mordants to produce a range of colours. Most often the product is yellow or gold, but depending on the part of the plant used and the choice of mordant, greens, browns or greys may result. Although it would be expected that flowers used as the dye source would always give a yellow or gold colour, this is not necessarily so; for example, *Acacia cunninghamii* flowers used with different mordants produced gold, brown, fawn, green and grey colours in wool.
Distribution: Some species in all States

Adenanthera pavonina   CORAL WOOD

Coral wood is one of our relatively few deciduous native trees. Found in this country only in the far north, it has been seen by many Australians in South-east Asia and India where it also occurs, and where it is frequently cultivated. A moderate-sized tree of the legume family, it has small yellow flowers something like those of *Acacia* but borne on stalks in a branched cluster. The pods are very distinctive, being about 15 cm long, strongly twisted when ripe, and splitting to reveal scarlet seeds.

The heartwood is red and produces a red dye, although this is not very much used for colouring cloth. However a paste prepared from the powdered wood is used in India for applying castemarks.

Distribution: Qld

Alstonia constricta   BITTER BARK, QUININE TREE

Widespread in subcoastal New South Wales and Queensland, *Alstonia constricta* is a small tree often found in close groups because of its suckering habit; it is a common species of softwood scrub. The leaves are narrow and pendulous, opposite, usually shiny although there is a hairy form; the leaf margins are pale, almost ridged, distinctly wavy so that a leaf will not lie flat. If the stem or leaf is broken a milky juice, the latex, is exuded. Small creamy yellow flowers are produced in a much-branched cluster; the flowers have a distinct waist which gives rise to the *constricta* part of the name.

This small tree is known for the extremely bitter taste of the bark. Possibly this led Baron von Müller to test the bark for its quality as a dye. He exhibited cotton and woollen materials dyed with bitter bark at the Intercolonial Exhibition of Melbourne in 1866. The cloths were dyed in different shades of yellow.

Distribution: Qld, N.S.W.

Baloghia lucida   SCRUB BLOODWOOD

Dark green, leathery, opposite, elliptical leaves make the scrub bloodwood one of the more easily recognized of the rainforest trees. On injury to the bark, a clear sap oozes out and turns red on exposure to air, hence the common name. No use seems to have been made of this exudate in Australia but, at one time, it was used in Norfolk Island as an indelible paint for marking bags and blankets and for staining the timber of the Norfolk Island pine.

To collect the sap, a cut was made vertically in the bark; it was reported that about a quarter of a litre could be obtained in twelve hours.

Distribution: Qld, N.S.W.

Calanthe triplicata   CHRISTMAS ORCHID, SCRUB LILY

This large ground orchid can be recognized even when not flowering by its tuft of broad lily-like leaves up to 90 cm long. Around Christmas time the sprays of pure white flowers appear on long stems; individual flowers are up to 3 cm broad and have a lobed lip. Plants are relatively common in some of the east coastal rainforests.

If the flowers are bruised it will be noticed that they turn blue. Both flowers and leaves contain indican, the same substance as is in indigo and woad; the bruising allows a chemical change to take place, transforming the colourless indican into the blue indigo. This is of theoretical interest only; no one would wish or be legally permitted to gather native orchids for the sake of extracting a small amount of blue dye.

Distribution: Qld, N.S.W.

Casuarina   SHE-OAK

Although much more important in tanning, the bark of some casuarinas can be used as a dye. Bark of *C. equisetifolia* has been used in India and some of the South Pacific islands as a fabric dye, producing a light reddish drab. The Australian variety of this species is the coastal she-oak, *C. equisetifolia* var. *incana*; it does not seem to have been used at all, but would probably produce a similar result.

Recently Australian craft dyers have used the foliage of *C. cunninghamiana*, the river oak, to produce gold, green and grey colours in wool with the use of different mordants.

Distribution: *C. equisetifolia* var. *incana*: Qld, N.S.W., N.T.
            C. cunninghamiana: Qld, N.S.W.

Ceriops tagal   ORANGE MANGROVE

The orange mangrove can often be picked out from a distance in the mangrove swamp by the yellow-green of its foliage. Often a smaller tree than the rhizophoras and avicennias which it accompanies, it has a strongly buttressed trunk with large lenticels — cork-filled air pores — in the bark. As in the related spider mangrove, the seed germinates while still on the tree, producing a curved projecting root 5 cm or more long.

Although now replaced largely by synthetic aniline dyes, the bark of this mangrove is one of the traditional dyes of Indonesia and Malaysia, having been used a great deal in batik-making. Used in varying proportions with indigo, colours from blue to black are produced; with different methods, browns and purples can be obtained. The bark extract has also been used for dyeing matting.

Distribution: Qld, N.T.

Clitoria ternatea   BUTTERFLY PEA

A woody climber with showy blue or white pea-flowers about 3 cm long, this plant is a tropical species which has escaped from cultivation in north Queensland and has become naturalized in the rainforest areas.

The blue colour of the flowers can be used to colour cloth but the dye is very impermanent. A more interesting use is the Malaysian practice of boiling the flowers with rice, for the rice takes up the blue colour. This blue dye can be used as a substitute for litmus as it changes colour in reaction to acid or alkali.

In India, a blue dye has also been obtained from the seeds. The juice of the leaves has sometimes been used in Indonesia as a green food colouring.

Distribution: Qld

Cudrania cochinchinensis (Maclura cochinchinensis) COCKSPUR THORN

A stoutly spined shrub, cockspur thorn produces long arching canes which either form untidy thickets or scramble over other plants; it is found in light rainforest, frequently along creek banks in east coast districts. The elliptical leaves have a short sharp point, and bear in their axils unpleasant spines which assist in the scrambling habit. Separate sexes of flowers are produced in small globose heads and those on the female plants develop into rounded orange compound fruits about 1.5 cm diameter.

This species occurs throughout south-east Asia and as far as India and Japan. It was known, especially in Malaysia and Indonesia, as a traditional dye. A considerable trade in the heartwood took place from Thailand and Malaysia to Java where the dye was one of those used for dyeing batik.

To use the plant, the inner part of older trunks is chipped and soaked overnight in water then boiled. The extract is strained, alum is added and the cloth to be dyed is boiled in the mixture, a yellow colour being produced. The dye has been used in combination with others to produce red or green.
Distribution: Qld, N.S.W.

Drosera whittakeri   SCENTED SUNDEW

An attractive small plant of damp places in southern States, the scented sundew has the sticky insect-trapping leaves characteristic of *Drosera*. The leaves form a red-tinged rosette from which arise single, short stalked white flowers nearly as large as the cluster of leaves; these flowers are sweetly perfumed.

D. whittakeri has a subterranean tuber 1-2 cm diameter, found 7-10 cm below the surface. Beneath the thin black skin of the tuber is a small amount of a brilliant red colouring matter which has been used to produce 'beautiful tints' in silk when used with various mordants. Although the plant is plentiful in some areas, the tedious procedure of digging for the tubers, the relatively small yield, and the fact that obtaining the dye entails destruction of the plant, makes this dye source unlikely to be exploited.

D. peltata, the pale sundew, is reported from India to provide a dye in a similar way; in this species a yellowish-brown pigment has been obtained and used to dye silk a fast rich brown.
Distribution: *D. whittakeri*: Vic., S.A.
            D. peltata: All States

Eclipta prostrata (E. alba)   WHITE TWIN-HEADS

This widespread tropical herbaceous plant has small white daisy-like flower heads produced usually in pairs in the axils of the opposite leaves. The plants are erect or prostrate; they frequently root at the nodes, and bear short stiff hairs.

Leaves of this plant have been used to produce a black hair dye in India, Malaysia, Indonesia and Brazil. In India the leaves are boiled with sesame or coconut oil and the preparation is used to anoint the head, while variations on this procedure are used in other countries. The leaves have also been used in India in tattooing.
Distribution: Qld, N.S.W.

Eucalyptus GUM TREE

Those who are interested in obtaining dyes from our native flora need not go beyond the genus *Eucalyptus* to obtain a range of colours from reds, yellows, browns, greens and greys to black. Most of the research in this area has been done in the last decade or so by Mrs Jean Carman who has experimented with more than 160 species of eucalypt, and used a variety of mordants to produce this array of colours in wool samples. She obtained a blue-grey colour using chips of the wood of the blackbutt, *E. pilularis*, and mainly light greys and browns from wood and bark of other species. Leaves are more convenient to obtain, and in general produce colours of greater interest; with different mordants applied to leaves of any one species, Mrs Carman obtained several different colours from the one batch of dye. *E. obliqua*, the messmate stringybark, with six mordanting methods gave yellows, greens and greys, while *E. diversicolor*, the karri, with four different mordants gave orange, yellow, green and golden-brown.

Some dyers obtain pleasing fast colours using eucalypt leaves without a mordant; results include a soft pinkish-tan by boiling wool directly with leaves of *E. melliodora* yellow box. With over 500 species of *Eucalyptus* in Australia, there is still ample scope for experiment.

Distribution: Some species in all States

Eucalyptus macrorhyncha RED STRINGYBARK

A coarsely stringy-barked eucalypt of the dry forests and savannah woodlands, *Eucalyptus macrorhyncha* occurs especially on the inland slopes of the Great Dividing Range in New South Wales and Victoria. It is a comparatively tall tree in favourable conditions, reaching about 30 m in height. As the common name implies it has a persistent, fibrous, dark reddish-brown bark.

This eucalypt is an important drug plant but it was as a source of dye that it first came to serious attention. Late in the nineteenth century H. G. Smith isolated a yellow crystalline substance from the leaves; he named it 'myrticolorin' and suggested it as a commercial possibility to replace dyes such as fustic which were imported at considerable expense. The colour produced by the dye was similar to khaki. However, with the widespread use

of synthetic dyes myrticolorin production did not become practicable. Following the discovery that this dye and rutin were identical, and the development of rutin as a useful drug, the idea of using the species commercially as a dye completely disappeared but it is still of interest as a craft dye. Mrs Carman has used it with an alum mordant to produce an olive green.
Distribution: N.S.W., Vic., S.A.

Haemodorum coccineum   BLOODROOT

This grass-like plant of the north has clusters of reddish flowers and a red-coloured underground stem which was used by the Aborigines as a source of dye. In north Queensland, Roth recorded the use of the roots (presumably the underground stem) for staining twine prepared from plant fibres. Species of *Haemodorum* have also been used to dye *Pandanus* leaves in the Northern Territory; in this case the stem base was used.
Distribution: Qld, N.T.

Hardenbergia violacea   FALSE SARSAPARILLA, CORAL PEA

A widespread twining or trailing plant of east coastal areas, the false sarsaparilla is conspicuous in the spring with its attractive violet pea-flowers. Sometimes found in great profusion, the flowers have been used as a source of dye; when mordanted with alum, they give a grey-blue colour to wool.
Distribution: Qld, N.S.W., Vic., S.A.

*Indigofera tinctoria   COMMON INDIGO, INDIAN INDIGO

Even a superficial student of history knows that when Julius Caesar invaded Britain in 55 B.C. he found a tribe who, amongst other uncivilized habits, painted themselves blue with a plant called woad, *Isatis tinctoria*. The blue dye obtained from woad was indigo, which occurs naturally in a number of plants, including several species of *Indigofera*.

Indigoferas are pea-flowered shrubs with pinnate leaves and cylindrical pods. Several species occur in Australia; *I. tinctoria*, which has become a naturalized weed, is the traditional Indian source of indigo, although it is not the most important of them; its distinguishing features are its red flowers and small pinnate leaves up to about 7 cm long, with nine to thirteen leaflets.

The dye is not present in its blue form in the growing plant, but is prepared by fermentation of the leaves. To extract it, the freshly picked leaves are steeped in warm water to ferment for 10-15 hours, then the greenish-yellow liquor is drained off. For commercial production, or for preparing a supply of the dye to keep, the liquor is then whipped up with paddle-wheels or whatever similar device is available; the reaction with oxygen produces the blue dye in the form of an insoluble residue which sinks to the bottom; it can then be collected and dried for storage. For use in dyeing, it must again be dissolved using an alkaline solution. The cloth is dipped in the virtually colourless liquid, and allowed to dry in the air, when the blue colour reappears in the fibres. It may be necessary to dip the cloth a number of times to obtain the required depth of colour.

Indigo is regarded as a dye better suited to cotton and rayon than to wool; a mordant is not needed in the process, which is referred to as vat dyeing. The blue colour produced is fast to light.

It is possible to dye cloth directly with *Indigofera* leaves, as has been done in Malaysia. The freshly cut leaves are soaked in water for some hours, then the cotton cloth is added with a little slaked lime. In this method the blue dye is deposited directly in the fibres.

Indigo is the dye traditionally used for Chinese cotton clothing; the enormous amounts used in that country help to make it the most widely used dye in the world. As the name suggests, production took place first in India from where the dye was exported even in the times of the ancient Egyptians; mummy clothes have been found dyed with it. The American Indians independently discovered how to produce the colour from indigoferas growing in that continent.

Synthetic indigo was first marketed near the end of the nineteenth century and has almost entirely replaced the natural product, although there were brief revivals of cultivation in India during the two World Wars.

In recent times synthetic indigo has been used in large amounts to dye denim cloth for jeans.

Distribution: Qld, N.T.

Indigofera australis   AUSTRALIAN INDIGO

Australian indigo is a widespread common shrub, varying greatly in height from about 30 to 250 cm. The pinnate leaves have nine to twenty one leaflets; short sprays of lilac-coloured pea-flowers are produced in early summer, and are followed by narrow cylindrical pods.

Of the native species of *Indigofera*, none has been significant as a dye source. In the early days of European settlement here, vigorous attempts were made to find native dyes, and the Australian indigo was one of the earliest plants investigated. Governor King, to whom the plant was recommended, had experiments carried out, but became convinced that 'all that could be produced from it was a dirty substance'. However, later experimenters must have had greater success; there is a record of good quality indigo having been prepared from this species at Bathurst in the first half of the nineteenth century.

Our experimental direct dyeing of cotton with *I. australis* produced a colour in keeping with Governor King's description, but with a distinct blue tinge in the 'dirty' product.

Distribution: All States

Lichens

Lichens are frequently grouped with mosses by the layman, who regards them all as small green plants growing on rocks and logs. There is, however, a vast difference between the two: mosses are plants with small but distinct leaves, whereas lichens, although having definite forms characteristic of the species, are non-leafy. Lichens take various shapes: they may form a closely adherent crust over the surface on which they grow; they may develop as a partly-attached, rather frilly sheet; they may even develop a small 'shrubby' branched form, or a long drooping stringy shape as in *Usnea*, the old man's beard, familiar in moist mountain forests. In colour they may be green, grey, yellow-green, orange or black. Each lichen is actually an association of two simple plants, an alga and a fungus, the two growing together with mutual benefit.

These remarkable plants yield amongst the most interesting of the vegetable dyes. They may be extracted by boiling with water in a similar way to the other plants described, and provide a variety of rich colours by this method; if wished, the wool or silk can be boiled gently with the powdered lichens for direct dyeing. A mordant is not necessary, although some dyers prefer to use one to obtain a deeper colour. The range of colours is usually in the yellows, browns and reds, although some are known overseas which give a pinkish colour.

A number of lichens have been used from remote times in a different dyeing process, the preparation of orchil. By this means rich reds, purples and blues are obtained from lichens which in their growing state give no hint of such colours. The plants are powdered or crushed and allowed to ferment in a strongly ammoniacal solution, which traditionally was putrid urine. The fermentation and reaction with acids in the lichen produced the colour which could then be varied between red and blue by altering the acidity of the solution. Different unrelated lichens can be used for the process, whose success depends on the presence of particular lichen acids. The famous royal purple, which was originally produced from a marine shellfish, was later prepared from lichens, while the distinctive character and odour of genuine Harris tweed is said to be due to the particular method of dyeing.

A number of Australian lichens contain lecanoric acid, the acid responsible for the orchil dye. To use them, it is not necessary to follow the original method in complete detail: the modern process is to soak the lichen in a 1:2 mixture of household ammonia and water in a glass vessel with a lid for 3 or 4 weeks, stirring frequently to allow oxygenation, and adding more ammonia if necessary. To find whether the lichen collected has lecanoric acid, a small amount can be soaked in diluted ammonia for a couple of days in a small jar with a lid to see whether any colour is produced. In one experiment we soaked separately four lichens removed from a fallen branch of narrow-leaved ironbark, *Eucalyptus crebra*, and found that three of these produced the red colour. As most people have difficulty in identifying lichens, this trial-and-error method of selecting material to use is probably as good as any. In general, the flat or frilled forms, rather than shrubby ones, are most likely to be of use.

Lichens are slow-growing plants, and heavy collection may

easily result in their permanent disappearance from an area. For this reason, lichen dyeing is not recommended to be done in any quantity. Most of the colours they produce are also obtained from eucalypt leaves which are more rapidly renewable. For those who wish to experiment it is, however, frequently possible to gather a considerable amount from fallen branches.

The one lichen, or group of lichens, which many people can recognize is *Usnea*, the old man's beard, with its pendulous grey-green tufts. *Usnea* does not contain lecanoric acid so will not give a red dye. It will, however, give a brown; if the lichen is soaked in dilute ammonia for a few days the dye produced is a richer colour than if it is used for direct dying without ammonia.

Distribution: Some lichens in all States

Mallotus philippensis KAMALA TREE

A rainforest tree widespread in tropical Asia from India to southern China, *Mallotus philippensis* extends through Papua to Australia, being a common tree of coastal forests as far south as the Northern Rivers district of New South Wales.

Although it may grow to a moderately large tree about fifteen metres tall, kamala is found frequently in a shorter, bushy form. The leaves which are leathery, smooth above, and softly hairy beneath, are produced on relatively long stalks. Young shoots usually have a rusty appearance due to the presence of red-brown hairs. Male and female flowers are produced on separate plants; flowers of both sexes are small and are produced in short branched clusters at or near the branch apices. Fruits are, of course, found only on female trees; they are three-lobed, about 1 cm in diameter, and contain three seeds; the capsules have a red, mealy covering of small hairs some of which are glandular, some minutely star-shaped and non-glandular. This powdery layer is the kamala, one of the traditional dyes of India used for silk and wool. The dyestuff is removed from the fruits by brushing or beating, or by shaking in water, when the red powder falls to the bottom as a sediment.

Kamala is insoluble in cold water, but soluble in alkali and some organic solvents, to give a deep red solution. For dyeing, a boiling alkaline bath with 4 parts of kamala, 1 of alum and 2 of sodium carbonate is used, the dry ingredients being mixed first with a little sesame oil. The flame colour produced fades some-what in sunlight but is fast to washing. Kamala dye has also been used to some extent for colouring foods and drinks.

Due to the small yield of dye for the amount of work entailed in preparation, production of kamala is no longer a commercial proposition, being largely replaced by synthetic dyes. However, for those who prefer the natural dyestuffs, *Mallotus philippensis* is a worthy addition to their store.

Distribution: Qld, N.S.W.

Morinda citrifolia   GREAT MORINDA

This small tropical tree, with bright green, large, elliptical leaves and egg-shaped, compound, odorous fruit, is common along Australia's northern shores and throughout southern Asia.

Young roots of morinda yield a very good dye, and the plants were cultivated on a considerable scale, especially in India and some of the Indonesian islands. The dye is obtained only from young roots of not more than 13 mm diameter; the bark of the root yields a red dye and the wood itself a yellow one, so the resulting colour depends on the relative proportions of the two. For good results a mordant must be used, when red, purple and chocolate brown colours may be obtained; the dye is satisfactory for wool, silk and cotton.

The use of morinda has been virtually abandoned in Asia with the introduction of synthetic dyes, but it was formerly used in large quantities for batik dyeing in Indonesia, and in India was used for carpets as well as textiles such as turbans.

Roots of several other species of *Morinda* have been used as sources of dyes in tropical Asia. Two which extend to northern Australia are *M. umbellata* and *M. reticulata* both of which are reported to yield yellow dye; the latter was used by Aborigines to colour their apron belts.

Distribution: Qld, N.T.

Olearia argophylla   MUSK DAISY-BUSH, MUSK TREE

The musk tree is one of the few members of the daisy family to grow to the size of a tree, reaching at times nearly 10 m tall; the finely toothed leaves are silver beneath, and numerous daisy-like heads are produced in large branched clusters.

It is recorded that Joseph Bosisto, the Melbourne pharmacist, obtained a brilliant sap-green dye from the tree, but unfortunately details of his method are not given. Craft dyers using the standard procedure with an alum mordant, have dyed wool yellow with the leaves.

Distribution: N.S.W., Vic., Tas.

Omalanthus populifolius　　　　　NATIVE BLEEDING HEART

A small well-shaped tree common along rainforest margins, the native bleeding heart, as its name suggests, has roughly heart-shaped leaves (poplar-shaped, according to the scientific name); before they fall the leaves turn a brilliant red which stands out at a distance.

Use of this plant as a dye could probably be described under 'Methods Nobody Wants to Try', but it is of some interest. In Indonesia a black dye was prepared by boiling together bark and leaves; the material to be dyed, which could be cotton, matting or cane, was soaked in the preparation, either before or after being buried in mud for an unspecified period. Presumably metallic salts in the mud provided a mordant so that the dye would take.

Distribution: Qld, N.S.W.

Piptoporus australiensis　　　　　CURRY PUNK

Wood-rotting fungi which produce dry, thick fruiting bodies jutting as brackets from living or dead trees are known colloquially as punks. The curry punk is distinctive amongst them as, although smooth and white above, it has a rusty undersurface penetrated by numerous shallow pores where the spores are produced, and a strong musty aroma; fruiting bodies are up to about 14 cm broad and 6 cm high. The species is found on fallen logs, often on ones that have been partly burnt.

When fresh, the punk exudes an orange-yellow juice which has been used as a dye for raffia and similar materials.

Distribution: Qld, N.S.W., Vic., Tas., S.A., W.A.

Pisolithus tinctorius　　　　　HORSE DUNG PUFFBALL

This puffball is almost world-wide in its distribution. Its common name gives a good idea of its appearance, enhanced by the fact that it frequently grows in the hard-packed soil at the side of the road. In contrast to other puffballs, the interior is divided into a honeycomb of small spore-filled chambers at maturity; as the puffball wears away the chambers of spores are successively exposed for dispersal.

Varying in size up to 15 cm or so in height, the puffball also varies in colour, being white and shiny when immature, becoming brown or black on ageing. The spore mass is usually yellowish brown, sometimes darker. It was formerly used as a fabric dye in southern Europe, a practice which caused it to be named *tinctorius*.

Distribution: All States

Polygonum aviculare   WIREWEED, KNOTWEED

Polygonums in general are known as smartweeds; they are acrid, astringent herbs with a reputation as minor stock poisons. The genus can usually be recognized by the tubular sheath around the stem above the base of the leaf. *P. aviculare* is a prostrate species with elongate wiry stems; the small flowers are followed by nuts which are dull because of minute wrinkles on the surface.

This introduced herbaceous weed is reported to yield a blue dye similar to indigo. In France it has also found some use as a substitute for mulberry leaves in feeding silkworms.

Distribution: All States

Polygonum barbatum   SMARTWEED

This tropical species is also reported to yield 'a good blue dye' similar to indigo. It is an erect species with small spikes of flowers followed by shining nuts; the sheaths at the leaf bases are distinctly hairy.

Distribution: Qld

Rhizophora   SPIDER MANGROVE

Mangrove bark is well known for tanning but can also be used for dyeing. In coastal Malaysia it was employed locally to give a deep brown or black colour. The leaves, too, have been soaked in water and the liquor used with alkali to give a reddish brown or black colour to cloth.

Maiden recorded that the sap, which is blood red, was used by the Fijians as a hair dye; mixed with the sap of *Hibiscus moschatus*, it was used to paint pottery. A minor use for the bark was to use a decoction to dye poor quality bêche-de-mer a deep red-brown so that they could be 'blended' with more valuable types for sale to the Chinese.

Distribution: Qld, N.S.W., N.T.

Semecarpus australiensis   MARKING-NUT, TAR TREE

The true marking-nut tree is an Indian species, *Semecarpus anacardium*, cultivated in a number of tropical countries; its economic use arises from the acrid blistering black juice, produced in the wall of the fruit. This resinous juice, when mixed with lime water, will make indelible marks on cloth. If used with alum and lime, it provides a dark grey dye. The Australian species is very similar with a blistering irritant juice in the wall of the fruit frequently streaking other parts of the plant with black. It does not seem to have been used for the same purposes as the Asian species, but from the close similarity it would be expected to have a similar action. Difficulties of handling the fruit, however, make it a somewhat unattractive proposition.

Distribution: Qld, N.T.

Thespesia populnea   PORTIA TREE, INDIAN TULIP TREE

A tree of tropical shores, *Thespesia populnea*, with its dark green heart-shaped leaves and yellow hibiscus-like flowers, has a strong resemblance to the well-known cottonwood, *H. tiliaceus*. In the latter species the leaves are hairy on the undersurface, those of *T. populnea* being hairless; the fruits are distinctive, *Thespesia* having a flattened-globose leathery fruit which does not split open at maturity, while that of *Hibiscus* splits into five or ten segments.

The wood of *Thespesia* has been used in dyeing; it gives an orange-yellow extract which has been employed to dye wool a deep brown, but is reported as useless for silk. Flowers and fruits were used in India to give a yellow water-soluble dye producing brown and yellow-brown tints in wool and silk.

Distribution: Qld, N.T.

*_Urtica Urens_ STINGING NETTLE

Urtica Urens is a European nettle which has become naturalized almost all over the world, including Australia, where it occurs from time to time in gardens and farm areas which may be rich in nitrogen. The plants are usually less than 60 cm tall with toothed, short, opposite leaves; stinging hairs are borne on both surfaces of the leaves, and on the stems.

A much-maligned yet very useful plant, the stinging nettle could be included in almost every chapter of this book. To use for dyeing, a decoction of the shoots is made by boiling in water; this has been used as a 'beautiful and permanent' green dye for woollen cloth in Russia. A yellow colour is produced by boiling the roots with alum; as well as being used in cottage industry dyeing of wool, the yellow was used in Russia to colour eggs on Maundy Thursday.

Distribution: All States

OTHER NATIVE PLANTS OF MINOR USE AS DYES

Alphitonia excelsa (red ash, red almond): timber containing a glucoside which, with chromium or aluminium mordants, dyes cloth red-brown or orange-yellow

Amanita muscaria (fly agaric): formerly used to produce a red dye

Auricularia polytricha (hairy jew's-ear fungus): reportedly used by Chinese as a dye

Cadellia pentastylis (solidwood): red dye obtained from the wood

Calophyllum inophyllum (Alexandrian laurel): fruit yielding a yellowish dye

Casearia tomentosa: bark used as adulterant for kamala

Cassia pruinosa: red dye from bark

Crotalaria pallida (rattlepod): said to be used in Madagascar to produce a black dye

Dianella sp.: blue berries said to be used by Aborigines as permanent blue dye

*_Fumaria officinalis_ (fumitory): flowers reported used to make a yellow dye for wool

Intsia bijuga (Johnstone River teak): wood reported to yield a purplish dye

Ludwigia octovalvis: black dye for cloth obtained from leaves on the island of Truk

Mallotus discolor: powder from seed capsules gives a bright yellow dye

Nauclea orientalis (Leichhardt tree): wood and bark reported to yield a good yellow dye

Petalostigma pubescens (quinine berry): bark said to give a brownish yellow dye

Rauwenhoffia leichhardtii: bark said to yield a brownish red dye

Rhodamnia trinervia: bark said to yield a black dye used in Malaysia

Zieria smithii (turmeric tree, stinkwood): yellow inner bark of tree suggested by Maiden for use as dye

4

Gums, Resins and Kinos

'. . . he swiftly made a pair of fine moustaches out of
dried grass and stuck them on with wattle gum.'

The Magic Pudding, Norman Lindsay

WHEN INJURED, the stems of many plants exude a clear, sticky fluid
which accumulates as a glistening globule or trickles slowly down
the stem, forming stalactites shedding occasional drops from their
ends. As the exudate ages it hardens, in some cases becoming
almost glassy. Three groups of substances, gums, resins and kinos,
make up these clear exudates and although superficially similar
they differ in chemical nature and in other ways.

Gums are commonly soluble in water although some swell in
water forming a gel rather than dissolving completely; they do
not soften on heating and are insoluble in common organic solvents. *Resins*, on the other hand do not dissolve in water but are
soluble in various organic solvents such as alcohol, ether and
some oils although not all are soluble in all of these solvents. They
soften on heating. In some cases, the exudate consists not of the
single substance but of a mixture of the two, sometimes with an
oil added also, so that it is possible to speak of gum-resins, oleo-
resins and oleo-gum-resins. Some of them are cloudy or milky
rather than transparent. *Kinos*, at least as known in Australia, are
complex mixtures of tannins with various other substances, and
vary considerably in their solubility in water and other solvents.
However, in spite of the differences between these three substances they have all commonly gone under the name 'gum'.

Another type of exudate is latex, a milky fluid containing a
mixture of substances such as resins, oils, proteins, sugars and
caoutchouc, this last mentioned being the source of rubber. Although some Australian latex-bearing plants have, in the past,
been suggested as a source of rubber, none seems likely to be of

any large-scale commercial value.

Today, synthetic materials have displaced or reduced the importance of many of the plant exudates for which man has found uses throughout recorded history and no doubt in earlier times. Gums have been used particularly in adhesives but also in foodstuffs, pharmaceuticals, cosmetics, paints, inks and matches. The chief use of resins has been in varnishes but they have figured also in waterproofing, adhesives, paints, linoleum, primitive torches, incense and embalming. Perhaps the two resins which are most widely known, at least by name, are those mentioned in the Bible, frankincense and myrrh, both valued greatly in ancient times for their fragrance. No Australian resins have achieved such fame but, to the Aborigines, some of the indigenous resins must have been at least as important as the Biblical resins were to the ancients.

Acacia
WATTLE

Probably the best known gum is gum arabic, derived from species of *Acacia*, particularly *A. senegal*, in arid regions of northern Africa, Arabia and India. The trees are commonly tapped by peeling off strips of bark to induce the flow of gum. This pale, high quality gum dissolves readily in water giving a clear, sticky mucilage, and has been an article of commerce for over 4000 years.

Many of the Australian species of *Acacia* exude gum from the trunks and branches, usually at the sites of injuries caused by insects. The exudate appears as glistening globules or rivulets which gradually harden as they dry. Some of the gums from Australian acacias are pale amber in colour, and commonly these are almost flavourless or with a slightly sweet taste. Some such gums were an important food for the Aborigines. Others have a much darker colour, and generally these contain tannin making them too astringent to be eaten. While a few species such as *A. dealbata* yield a gum which is claimed to rival gum arabic in quality, on the whole the gums of Australian members of the genus are of poor quality, either because of the presence of excessive tannin and colouring matter or because they do not dissolve completely in water but swell considerably, forming a gel. As a rough generalization, the better gums are produced by trees in

△ *Thespesia populnea* (Portia tree, Indian tulip tree) pp. 76, 98, 209

▽ *Lichen (parmelia)* p. 70

Rhizophora stylosa (spider mangrove) p. 58 △

Mallotus philippensis (kamala tree) pp. 43, 72 ▽

the drier regions. *A. microbotrya* from Western Australia is an example of one such species which has been exploited.

In the early days of settlement it was hoped that *Acacia* gum would become an important export from the colony and in 1827 it was suggested that gum collecting would be a useful occupation for 'the very idle children, and the hordes of lazy fellows who hate hard work'. However, because of lack of overall high quality and probably because of competition from areas where labour was cheaper, the vast *Acacia* flora of Australia has never been an important commercial source of gum.

Distribution: Some species in all States

Agathis   QUEENSLAND KAURI, KAURI PINE

The kauri pine is represented in Australia by three species confined to Queensland: *A. robusta* in the Wide Bay district and northern Queensland; and *A. atropurpurea* and *A. microstachya* found only in northern Queensland. *A. robusta* is probably the best known species and is the one most often seen in cultivation. It is a tall tree with smooth bark shed in flakes, and commonly has a long length of main trunk without lateral branches, even when growing in isolated positions.

Injury to the bark often leads to a copious flow of milky latex-like material which is an oleo-gum-resin. The oil can be removed from this exudate by steam distillation and consists almost entirely of pinene or oil of turpentine. It was at one time suggested as a source of this material but was never exploited. In fact, there seems to be no record of the resin, 'kauri gum', having been used in Australia, although the resin of species from other areas has formed an important item of commerce. In New Zealand, most of the resin collected was in what was generally described as a semi-fossilized condition. This resin, in pieces varying in size from small flakes to lumps up to 45 kg, was dug from the ground on the sites of present and former kauri forests. The better grades were used for high quality spirit varnishes and the poorer grades for linoleum.

A similar resin was found in Queensland towards the end of the last century but the finder did not publicize the site of his discovery.

In South-east Asia and Irian Jaya, kauri pines are tapped for their resin but labour costs and the availability of synthetic substitutes make it unlikely that the Australian species will be exploited in this way.

Distribution: Qld

Angophora   APPLE

Species of *Angophora* often go under the general name of 'apple'. There is a strong resemblance to eucalypts but the flowers lack the cap or operculum which distinguished those of *Eucalyptus*. *Angophora* trunks produce a kino which, at least superficially, resembles the kino from some eucalypts. That from *A. costata* has been used medicinally as an astringent to a limited extent in the same way as *Eucalyptus* kino, while *A. floribunda* (*A. intermedia*) kino was once used by fishermen to tan their nets.

Distribution: Qld, N.S.W., Vic.

Araucaria cunninghamii   HOOP PINE

The hoop pine, well known as a timber tree (p. 108), exudes a milky oleo-gum-resin from injuries in the bark. On ageing, the material often becomes yellowish. Usually, only small quantities are produced; the largest quantities are formed on the stumps of felled trees. The exudate seems to have no commercial value but the Aborigines of the Moreton Bay district used it as a cement which 'was warmed and worked up with the fingers'.

Distribution: Qld, N.S.W.

Callitris   AUSTRALIAN CYPRESS PINE

One of the well-known resins of commerce is sandarac, obtained from *Tetraclinis articulata*, a small cypress-like tree of Algeria, Morocco and southern Spain. This resin was used in spirit varnishes, particularly on metal surfaces, but was also put to several other interesting uses. These included the manufacture of pounce, a powdered material used for preparing the surface of parchment for ink; as incense; for varnishing pills; and as a temporary filling for teeth, for which purpose an alcoholic solution of the resin was mixed with cotton wool.

In Australia, species of the closely related genus *Callitris* (p. 53) produce a very similar resin, variously known as cypress pine resin or Australian sandarac, which could be used for similar purposes. The resin exudes from injured points of the bark as clear, glistening drops sometimes known as cypress tears. Gradually the drops harden and, due to a fine cracking of the surface, the tears take on a powdery or mealy appearance.

Quantities were, from time to time, exported to Europe but there seems to have been no well-developed industry based on the product. Possibly the fact that the tree did not respond well to tapping, as *Tetraclinis* did, militated against the success of the enterprise. However, as late as 1907 the Government Botanist of New South Wales was urging collection of this resin and claiming, 'Seventy shillings per hundredweight leaves a handsome sum to the collector when all expenses are paid . . . '.

Two interesting local uses for the resin are recorded. In the Snowy River area, settlers mixed the resin with fat to make their candles; this may have been an unusual, soft resin reported from some *Callitris* in this area and said to resemble Manila elemi, a soft resin which has been used in the Philippines for torches. Aborigines in Victoria used the resin to consolidate the lashing used to join a hardwood head to the reed shaft of a spear.

Distribution: Some species in all States

Canarium muelleri   QUEENSLAND ELEMI TREE

Manila elemi is a useful oleo-resin obtained by tapping the bark of *Canarium luzonicum* in the Philippines. It is a valuable substance used in various products such as lacquers for metal, inks for non-paper surfaces and perfumes; some was once exported to China for making transparent paper for window panes. *C. muelleri* (Queensland elemi tree) is a large rainforest species of northern Queensland producing an oleo-resin with considerable resemblance to Manila elemi, but no use seems to have been made of it by Europeans other than as a 'healing agent for cuts, sores, and chronic ulcers'. However, the Aborigines of the Bloomfield River collected it for use as a cement and bartered it with tribes that had no other supply.

The exudate from *C. australasicum* (mango bark) also was used as a cement, either after warming and pounding or after boiling with stingray fat in a baler shell.

Distribution: *C. australasicum* — Qld, N.S.W.
                C. muelleri — Qld

Eremophila fraseri   BIRO BUSH

Eremophila is a large genus of shrubs and trees, with curved two-lipped flowers, confined to arid regions of Australia. *E. fraseri* is a small shrub which provided a cementing material for those Western Australian Aborigines who lived between the coastal areas where *Xanthorrhoea* resin was available and the inland areas where spinifex resin was used. The leaves, which are covered with sticky material, were placed on a flat stone and covered with another stone to press them down. Further leaves were added, and eventually the resinous material collected on the lower stone and could be melted for use.
Distribution: W.A.

Erythrophleum chlorostachys   IRONWOOD, COOKTOWN IRONWOOD,
                                              CAMEL POISON

The ironwood which the Aborigines of northern Australia used for weapons and drone pipes (p. 121) provided them also with a resinous cement. Roots of a young tree were cut into convenient lengths, the outer sticky layer removed, roasted lightly over a fire, and hammered between stones greased with the oily seed of *Calophyllum inophyllum*. Alternate roasting and pounding eventually produced a lump of resin.
Distribution: Qld, W.A., N.T.

Eucalyptus   GUM TREE

When William Dampier landed on the shores of Western Australia in 1688 he noted that in some species 'the gum distils out of the knots or cracks that are in the bodies of the trees'. This is the first reference to the substance which later gave the genus *Eucalyptus* its generalized common name. This material is now called kino and is a complex mixture of tannins and other substances of which gum is not one. The composition of kino and the ease with which it dissolves in water varies considerably between different species.

   Kino often exudes at points of injury as a syrupy red fluid which darkens on exposure and eventually becomes rigid and brittle so that it may powder between the fingers when removed from the trunk.

The well-known Botany Bay kino exported to England at least as early as 1810 came from *E. fibrosa* (often known as *E. siderophloia*) but for a long time the export material has come from *E. camaldulensis* in New South Wales and Victoria. Kino was obtained by tapping cavities in the trees, diluting it with water to allow filtration, then evaporating to dryness. In Europe it was used mainly in pharmaceutical preparations for diarrhoea and dysentery and for throat gargles. A small amount was used in the French wine industry. However, the industry has been a declining one, and even about twenty years ago the annual production was down to not much more than 200 kg. The tannins present in the kino produce a deep green or blue colour with some iron compounds; a minor use for this among the early settlers was to boil some kino with a little water in an iron vessel to produce a makeshift ink.

The Aborigines seem to have made little use of *Eucalyptus* kino although there is a record of the use of *E. gummifera* in New South Wales: 'Fishing lines were soaked in the sap to prevent them from fraying.'

Distribution: Some species in all States

Flindersia maculosa   LEOPARDWOOD

Leopardwood is one of the distinctive small trees of inland areas in Queensland and New South Wales. For several years it grows as a spiny intricate shrub but eventually an erect trunk arises from this tangle. The bark is shed in irregular, rounded flakes giving the trunk an attractively dappled appearance.

A clear, amber gum exudes freely from damaged areas of the trunk and this formed an item of food for the Aborigines. It dissolves completely in water and forms a good quality adhesive mucilage which could probably be used commercially if it could be collected economically in sufficient quantity.

Distribution: Qld, N.S.W.

Grevillea striata   BEEFWOOD

Beefwood is a rough-barked, small to medium tree, widespread in arid regions of eastern Australia. The tough, ribbon-like leaves are 15-45 cm long.

A resin sometimes exudes from the trunk and it is possible that the Aborigines utilized this as a cementing material. However, according to W. E. Roth, they obtained their supply from the roots of young trees. Lengths of these roots were heated over a fire and the outer sticky bark scraped off. This material was then tied in a sheet of tea-tree bark and baked for about ten minutes. The small pieces of resin were pressed together and alternately pounded between two stones greased with *Calophyllum* seeds and heated on a stick over the fire until the mass reached the required consistency.
Distribution: Qld, N.S.W., N.T.

Leschenaultia divaricata

Leschenaultia divaricata is a small shrub 30-60 cm high with fan-shaped yellow flowers, growing in some of the most arid regions of Australia. Sand grains are firmly cemented to the roots, apparently by some resinous material. The Aborigines extracted this resin by heating roots in the ashes and rubbing the material on to a stick as it exuded. It was then used as a cementing material for attaching stones to handles in making implements.
Distribution: N.S.W., S.A., N.T.

Melicope octandra   DOUGHWOOD

This is a small rainforest tree of the orange family with opposite, trifoliate, oil-dotted leaves. It provided the main cementing material for Aborigines in the Tully district of northern Queensland. The resin was collected from one or two-day old splits in the bark, warmed, pounded, mixed with charcoal and pounded again.
Distribution: Qld, N.S.W.

Myoporum platycarpum   SUGARWOOD

Sugarwood is a small tree with pendulous branchlets, narrow slightly toothed leaves, and groups of small white flowers in the leaf axils. Stems sometimes produce small nodules of resin quite different from the manna for which the tree is well known. This resin was collected by the Aborigines and mixed with fat to produce a wax-like substance which was applied to the twine used for attaching stone tomahawk heads to handles, and spear heads to hafts.

Probably because of the resin it contains, the dry timber burns very readily giving off a pleasant perfume. At one time it was exported to Asia as a sandalwood substitute.
Distribution: Qld, N.S.W., Vic., S.A., W.A.

Sloanea australis   MAIDEN'S BLUSH

The maiden's blush, named for the pinkish tinge in its timber, is a rainforest tree sometimes producing gum from the trunk. Its only recorded use was as a stiffener for straw hats in northern New South Wales many years ago.
Distribution: Qld, N.S.W.

Tieghemopanax murrayi (Polyscias murrayi)   PENCIL CEDAR

One of the fairly easy trees to identify in the rainforest, *Tieghemopanax murrayi* is distinctive in often reaching a height of about 6 m before branching so that, with its crown of large pinnate leaves, it has a somewhat palm-like appearance. The resin exuding from damaged parts of the bark was alternately heated and pounded by the Aborigines to prepare it for use as a cement.
Distribution: Qld, N.S.W.

Triodia   PORCUPINE GRASS

Triodia irritans and *T. pungens* are both known as porcupine grass or spinifex, although the latter is the generic name of a different grass and therefore probably better avoided for *Triodia*.

Porcupine grasses are prominent plants of much of the desert region of Australia. They are harsh, rigid, spiky grasses forming dense hummocks, often a metre or more in diameter, sometimes ring-shaped in the case of old colonies. The base of the leaf which forms a sheath round the stem exudes small globules of resin, very sticky when fresh but drying hard. This material was highly valued by the Aborigines who used it as a cement to fasten spear heads to hafts, and for other similar purposes.

Spencer, in his *Wanderings in Wild Australia* described the Aboriginal collection of the resin in this way: 'They chop the stalks up into little pieces, burn them and, in this way, make lumps of black resin, that sets hard but can easily be softened again by heat.' One might expect such treatment to destroy much of the resin but perhaps a very gentle fire would leave some of it intact. The method of preparation described by Chewings in *Back in the Stone Age* seems less destructive of the resin: 'The women root out the stems with a yam-stick, and with it beat them on a flat bare rock if such be near, or failing that, on a hard bare patch of ground. The stems are thrown away and the chaff and most of the dirt are winnowed from the gum. The residue is melted by holding a fire-stick above it and pressing it into a lump. This is then worked up on a stone by ironing it out, doubling it, and so forth, with another hot stone, until a pitch-like substance results that will set like a rock. This is the substance with which they fix handles on stone axes and stone knives, set cutting-stones in adzes, fasten spears, and use for many other purposes: for example, plugging holes in their water troughs. As it can be softened by heat it can be pressed into any shape. The natives carry a reserve stock about with them.' In the Warburton Range, the practice was to set fire to the clump of grass after which the women winnowed out the minute globules of resin from the ashes.

According to one early report, the Aborigines of the Napier Range, inland from Derby, obtained the resin from the roots of *Triodia*. A sample of this resin was said to have a disagreeable and persistent odour.

Distribution: All mainland States

Xanthorrhoea   GRASS TREE, BLACKBOY, YACCA

The grass tree is a most distinctive plant, confined to Australia, and one of the plants which gives what is often considered to be the typically Australian appearance of considerable areas of the countryside. Although there are some species with no above-ground stem, several have stout trunks, either simple or sparsely branched, which in large specimens reach a height of 4 m. At the end of each branch is a dense crown of long narrow leaves arching outwards and eventually drying to form a grass skirt enveloping the top of the trunk. When these leaves fall they leave behind their broad bases which form an armour-like layer over the soft, fibrous core. Bushfires sweep through most grass tree country at fairly frequent intervals quickly disposing of the grass skirt and leaving the trunk charred, so that the term blackboy, applied particularly in Western Australia, is an appropriately descriptive one. However, the leaf base armour is an effective protection, charring only slowly; and the grass tree is often the first species to show signs of renewed growth after a bushfire.

Cementing the leaf bases together is a brittle red or yellow resin which, in some cases, accumulates on the outside of the trunk in rounded lumps up to 5 cm across. There is little doubt that this grass tree resin, sometimes called grass tree gum, has been the most important Australian resin for both Aborigine and white man.

For the Aborigine the resin was a very important cementing material, used for attaching stone axe heads to wooden handles and spear points to hafts. For this purpose it was sometimes mixed with native beeswax or with fine sand and dust. Careful heating would soften the material sufficiently to allow it to be moulded. It was a useful item to trade with those tribes who did not have access to the plants.

The resin has been collected widely by the white man in Australia, the main supplies coming from *Xanthorrhoea resinosa* in New South Wales and Victoria, *X. preissii* in Western Australia, and *X. tateana* on Kangaroo Island where a small amount is still collected. *X. resinosa* yields a yellow resin, the others a red resin. Recently, the price paid for the Kangaroo Island resin was $882 per tonne.

A common method of collection is to spread a sheet round the base of the trunk to catch the leaf bases as they are chopped off. The material is flailed to separate resin from leaf, then sieved, the fine resin particles passing through the sieve and most of the leafy material being retained. Another method which has been used is to spread the mass of leaf bases and resin on a shaking table over which water runs, washing away the leafy material and leaving the resin. Still another method of extraction was to heat the leaf and resin in a vat with steam causing the resin to melt and run into trays. This process recovered considerably more resin than the sieving method. In the year 1934 approximately 2000 tonnes of resin were processed on Kangaroo Island but the current production is very small. The resin dissolves readily in alcohol, and probably its main use has been in the preparation of cheap spirit varnishes used for furniture and floors. Its strong red colour has led to its use for giving cheap timbers the appearance of red cedar. Although it has been used as a substitute for shellac in French polishing, it produces an inferior surface on which water will leave opaque patches. We once varnished a desk with grass tree resin dissolved in methylated spirits and although the result was at first reasonably satisfactory the surface eventually developed a strong tendency to crack and flake. It is said that the addition of a small amount of castor oil will reduce this tendency and give a tougher surface. For commercial preparations the resin was sometimes mixed with shellac, softer resins or linseed oil.

As well as being used on wooden surfaces, grass tree resin varnish has been used as a metal coating on brass instruments and for preserving tins for meat canning. Considerable quantities were used in Australia in one brand of stove polish.

When the yellow resin burns it gives off a pleasant scent, and this has led to its use in incense in churches in both Australia and Europe. Another minor use has been in manufacturing sealing wax, for which purpose it was mixed with turpentine and chalk. Small amounts were once used in sizing paper, perfumery, soap making and gramophone records.

On treatment with nitric acid the resin yields a considerable quantity of picric acid, up to 50% in the case of the yellow resin. In the three years immediately prior to World War I, Germany imported approximately 1500 tonnes of grass tree resin and it was suspected at the time that the material was being converted to picric acid for explosives manufacture although there seems to be no good evidence for this. Picric acid made from *Xanthorrhoea* resin is difficult to purify and its manufacture from phenol obtained from coal tar is more satisfactory. Although there was a report that fine dyes had been produced in Germany from this resin, investigations in London showed that neither the red nor yellow resin was a useful dye for wool or cotton.

In 1854 a report was presented to the Western Australian Government on the use of *Xanthorrhoea* resin for the production of illuminating gas 'at one-third the expense of lighting with oil and candles'. The mixture of leaf bases and resin was distilled, producing gas, tar and coke, the latter being suitable as a substitute for lamp black in paints. We have no information on whether or not this enterprise ever passed the experimental stage.

Distribution: Some species in all States

5

Fish Poisons

'A stunned mullet'

Australian expression

THE ABORIGINES caught fish by spearing, with line and hook, with nets and in wood or stone fish traps of varying complexity. An additional method, by no means limited to Australia, was to poison the water with some plant which killed or stupefied the fish so that they floated to the surface and could be easily captured. This method is perhaps akin to the more modern and reprehensible technique of fishing with dynamite since juvenile as well as adult fish must have been affected.

Toxins in the plant material used include alkaloids, saponins and tannins. Although some are toxic also to man, the amount absorbed by the fish was insufficient to affect their edibility.

Plant material was generally thoroughly pounded so that the toxic material would be released more readily. The material was then thrown into the water and after a wait of from half an hour to a few days, the fish were collected.

Acacia   WATTLE

Either bark or leaves of various species of wattle have been used as Aboriginal fish poisons. The nature of the substance which affects the fish is not known but both tannins and saponins are common in acacias and it is possible that one or both of these are active in stupefying the fish.

The following species are recorded as being used by the Aborigines: *A. binervata* (leaves), *A. decurrens, A. falcata* (bark), *A. longifolia* (leaves), *A. melanoxylon* (bark and twigs), *A. penninervis* (bark and leaves), *A. salicina* (bark).

Distribution: Some species in all States

Asclepias curassavica   RED-HEAD COTTON-BUSH

This widespread weed of eastern Australia is a native of the West
Indies, thought to have been introduced during the 1880s to
Queensland. It is interesting that the Aborigines of the Don River
should have used the introduced plant as a fish poison, presumably without prior knowledge of its toxic properties.

The plant is a small erect shrub with a milky latex and handsome clusters of red and orange flowers. The larva of the wan-
derer butterfly often feeds on the leaves.
Distribution: Qld, N.S.W., Vic.

Barringtonia asiatica   BARRINGTONIA, SQUARE COCONUT

The most distinctive feature of this coastal tree of the tropical
Pacific area is its large, sharply four-angled fruit with a spongy,
fibrous layer surrounding the single large seed. These fruits are
common objects among beach drift in Queensland, particularly
in the central and northern parts of the coastline.

The species has been widely used as a fish poison in Australia
and overseas. Generally, it seems, the seed was used after pounding or grating. However, the bark also has been used.
Distribution: Qld

Barringtonia racemosa   FRESHWATER MANGROVE

The large leaves, about 30 x 7 cm, and the long pendulous ra-
cemes of flowers help to distinguish this small tree of tropical wet
places. Small pieces of bark were pounded on a stone before being
thrown into the water to stupefy fish. In Fiji, the outer part of the
fruit rather than the bark was used for this purpose.
Distribution: Qld, N.T.

Derris trifoliata

Species of *Derris* are woody creepers probably best known for the
insecticide, derris dust, prepared from the roots of some species.
D. trifoliata is commonly found between mangroves and rainforests in northern Queensland. Its leaves may be trifoliate or
pinnate with five leaflets 6-12 cm long. The pea-like flowers are
followed by distinctive, very strongly flattened pods 3-5 cm long,
often kidney-like in outline. Pounded stems and leaves of this

species have been used in both Australia and South-east Asia and, in the latter region, have been used also as an insecticide. Many of the fish poisons were used only in fresh water but *D. trifoliata* was used also in salt water.

In the New Hebrides, arrowheads which had been poisoned by being dipped into a corpse were given that little extra something by adding an infusion of *D. trifoliata*.

Distribution: Qld

Diospyros hebecarpa TULICAN

In appearance, the fruit of *Diospyros hebecarpa*, a north Queensland rainforest tree, is very similar to a small persimmon fruit 2-3 cm across; the persimmon is a species of *Diospyros*. However, this similarity having prompted one of us to sample very cautiously the possible edible qualities, it can be reported that its flavour is entirely in keeping with its use as a fish poison and its reported skin-blistering properties.

The Aborigines pounded the fruits, placed the pulp in a dilly bag and dragged it through the water to disperse the toxic material. Fresh water was reported to be turned yellow and salt water red.

Distribution: Qld

Entada phaseoloides MATCHBOX BEAN

Widespread in the tropical Indo-Pacific region, this large climber bears enormous pods up to about a metre long. The large, dark brown flattened seeds, about 5 cm across, are often washed up on beaches hundred of kilometres from areas in which the vine grows.

Both the seeds and bark have been used in tropical countries outside Australia as fish poisons. There seems to be no record of the Aborigines using the plant for poisoning fish; in fact they ate the seeds after prolonged soaking.

Distribution: Qld

Eucalyptus microtheca COOLIBAH

The well-known coolibah which lines many inland watercourses was widely used by the Aborigines as a fish poison. Small branches with their leaves were thrown into the water in considerable quantity. The action of the poison, possibly a tannin, was slow and it apparently took one to several days for the fish to come to the surface.

Coolibah may well have been the eucalypt which deprived Sir Thomas Mitchell of an expected fish meal on his expedition of (1835-6.) Writing of the Lachlan River he stated, 'There the river contained some deep pools, and we expected to catch fish, but Piper [the Aboriginal interpreter] told us that the holes had been recently poisoned, a process adopted by the natives in dry seasons . . . All these holes were full of recently cut boughs of the eucalyptus, so that the water was tinged black.'

Distribution: Qld, N.S.W., S.A., W.A., N.T.

Faradaya splendida

This widespread climber of tropical rainforests has entered cultivation to some extent because of its attractive terminal clusters of white flowers. The large leaves 15-30 cm long are rounded or heart-shaped at the base.

Use of this plant as a fish poison was reported by E. J. Banfield of Dunk Island, well known as the author of *Confessions of a Beachcomber*. The stem was cut into lengths of about 30 cm, the outer bark removed and discarded, and the inner bark scraped off and collected. This material was then rubbed on stones which had previously been heated in a fire, and the stones were then thrown into a marine pool or creek 'with fatal results to all fish and other marine animals'.

The active principle of the plant is reported to be a saponin. Laboratory experiments with an infusion of the plant caused fish death within one hour. It is not clear why the Aborigines should have applied the scraped bark first to hot stones rather than adding it directly to the water.

Distribution: Qld

Jagera pseudorhus   FOAM-BARK

The foam-bark, so called because of the strong frothing action shown when an extract of the bark is shaken, was a well-known Aboriginal fish poison.

This fairly common tree is found mainly in rainforests and

along creek banks. The leaves are pinnate, with twelve to eighteen leaflets with toothed margins and hairy undersides. Young twigs are densely covered with rusty brown hairs. Handling the yellow fruits can be an unpleasant experience since the numerous rigid hairs which cover them readily become embedded in the skin.

The fish are poisoned by saponin abundant in the inner bark. In a laboratory test, bark added to the water at a concentration of 1:1000 caused death of fish in less than one hour. Aborigines used the plant for poisoning both freshwater and marine fish. One report stated that the bark scraped from the trunk and branches was cooked in native ovens for half an hour before use but whether or not this was a widespread practice is not known. It is unlikely that such treatment was essential but it may well have led to the more rapid release of the toxic material from the cells.

Distribution: Qld, N.S.W.

Melia azedarach   WHITE CEDAR

White cedar, a native species with bipinnate leaves and yellow elliptical fruits, is now a well-known ornamental tree of cultivation. Aborigines of the Tully River area used the bruised bark and leaves as a fish poison which was reported to act fairly rapidly.

Distribution: Qld, N.S.W., N.T.

Petalostigma pubescens   QUININE BERRY

P. pubescens is a small, spreading, crookedly branched tree with pendulous branchlets. Its elliptical leaves, mostly 2-4 cm long, are pale on the underside because of the presence of densely placed hairs. The hard, fleshy, yellow fruits about 12 mm broad are intensely bitter.

There is a report of Aborigines in the Marlborough (Qld) area pounding the fruits and throwing them, together with the leaves of an unidentified broad-leaved plant, in a waterhole where the mixture acted as an effective poison for mullet and garfish. Fruits alone, tested in the laboratory, produced only minor effect on fish. Whether the laboratory test was on fresh or dried fruits was not stated; there is a report that once the fruits have dried they lose their supposed medicinal virtue.

Distribution: Qld, N.S.W.

Planchonia careya   COCKY APPLE

The cocky apple is a small tree with crooked branches that resembles the swamp mahogany, *Tristania suaveolens*. Its buds open at night to produce a beautiful brush of long stamens, white above and pink below. Unfortunately, most of the flowers have fallen not long after dawn so it is only the early riser who can fully appreciate the beauty of this tree.

In coastal Queensland the bark of this species was thoroughly pounded before being used to poison both freshwater and salt-water fish. James Murrell who lived with Aborigines during the years 1846-63 after being wrecked at Cape Cleveland reported that the bark of the stems was used in fresh water and the bark of the root in salt water. It is not known whether this distinction was widespread nor whether it had any logical basis.

Distribution: Qld, N.T.

Polygonum hydropiper   WATERPEPPER, SMARTWEED

One of several species of *Polygonum* inhabiting creek banks and swampy positions, *P. hydropiper* owes its common names to its juice which can cause considerable irritation to lips and eyes. It is a herbaceous plant, up to about 1 m high, and, like other species of the genus, has a membranous sheath extending up round the stem above its junction with the leaf stalk. The slender flowering spike has the greenish white flowers relatively widely spaced for a *Polygonum*; many of the flowers are not in contact with their nearest neighbours while in most of the Australian species the flowers are densely crowded.

In *Tom Petrie's Reminiscences of Early Queensland* the method of catching fish by poisoning the water with *P. hydropiper* was briefly described. The plant 'was pounded up with sticks, and then thrown into the waterhole, and the water stirred up with the feet'.

Species of *Polygonum* are used for this purpose outside Australia and it is likely that the Aborigines used also species

△ *Melia azedarach* (white cedar) pp. 95, 140, 219

▽ *Grevillea robusta* (silky oak) p. 137

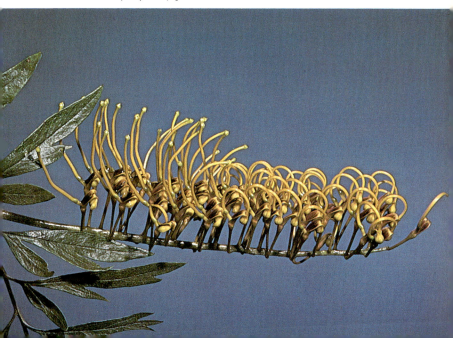

Triodia (porcupine grass) p. 87 △

Diospyros hebecarpa (tulican) p. 93 ▽

other than *P. hydropiper*. One used in the Port Curtis district was
possibly *P. orientale*.
Distribution: Qld, N.S.W., Vic.

Pongamia pinnata   INDIAN BEECH

This is a small, spreading, attractive tree of coastal tropical
Queensland and the tropical Indo-Pacific region. Leaves are pinnate, and the small lavender and white pea flowers are followed
by broad pods up to 5 cm long. W. E. Roth, who was Protector
of Aborigines in Queensland, described its use as follows: 'After
being roasted, the roots are beaten upon a stone, tied in bundles
and thrown into the water which turns somewhat greenish; it is
put in of an evening and left there all night.'
Distribution: Qld

Stephania japonica   TAPE VINE

In the moister eucalypt forests and along rainforest margins tape
vine is a common slender twiner easily recognized by its small red
fruits and pointed egg-shaped leaves with the leaf stalk inserted
some distance from the margin. Lengths of pounded stem about
60 cm long were thrown into a suitable waterhole. Reports on the
action of the toxin, probably an alkaloid, vary. Towards the end
of last century, it was reported that its action was very rapid but
that fish left in the poisoned water eventually recovered. However, later laboratory tests indicated that the action was certain, but
comparatively slow.
Distribution: Qld, N.S.W.

Tephrosia purpurea   WILD INDIGO

Species of *Tephrosia* have been widely used as fish poisons both
within and beyond Australia. *T. purpurea* is a low spreading shrub
with pinnate leaves and pink or purple pea-like flowers. It is
widely distributed both in Australia and in India and South-east
Asia where it is regarded as a medicinal plant. The Aborigines
used this plant not only as a fish poison but also to stupefy emus
by placing the plant in water likely to be drunk by the birds. A
poisonous substance from this plant, diluted to one part in a
million was deadly to fish in half an hour. The poison is reported

to be rotenoids, similar to the insecticide rotenone.
Distribution: Qld, N.S.W., S.A., W.A., N.T.

Tephrosia rosea   FLINDERS RIVER POISON

Reputedly a stock poison, this small shrub with silky pinnate
leaves has been regarded as one of the most effective fish poisons
used by the Aborigines of the Cape York Peninsula. A poison,
probably the same as that isolated from *T. purpurea*, has been
found in this species.
Distribution: Qld

Thespesia populnea   PORTIA TREE, INDIAN TULIP TREE

This hibiscus-like tree was used by Aborigines of the Normanton
district as a fish poison. Laboratory tests indicate that it is
effective only at fairly high concentrations.
Distribution: Qld, N.T.

OTHER SPECIES USED AS FISH POISONS

Acacia auriculiformis

Acacia holocarpa

Acacia verniciflua

Adenanthera abrosperma

Albizia procera

Alocasia macrorrhizos

Barringtonia acutangula

Barringtonia calyptrata

Callicarpa longifolia

Calophyllum inophyllum

Canarium australasicum

Cathormnion umbellatum

Derris involuta

Derris koolgibberah

Eucalyptus corymbosa

Eucalyptus polycarpa

Eucalyptus resinifera

Euodia vitiflora

Indigofera australis

Luffa cylindrica var. peramara

Nauclea orientalis
     (*Sarcocephalus coadunatus*)

Pleiogynium timorense

Tephrosia arnhemica

Tephrosia astragaloides

Tephrosia lamproloboides

Terminalia sericocarpa

Ternstroemia cherryi

Wikstroemia indica

6

Timbers

'And their weapons were the cross-cut
and the wedges and the maul.'

Henry Lawson

WOOD HAS PLAYED a unique role in man's advance to civilization
from his ape-like beginnings. Early man found wood a material
that was easy to work with primitive tools and which occurred
with such a diversity of properties that it could be used for
purposes ranging from weaponry to shelter and transport. Until
recent times, moreover, it has been almost his only fuel. Even
today when metals and plastics have replaced wood in many of
its traditional uses most people still have daily contact with wood.
And even though laminated plastic may be more practicable
than wood for some kitchen surfaces, such is the attraction
of wood that commonly the plastic is made to simulate the
traditional material. For high quality furniture, wood has an
indefinable attraction which seems to ensure it an honoured place
well into the future.

Wood is a remarkable substance. It is made up entirely of
microscopic cells, and consists mainly of a mixture of carbo-
hydrates, particularly cellulose, and the very complex substance
lignin which, to a large extent, is responsible for its strength and
durability. Differences in size and arrangement of the cells and in
the composition of their walls are responsible for the characters
of different woods — heavy or light, strong or weak, tough or
brittle, plain or ornamental.

The fact that wood is made up of hollow cells is responsible or
partly responsible for many of its characteristics. It is relatively
light, and most woods will float when dry. On the other hand it
is strong, and, weight for weight, many timbers compare favourably with steel for strength. The porous nature of wood is also
partly responsible for its good insulating properties, the fact that

it can be screwed and nailed, and its ability to hold paint and glue well. And, although it is flammable it does not soften at high temperatures so that a large beam will char slowly where a steel support may soften and collapse.

One prominent feature of some timbers is the presence of medullary rays. These are ribbon-like strips of soft tissue radiating outwards from the centre of the trunk. If the trunk were sawn lengthwise through the centre the rays would be expected to appear as bands running horizontally across the wood. However, because of irregularities in the timber and because, in any case, the cut is seldom made exactly through the centre, the bands, in practice, are very much broken up. Planks cut from near the edge of a log have wood rays appearing as scattered, spindle-shaped patches. Silky oak is a timber in which these rays are particularly prominent.

Terms applied when in describing timber are texture, grain and figure, terms often used rather loosely. Strictly speaking, texture refers mainly to the size of the cells and grain to the direction in which the cells lie. Figure is the pattern on the surface of cut timber and is dependent partly on texture and grain. Some figures occur as the result of growth rings, while fiddle-back is a type of figure caused by an undulate course of the cells. Bird's eye figure is caused by indentations at the surface of the wood or by the presence of numerous dormant buds.

While use of Australian plants for many purposes such as dyes, medicines and fibre is today insignificant, timber production is still of great importance in the economic life of Australia and employs thousands of workers. In spite of this importance, the area under forest in Australia is very low compared with that in many other important timber-producing countries. This is largely because such a high percentage of the continent is arid. The area of reserved forest in Australia is only 1% of the continent's total area, and only about 0.6% is regarded as good forest country. While in most timber-producing countries there is a preponderance of softwoods, the position is different in Australia. Here the enormously important genus *Eucalyptus* is responsible for a great preponderance of hardwoods. The country is deficient in naturally occurring softwoods, natural stands of which have mostly been cut out, so that Australia is dependent for softwoods mainly on plantations of pines introduced from other countries.

This chapter cannot hope to be comprehensive. To describe all the timbers which are or have been used in Australia would require a large book to itself. All we can hope to do here is to pick out some of the species which are economically important and some which have or have had uses which, to us, are of interest.

Acacia   WATTLE

In Australia, *Acacia* is a very large genus of over 700 species. The plants are mainly shrubs and small trees which range from the coastal rainforests to the arid interior.

Acacias fall into two groups on the basis of leaf type; in one group the leaves remain bipinnate throughout life — these species are mostly those in relatively moist habitats; in the other, larger group, the bipinnate nature of the leaf becomes progressively reduced with successive seedling leaves so that the leaf is eventually reduced to its leaf stalk and axis which is commonly much flattened to resemble a simple leaf. This structure is termed a phyllode.

Since most of the species are shrubs or only small trees the genus as a whole is relatively unimportant as a timber producer. A few of the best known species are noted here.

Acacia acuminata   RASPBERRY JAM

Much of the *Acacia acuminata* of Western Australia has been cleared for wheat and sheep production. It is a shrub or small tree to about 8 m high and has been put to much the same use as mulga — Aboriginal implements, fencing material and fancy articles. The timber is extremely hard and at one time was even used for machinery bearings. Perhaps the timber's most distinctive feature is the strong scent of raspberry jam given off by the freshly cut wood.
Distribution: W.A.

Acacia cambagei   GIDGEE

This inland *Acacia* is notorious for the strong and peculiar odour, regarded by many as highly offensive, which it gives off in humid weather, particularly just before rain and just after a light shower. The odour has been likened to that of rotten cabbage and although this is probably a reasonable description there is nothing else quite like it.

It is a small tree with leathery grey phyllodes about 10 cm long. Although it forms fairly extensive scrubs in some areas in the Channel country it mainly lines the channels.

As with many acacias, the small size of the logs available limits the usefulness of the timber, which has been used mainly in very durable fencing, claimed to last up to fifty years. The heartwood is often very dark brown, and particularly those pieces with a fiddle-back figure have been used in fancy articles. It is a very hard, heavy wood, in fact one of the heaviest woods in the world, and has had a very minor use in the manufacture of xylophones.

The sawdust is said to produce dermatitis in those working the timber, and where the logs have been used in lining wells the water is reported to have taken on an unpleasant taste for several years. Gidgee is highly regarded as firewood, producing an intense heat.

Where it was available, gidgee was probably the favourite timber for Aboriginal weapons. Boomerangs, nulla-nullas, fighting poles, woomeras and spears, some about 4 m long, were made from this species.

Distribution: Qld, N.S.W., Vic.

Acacia harpophylla   BRIGALOW

Brigalow is one of the larger species of *Acacia*, the more robust specimens reaching a height of about 12 m. At one time it occurred in extensive, dense stands in parts of sub-coastal and central Queensland and was difficult to eradicate for the establishment of pasture because of its strong tendency to sucker from the roots. However, with the introduction of large-scale clearing machinery much of the once extensive brigalow scrub has disappeared.

Although some specimens near the coast are a dull green colour, the sickle-shaped phyllodes of brigalow typically have a silvery, blue-grey sheen.

The timber is a hard, heavy, dark brown durable one which splits readily, making it a useful fencing timber. It is not extensively sawn because of the relatively small size of its logs. A faint odour of violets is reported from the wood.

Aborigines used the timber for spears, boomerangs and clubs. For these purposes a strong, elastic timber which does not readily shatter on impact is desirable and brigalow fulfilled these requirements well. These attributes made the timber suitable also for fishing rods and it has been claimed to be one of the best timbers in the world for this purpose. However, with the advent of fibreglass only the most dedicated wood fancier is now likely to use a brigalow rod.

Distribution: Qld, N.S.W., Vic.

Acacia aneura   MULGA

More book ends, serviette rings and ink stands must have been made from mulga than from any other Australian timber. In souvenir shops these ornamental mulga articles are as ubiquitous as toy koalas.

Mulga, like brigalow, often occurs in fairly dense stands but is a species of drier areas, being found mainly in the 200-400 mm annual rainfall belt. It has been estimated that it is a major species in over 130 million hectares of Australia and a minor species over a similar area.

The plant is a shrub or small tree, with blunt, blue-grey phyllodes mostly 4-8 cm long. Since branching is mainly from near the base the logs available are of only small size. Its value as an ornamental timber for small articles is due to the fact that it turns well, takes a high polish and shows an attractive contrast between the dark brown heartwood and the yellow sapwood. The bark adheres tightly to the wood and is left in position for some fancy articles.

Mulga has been used also as a fencing timber and was used by the Aborigines for boomerangs, spears, clubs and digging sticks. Its common name is derived from the Aboriginal name for a shield which they made from the tree. The Aborigines found the plant useful also as a source of tinder; it has been suggested that in inland areas firemaking by friction is difficult because of the scarcity of soft wood and that, consequently, it was the Aboriginal practice to maintain and transport fire, once produced, on mulga bark.

In the early days, mulga had a bad reputation among inland bushmen as a cause of Barcoo rot, the belief being that wounds caused by mulga were likely to develop into the sores and ulcers which were characteristic of the disease. It is now known that Barcoo rot is scurvy, and results from lack of vitamin C in the diet. Being such a common plant it was commonly responsible for the skin breaks which often developed into Barcoo rot. There seems to be no evidence of any poisonous principle in the wood being the cause of sores.

Distribution: Qld, N.S.W., S.A., W.A., N.T.

Acacia melanoxylon   BLACKWOOD

This is the tallest species of *Acacia* in Australia, reaching heights of about 30 m in rainforests of Victoria and Tasmania. It extends northwards into Queensland but there it is a relatively small tree. Leaves are of the phyllodineous type, and flower heads are followed by much curved pods, about 6 mm across, in which the seeds are encircled by a red, stalk-like structure.

Blackwood is commonly regarded as one of the best cabinet timbers in Australia. It has an attractive golden brown colour, and dresses and polishes well. Some samples have a waxy grain which results in the very pleasant sheen and fiddleback figure for which blackwood is well known. Unlike some *Acacia* timbers it is not particularly hard to cut.

The timber has been used not only for cabinet work but also for ornamental interior work and panelling of railway carriages. Because it is a very good steam-bending timber it was used extensively in coach and boat building. Barrel-making has declined since the introduction of stainless steel beer kegs but, at one time, blackwood was used extensively in beer barrel construction and, in fact, has been regarded as the best Australian timber for this purpose. It was used also for casks to contain whale oil from Tasmania. Minor uses to which it has been put include manufacture of walking sticks, fancy boxes, tennis racquet frames, gun stocks (in 1844-5, 430 gun stocks were exported from Launceston to Great Britain) and sounding boards of pianos.

Distribution: Qld, N.S.W., Vic., Tas., S.A.

Acacia pendula   MYALL, WEEPING MYALL

Myall is a distinctive tree of inland parts, readily recognized by its attractive, pendulous branchlets and silver-grey phyllodes. The wood is dark, attractive and particularly hard. Its relatively strong odour of violets, which it continues to release for some years if left unpolished, led to its use in small ornamental boxes for gloves and handkerchiefs. In 1894 a shipment of the timber was sent to Great Britain for use in spokes of gun carriages; the Aborigines had earlier also used the timber in weapons.
Distribution: Qld, N.S.W.

Aegiceras corniculatum   RIVER MANGROVE

Among the several mangroves in Australia, *Aegiceras corniculatum* is one of the smaller species, seldom exceeding the size of a shrub. It can often be distinguished by the crystals of common salt that occur over the leaves, the result of evaporation of salt solution excreted from glands sunken in the leaf surface.

The trunks do not reach a size which can be sawn but sticks cut from the plants have been used as oyster stakes, driven into tidal flats at suitable levels.
Distribution: Qld, N.S.W.

Agathis robusta   QUEENSLAND KAURI, KAURI PINE

A. robusta is probably the best known of the three Australian species of *Agathis* since it is the one most commonly cultivated as an ornamental.

Large specimens are magnificent trees, some known to have reached a height of nearly 50 m with a trunk of 27 m before the first branch. There is a strong tendency to shed lateral branches cleanly so that even isolated trees commonly develop the characteristic tall clear trunk before the first branch. The bark is shed in irregular flakes leaving a smooth, mottled trunk. Leaves are unusually large for a conifer, being up to about 10 x 4 cm with numerous fine parallel veins, and may have a life of several years.

Kauri timber is a creamy white to pale brown softwood of very even texture. When it was available it was used in cabinetmaking, for general indoor work including floorings, and for butter boxes. Unfortunately, natural stands of *A. robusta* have been mainly cut out and the tree does not perform well in plantations.

Two northern Queensland species, *Agathis atropurpurea* and *A. microstachya* are still cut to some extent.
Distribution: Qld.

Aleurites moluccana   CANDLE-NUT

Candle-nut is a tree of north Queensland rainforests, extending widely into south-east Asia and the Pacific. Its entire or three-lobed leaves are drawn out to a slender point and have a distinctive, silvery appearance.

The timber is silvery white, very plain, and although light and soft is fairly tough. When draining boards were of wood and kitchen shelves were often left unpainted, Candle-nut was popular for these purposes because it retained its whitish colour for a long time. Today the timber is used mainly for cases.

It is reported that the Aborigines ringbarked the trees to allow the growth in the decaying trunk of large white grubs which were a popular item of diet.
Distribution: Qld

Alphitonia excelsa   RED ASH, RED ALMOND

Red ash is a common tree in both rainforests and eucalypt forests, in some places extending into surprisingly dry areas for a species at home in the rainforest. It is fairly easily distinguished by its smooth, pale bark and alternate, non-serrate leaves with their white undersurfaces. A well-grown specimen makes an attractive tree but the appearance is often ragged because the leaves are so heavily chewed by insects.

The timber is a minor one, used to some extent for cabinet work and general indoor work and, because of its durability, also for fencing and house stumps. Its particular feature is the pink, orange or red colour which gradually develops on exposure to air. The coloured layer is only shallow but if it is removed the newly exposed surface will gradually regain the attractive colour over a few months.
Distribution: Qld, N.S.W.

Alstonia scholaris   WHITE CHEESEWOOD,
                                          MILKY PINE, DITA BARK

White cheesewood is a large tree of tropical rainforests, easily recognized by its copious milky latex and by the arrangement of the leaves, 10-15 cm long, in whorls of up to seven.

As the common name suggests, the timber is a soft one. With some resemblance to pine, it is creamy white, lightweight and easy to dress. Although used to a limited extent in furniture making and general building, its lack of durability in the weather, and its susceptibility to borer attack and to the fungus causing blue stain limit its usefulness. It is regarded as a good carving timber but its main use has been for packing cases and fruit boxes.

Distribution: Qld

Angophora costata   SMOOTH-BARKED APPLE,
                                       CABBAGE GUM, RUSTY GUM

In its trunk this species looks much like the spotted gum, *Eucalyptus maculata*, but can be distinguished by having opposite leaves, those of the spotted gum being alternately arranged. Usually about midsummer the old bark is shed leaving a most attractive, smooth, salmon-pink new bark exposed. On some trees small patches of old bark remain producing a mottled appearance and it is these specimens particularly which resemble spotted gums. Over the months the bright colour of the newly exposed bark gradually fades to grey.

The strong development of concentric gum veins in the timber and its lack of durability in the ground have limited the use of the timber mainly to rough slabs and fence rails. However, it is now used to some extent for the manufacture of hardboard.

Distribution: Qld, N.S.W.

Anodopetalum biglandulosum   HORIZONTAL

Well known to Tasmanians, this small tree with opposite yellow-green leaves is common in some of the rainforests of the central and south-western parts of the island. It is distinguished by a most unusual growth form; the slender trees commonly bend over more or less horizontally and from them arise erect branches which in turn also bend over. In this way there may be formed a dense tangle of branches over which one may walk, rather hazardously, several metres above the ground. Although not an important timber tree the wood has been used for tool handles.

It is claimed to be almost impossible to break in its green state.
Distribution: Tas.

Aphananthe philippinensis   NATIVE ELM, AXE-HANDLE WOOD,
GREY HANDLEWOOD

Rainforests fringing creek banks and the drier types of rainforest
are the areas in which this medium-sized tree is most commonly
found. The elliptical, pointed leaves with toothed margins have
a sandpapery surface. Leaves on coppice shoots have more
prominent marginal teeth and may be almost holly-like.

The cream to grey timber is available only in small sizes. Its
main virtue lies in its toughness, elasticity and resistance to
splitting. As a consequence, it has been used mainly for tool
handles, mallets and baseball bats.
Distribution: Qld, N.S.W.

Araucaria cunninghamii   HOOP PINE

Hoop pine is Australia's most important native softwood. It is
found mainly in the lighter types of rainforest, extending from
Coffs Harbour in N.S.W. to northern Queensland and Papua
New Guinea. Large specimens reach a height of 60 m. Branches
are produced along the trunk in whorls, and specimens in a forest
where there is heavy shading shed these branches early leaving a
good length of knot-free timber; trees grown in isolation retain
most of their lateral branches and their timber, like that of the
tops of forest specimens, is very knotty.

There is much variation between specimens in the spacing of
the whorls of branches, in the angle the laterals make with the
trunk and in general appearance, so that in some cases it may be
hard to believe that two adjacent specimens of hoop pine belong
to the one species.

The small, rigid, sharply pointed incurved leaves are densely
placed and overlapping so that they produce a snakeskin-like
effect along the branchlets.

In young specimens the copper-coloured bark is smooth,
somewhat papery, tightly adherent and with clear horizontal
banding. As it breaks, due to expansion of the tissues within, the
broken ends curl back tightly. In old specimens the bark becomes
rougher but still retains the horizontal orientation. The bark is

heavily impregnated with resin and, in a fallen tree, is much more resistant to decay than the wood. This results in the wood gradually rotting away and leaving a row of irregular bark hoops — the origin of the common name.

The wood is a first-class softwood varying from almost white to cream or light brown. It is a plain timber of even texture without prominent grain or growth rings and is easily worked. Large amounts have been used for a great variety of indoor purposes including cabinet work, floorings, mouldings and linings, and panelling in railway carriages. Chamfer boards are satisfactory if painted. It has been used successfully in building small boats and for match splints. The timber peels easily, and the Australian plywood industry was founded largely on hoop pine. At one time, wrapped packets of butter were packed in 56lb wooden boxes; butter very readily picks up taints so the timber used for the boxes had to be virtually odourless; hoop pine is such a timber and was the one used mainly for butter boxes.

At one time hoop pine was the major softwood in plantation in Queensland but has now been outstripped by the exotic conifers which can be grown on relatively poor soil; hoop pine grows satisfactorily only on rainforest sites. The plantations are first thinned after 12-14 years and the thinnings are used for case timber, wood wool, particle board and paper pulp. Final harvesting occurs after about 60 years.
Distribution: Qld, N.S.W.

Araucaria bidwillii   BUNYA PINE

The bunya pine is well known as a once important source of food for Aborigines. It is a distinctive tree with cylindrical outline, the apex conical in young specimens, dome-shaped in mature ones. Lateral branches, with the foliage of dagger-like leaves crowded near their ends, eventually fall and are replaced by a new set of branches which form a second crown some distance down the trunk. The species occurs in two areas of Queensland, the Bunya Mountains-Blackall Range area in the south and the Mount Molloy area in the north, but little millable timber remains outside national parks. It has been grown in plantations but to only a small extent compared with hoop pine.

Timber is very similar to that of hoop pine, and in the timber

trade commonly no distinction is made between the two.
Distribution: Qld

Argyrodendron trifoliatum   BOOYONG, CROWSFOOT ELM,
                                           BROWN TULIP OAK

Buttressing of the trunk base is well developed in several rainforest species and is particularly noticeable in booyong, where the
upper edge of the buttress is typically concave in outline. Leaves
are trifoliate and easily recognized by the silvery brown
appearance of the undersurface.

The timber is fairly heavy, brown with sometimes a purplish
tinge, and has broad medullary rays which give it a handsome
figure with some resemblance to that of silky oak. It is used in
general indoor work, particularly for panelling, and at one time
considerable quantities were used for panelling in Queensland
railway carriages. Because it splits well it was once used to some
extent for shingles but it lacks durability in the open. Its
flexibility and elasticity makes it reasonably suitable for tool
handles and even sail battens, but there are other better timbers
for these purposes.

A. actinophyllum, the black jack, has leaves with three to nine
radiating leaflets. Its timber tends to be pinkish but otherwise is
similar to that of *A. trifoliatum*.
Distribution: Qld, N.S.W.

Arthrotaxis selaginoides   KING WILLIAM PINE,
                                         KING BILLY PINE

Although King William pine is the standard trade name of this
Tasmanian tree it is far more commonly referred to as King Billy
pine or just King Billy. The species is found mainly in
mountainous regions of the central and western part of the island.
Largest specimens reaching about 40 m high occur in rainforests
while those on bleak, windswept open areas are relatively stunted.
The small, incurved, sharply pointed leaves give the branchlets
something of the appearance of those of the hoop pine. *Arthrotaxis*
belongs to the same family as the giant Californian redwoods and
its timber is somewhat similar, but it cannot match those trees in
height.

The softwood timber is pale pink to yellow-pink with

prominent growth rings, is light in weight, bends well and is durable. It has been extensively used for joinery, windowsills and weatherboards. Less extensive uses include slats for venetian blinds, sounding boards for pianos and battery separators. It is highly regarded as a timber for small boat construction.
Distribution: Tas.

Atherosperma moschatum   SOUTHERN SASSAFRAS

Although southern sassafras has a fairly wide distribution in rainforests of south-eastern Australia, its main exploitation has occurred in Tasmania where the trees commonly reach a larger size than in the mainland States. Opposite leaves with very pale undersurface and a distinctive aromatic scent in the cut bark are distinguishing characters.

The timber is white to light brown, fairly soft and of uniform texture. In addition to use in cabinet work and carving it has some interesting minor uses. These include manufacture of high heels for shoes, toys, wooden screws, sounding boards of musical instruments, clothes pegs and brushes. Its suitability for the last two articles is due partly to a very low tannin content; tannins in contact with iron produce an unsightly blue-black stain so a timber with appreciable tannin content would be unsuitable in contact with a wire clothes line or the staples holding the bristles of a brush.
Distribution: N.S.W., Vic., Tas.

Avicennia marina   GREY MANGROVE

Grey mangrove is one of the commonest mangroves in Australia and the only one to extend southward as far as the Victorian coast. It is easily recognized by the numerous, pencil-like roots protruding above the surface of the mud.

The timber is hard, strong and light and not now important although it was once used to a limited extent for mallets, wheel hubs and boat knees. *Avicennia* was the favourite timber for shields among the Aborigines who had access to it. The wood has an unusual structure with the fibres in adjacent growth rings running at different angles so that, to some extent, it resembles plywood. Splitting occurs very readily between the rings but not at right angles to them. To make a shield the desired shape was outlined on the trunk and a broad groove 5-7 cm deep was cut round it. Stone wedges were driven into this groove causing the shield-shaped piece to separate from the rest of the trunk. Final shaping and smoothing and the attachment of a handle completed the shield.

Distribution: All mainland States

Backhousia myrtifolia   CARROL, IRONWOOD

This is a small tree, sometimes not much more than a shrub, commonly found at the junction of eucalypt forest and rainforest, particularly in sandy areas. Its opposite leaves when crushed have a pleasant and distinctive spicy odour.

As a timber tree this species is of little significance being too small and irregular for normal milling. However, it is of some interest because of its very fine grained, exceptionally hard and tough timber. It has found limited application in manufacture of tool handles and, mainly by amateurs, in the construction of fishing rods and bows.

Distribution: Qld, N.S.W.

Banksia

Banksias are shrubs or small trees with a characteristic rigid bottlebrush of small, generally cream to orange flowers. Even well-grown specimens tend to be gnarled and irregular and yield only small logs, so the group is of only minor value for timber. However, the wood is highly decorative, being of the same general type as silky oak but usually redder. It has been used to a limited extent for cabinet work and small fancy articles, and, at one time, for bullock yokes. Natural bends of *B. integrifolia* were highly regarded for use as boat knees.

Distribution: Some species in all States

Callicoma serratifolia   CALLICOMA

Saw-toothed margins and pale densely hairy undersides to the opposite leaves distinguish this shrub or small tree usually found in the lighter types of rainforest or moister eucalypt forests. The name *Callicoma* means beautiful hair and was apparently applied because of the plant's fluffy flower-heads.

Some of the early buildings erected by the first arrivals at

Sydney Cove were of wattle and daub and it was *Callicoma* that was used to form the wattle framework on which the clay was plastered. As mentioned earlier (p. 51) the name wattle, appropriately applied to this plant, was eventually transferred to species of *Acacia*.

Distribution: Qld, N.S.W.

Callitris columellaris   WHITE CYPRESS

Of the several species of *Callitris* in Australia, *C. columellaris* is the most widely distributed and the most important timber species (p. 54). It occurs mainly on sandy soil in inland areas with an annual rainfall of 400-700 mm. Many of the once extensive forests have now been cleared to allow grazing or agriculture.

Foliage commonly has a grey-green colour which is responsible for the name *C. glauca* under which the species was known for a long time. Specimens growing on the coastal sand dunes in southern Queensland and northern New South Wales have dark green foliage. Large specimens reach a height of 30 m but 15-20 m is a more common height.

The resinous, aromatic wood is yellow to dark brown and is knotty. Knots are generally regarded as flaws in timber but those of *Callitris* are held tightly, and since the timber takes a good polish the knots have sometimes been regarded as an ornamental feature in polished surfaces.

Particularly in inland areas where it occurs in quantity, the timber has been extensively used in building construction, and for fencing posts and telegraph poles. A particularly useful feature is its complete resistance to termite attack and its high degree of resistance to fungal decay. A disadvantage in building construction is its brittleness and tendency to split on nailing when dry; it is therefore often used green or after only partial drying; this is possible because the degree of shrinkage on drying is small. Another disadvantage in building construction is that it is very flammable and burns fiercely with a spluttering flame. Because the timber is so flammable it was used by Aborigines in northern Australia for torches by which to spear fish at night.

The timber is fairly resistant to shipworm and is listed number four among Australian timbers tested against this pest.

Distribution: All mainland States

Castanospermum australe   MORETON BAY CHESTNUT,
                                              BLACK BEAN

The Moreton Bay chestnut, better known in the timber trade as black bean, is one of the best known rainforest species because of its common cultivation as a street tree and in home gardens. Attractive, rather fleshy flowers are borne in short sprays along mature branches, yellow-green at first but changing through yellow to orange-red. These are well loaded with nectar and are attractive to several nectar-seeking birds. The flowers are followed by large green beans which, given a sharp whack on a rock, will split open to reveal up to five large brown seeds embedded in a white pith. After removal of the seeds the half pods make good toy boats. The tree bears a dense crown of dark green, glossy, pinnate leaves. If there is any doubt about the tree's identity a scent of cucumber in the cut inner bark or even the broken leaf base will confirm it as Moreton Bay chestnut.

The timber is dark brown, sometimes almost black with a rather coarse grain and attractive figure. It dresses well and although heavy is highly regarded as a cabinet timber. Carvings and fancy articles also have been made from it. Before synthetic materials came into common use black bean was used for electrical switchboards because of its particularly high resistance to the passage of electric current.

Distribution: Qld, N.S.W.

Casuarina   SHE-OAK

The species of *Casuarina* are all alike in being virtually leafless trees and shrubs. Leaves, although present, are reduced to a small whorl of four to fifteen scale-like teeth at each joint; what may appear to be cylindrical leaves are simply branchlets which have the function of leaves and, in time, fall just as leaves do rather than persisting and gradually increasing in size. The small winged fruits are contained in hard, rough, cone-like structures.

The name *Casuarina* was applied because of the supposed resemblance of the slender, pendulous branchlets to the feathers of the cassowary. The common name, she-oak, applied to many of the species, has an origin which may be unacceptable to half the population: the timber resembles, but is inferior to, English oak and the addition of the prefix 'she' was simply the bushman's method of indicating inferiority.

The genus is mainly confined to Australia where there are approximately forty species occurring from coastal sand dunes to the arid interior.

A distinctive feature of the timber is the prominent development of medullary rays which are responsible for its general similarity to that of English oak and silky oak, and make it an ornamental timber for fancy articles. These rays lead to the timber splitting readily in the direction in which they run. This ready splitting was exploited early in the white settlement of Australia; Captain Phillip recorded the use of *Casuarina* shingles for roofs during the first year of settlement at Sydney Cove.

Casuarina cristata (C. lepidophloia) BELAH

Belah is a widely distributed inland tree growing generally on heavy soils and avoiding the ridges. Its branches are distinctly erect. The timber is chocolate brown, very hard and takes a good polish. Unlike other casuarinas it is a fairly plain wood, lacking the rays of exceptional width which characterize most species of the genus. Its main use has been in fencing but, in spite of its hardness, it is of only moderate durability in the ground. Casuarinas, in general, are regarded as good fuel, and belah is one of Australia's best firewood timbers.

Distribution: All mainland States

Casuarina cunninghamiana RIVER OAK

This is the largest of the casuarinas, reaching a height of about 30 m although the branchlets are among the finest and the cones among the smallest in the genus, only a little over 1 cm long. The tree characteristically lines freshwater streams where, because of its suckering habit and ready regeneration from seed it is a valuable stabilizer of banks. Its timber is not as heavy as that of some other species of *Casuarina*. Heartwood is light chocolate, sapwood pale pink. As well as being used for axe handles, heads of spirit casks and fancy articles it was the favourite timber in Queensland for bullock yokes. *C. torulosa* (forest oak) and *C. stricta* (drooping she-oak) also have been used for bullock yokes.

Distribution: Qld, N.S.W.

Casuarina glauca SWAMP OAK,
SWAMP SHE-OAK

Casuarina glauca is a rather scraggy member of the genus, with relatively thick branchlets, generally growing in swampy localities, in some places subject to some marine influence. Its tough timber has been used successfully in northern New South Wales for axe handles which were found to be more durable than those made from the traditional axe-handle timber, American hickory.

Distribution: All mainland States

Casuarina luehmannii BULL OAK

Bull oak is one of the casuarinas with a mainly inland distribution. The branchlets are erect and wiry and the cone very distinctive, almost disc-like in form.

The timber has been used for fencing, small fancy articles and as an excellent firewood. Some years ago it enjoyed a brief period of potential glory when stiletto heels were causing considerable damage to many wooden floors. The exceptional hardness of bull oak suggested it as a suitable timber for parquetry floors. However, before it was widely introduced for this purpose fashions in footwear changed. It has little value as plank flooring because of the small size of the logs available and its tendency to split when nailed. The rose she-oak or forest oak, *C. torulosa*, was also under consideration for parquetry and although very hard is not quite as hard as *C. luehmannii*.

Distribution: Qld, N.S.W., Vic., S.A.

Ceratopetalum apetalum COACHWOOD

Coachwood is a close relative of the New South Wales Christmas bush, *Ceratopetalum gummiferum*, a well known native plant in cultivation, particularly in the Sydney area. Although less ornamental, *C. apetalum* is rather more valuable. The tree is a very common one in some rainforests, particularly in gullies, where it may be the dominant species. Its bark is smooth and pale grey to white, covered with thin encrusting lichens, although old trees may develop very rough bark at the base. The freshly cut bark contains coumarin, the substance giving new-mown hay its characteristic scent. Leaves are opposite, bluntly serrate, with a joint at the junction of stalk and leaf blade.

The timber is light pinkish brown with an ornamental figure and has a faint odour of caramel. Its main use today is in cabinet work and general indoor work although at one time it was one of the chief Australian timbers used in coachbuilding. Other uses to which it has been put are in gun stocks, broom handles, dowelling and shoe heels. It is regarded as a particularly good timber for marine plywood.

An important use was found for the timber during World War II. Mosquito fighter-bombers were built in Australia using a layer of imported balsa wood sandwiched between plywood sheets made from coachwood.

Distribution: Qld, N.S.W.

Cinnamomum oliveri   OLIVER'S SASSAFRAS, CAMPHORWOOD

The strong scent of camphor emitted from crushed leaves immediately distinguishes this rainforest tree with simple, opposite leaves. The timber has been used for general indoor work but has no special distinction apart from its scent which is retained for many years. This would make it suitable for the manufacture of boxes, such as those for which camphor laurel is used, and which are claimed to deter clothes moths and silverfish.

Distribution: Qld, N.S.W.

Cryptocarya erythroxylon   SOUTHERN MAPLE, ROSE WALNUT,
                                   PIGEONBERRY ASH

There is no outstanding distinctive feature to help in the recognition of this rainforest tree, although the pale grey or whitish undersurface of the alternate leaves narrows down the possibilities.

It is a strong, tough, durable wood which dresses well and is used in general indoor construction. Although a little on the heavy side it has been used in cabinet work, where its often fiddle-back figure and surface sheen produce a very attractive appearance.

Distribution: Qld, N.S.W.

Dacrydium franklinii   HUON PINE

The Huon River area was the site of discovery of this tree by Alan Cunningham. It has the slender, conical form of most conifers and its more or less pendulous branchlets bear small, densely placed, overlapping leaves.

Huon pine has a very high reputation as a softwood but, unfortunately, only small supplies of millable trees now remain. The timber is pale yellow, lightweight and dresses well. Its notable resistance to decay and to termites and borers is due to the presence of an essential oil which makes the surface oily to touch. As well as being highly esteemed as a cabinet and joinery timber, Huon pine has been used extensively in boat building and is regarded as one of the best timbers for this purpose.
Distribution: Tas.

Daphnandra micrantha   SOCKETWOOD, CANARY SASSAFRAS

Daphnandra micrantha is a rainforest tree, fairly easily recognized by its opposite, toothed leaves and the commonly pronounced flattening of the twig at the point where the leaves join it.

The timber is pale, yellowish, lightweight and fine-grained, with considerable resemblance to hoop pine, although tougher, and is used for general indoor work and to some extent as a cabinet wood. Because it is light and holds staples well it is an excellent timber for brush backs and mousetraps. *Doryphora sassafras*, a close relative, has somewhat similar timber.
Distribution: Qld N.S.W.

Diospyros ferrea var. *humilis (Maba humilis)*   QUEENSLAND EBONY

Queensland ebony is a small, gnarled tree found mainly in the dry savannah country of northern Queensland. Its heartwood is very like true ebony, being black, extremely heavy, hard and difficult to work although dressing with a very clean surface. However the logs are often faulty and the timber has had difficulty in competing with the imported material. It can be used for the same purposes as the Indian and South-east Asian ebonies have traditionally been used — small fancy articles, piano keys, rulers etc.
Distribution: Qld

Dysoxylum fraseranum   ROSEWOOD, ROSE MAHOGANY

Rosewood is one of several rainforest trees with large pinnate leaves with five to ten leaflets. When the leaves are held up against the light and viewed with a lens numerous elongate or streak-like oil glands can be seen, and the distinctive form of these structures gives a good clue to the plant's identity.

The generic name *Dysoxylum* is derived from the Greek and means 'bad wood', a name justified by the unpleasant odour of the wood of one species. However, *D. fraseranum* wood has a pleasant rose-like perfume which is persistent for a long time. In general, the pink-brown to red-brown timber is similar to red cedar although it is harder and heavier and a little finer grained. Occasionally the surface 'sweats' and spoils a polished surface but in general it polishes well and is regarded as a good cabinet timber. At one time, when supplies were ample, it was used extensively in general indoor work and even, because of its resistance to fungus and termite attack, for house stumps.

Although the making of cases for lacquered brass instruments must have consumed only an insignificant amount of timber early accounts stressed the unsuitability of rosewood for this purpose; the surface of the instruments became sticky after a few weeks.

Distribution: Qld, N.S.W.

Dysoxylum muelleri   RED BEAN, ONIONWOOD,
                                                     MIVA MAHOGANY

The pinnate leaves of this species are larger, up to 60 cm long and have more leaflets (11-21) than those of *D. fraseranum* but perhaps the plant's most distinctive feature is the strong odour of onions apparent when the inner bark is cut.

The heartwood is reddish and resembles red cedar although it is harder and heavier. The timber is used mainly for cabinet work and interior construction although, like *D. fraseranum*, it was once used also for house stumps because of its durability in the ground. A disadvantage of the timber for those who have to work with it is that the dust produced during sandpapering is very irritating to the nasal passages and likely to induce violent sneezing.

Distribution: Qld, N.S.W.

Elaeocarpus grandis   QUANDONG, BLUE QUANDONG,
                                         WHITE QUANDONG

Elaeocarpus grandis is one of the large trees of the rainforest and has
the base prominently buttressed. The trees are often found in
parts of the rainforest where soil moisture is particularly high,
commonly in association with piccabeen palms. Two features
help to identify it: the leaves become brilliant orange-red before
they fall, and there are usually a few of these spectacular leaves
scattered through the canopy; as the fleshy, blue layer of the fruit
decays the deeply pitted stone is left and these can usually be
found on the ground in the vicinity of the tree.

The timber is pale, some pieces almost white, others pale
brown to light grey. Although there is some resemblance to hoop
pine it is stronger, lighter and more porous. Most supplies go into
general interior construction and cabinetmaking but small
quantities have been used for racing sculls and oars and in
aircraft construction.

Distribution: Qld, N.S.W.

Endiandra palmerstonii   QUEENSLAND WALNUT, WALNUT BEAN

Apart from being one of the largest trees of northern Queensland
rainforests this species has no particularly distinctive features to
aid identification.

It has a hard, fine-grained timber attractively figured in
various shades of brown. A high silica content leads to its
blunting saws quickly. The timber is used extensively for indoor
work, furniture and plywood. It is particularly suitable for
decorative panelling and has been used extensively in some
banks. Some of the panelling in the once well-known passenger
liners *Strathmore* and *Queen Mary* was of Queensland walnut. One
firm in Australia used it for piano veneers. It is suitable also for
small fancy articles, and was recommended at one time for
electrical switchboards because of its high electrical resistance.

Distribution: Qld

Eremophila mitchellii   BUDDA, BASTARD SANDALWOOD

Budda is an attractive small tree with a dense crown of dark green pointed leaves 2-3 cm long, and white two-lipped flowers. It is widely distributed in inland regions where it has often been known as sandalwood or bastard sandalwood. Although not closely related to true sandalwood these names have been applied because the wood contains about 3% of essential oils which produce an incense-like aroma when the timber is burnt. It has, at various times, been exported as a sandalwood substitute; in 1957-8, approximately 55 tonnes were shipped. However, the main uses of the timber have been as fencing posts which are durable and termite resistant, and as an excellent fuel.

It has been used to a limited extent for small fancy articles and carving.

Distribution: Qld, N.S.W., S.A.

Erythrophleum chlorostachys   IRONWOOD, COOKTOWN IRONWOOD, CAMEL POISON

Ironwood is a widespread tree of open forest country in tropical Australia. It has pinnate leaves of four to nine leaflets, small yellowish flowers, and flattened pods 2.5 - 4 cm broad. As one of its common names suggests, it is a poisonous plant, and not only camels but sheep, cattle, horses and goats have been poisoned by it.

The red-brown timber is exceptionally hard, heavy, strong and durable. Its main use has been as house stumps, railway sleepers and fence posts. The great difficulty of working limits its use for other purposes. It is reported suitable for xylophones, a market of limited potential.

Ironwood was a favourite timber among Aborigines for drone pipes. A branch a metre or a little more in length but not over 5 cm thick, which had been hollowed out by termites, was chosen. The walls of the pipe needed to be thin enough to give the instrument a good resonance. A mouthpiece of beeswax and resin was added and any cracks sealed with resin. When not in use the instrument was stored under water.

Aborigines also used the timber for woomeras and spearpoints. Those of the Prince Charlotte Bay area made fish hooks from tapered slivers of ironwood with a slip of bone attached at an acute angle at the narrow end.

Distribution: Qld, W.A., N.T.

Eucalyptus   GUM TREE

The genus *Eucalyptus* is the world's major hardwood genus. Of over 500 species only about six occur naturally outside Australia and these are limited to islands to the north of the continent. Eucalypts dominate most of the forest area of Australia and are largely responsible for the distinctive aspect of the Australian countryside. This aspect is well appreciated by many Australians although some overseas visitors find the sparse, greyish foliage a little monotonous and uninteresting after being used to a generally deeper green and more densely foliaged forest.

From such a large group it has been possible to select here only the most important species.

Eucalyptus acmenioides   WHITE MAHOGANY,
                                              YELLOW STRINGYBARK

Fibrous bark extends over the trunk and to the small branches in this species. It is a medium size eucalypt with its main occurrence in coastal and subcoastal southern Queensland and northern New South Wales. The cap of the bud is sharply pointed and the capsule is more or less hemispherical.

The timber is yellow-brown, hard and durable with an interlocked grain, and is used particularly for heavy work such as bridge construction, poles, sleepers and weatherboards.
Distribution: Qld, N.S.W.

Eucalyptus astringens   BROWN MALLET

Brown mallet is a small, smooth-barked eucalypt of the south-western part of Western Australia, inland of the jarrah forests. Supplies are now much reduced because of clearing and because of bark stripping for tannin extraction in earlier times.

The timber is very tough with a high shock resistance and so is particularly suitable for the manufacture of handles for axes and other tools. In fact, it has been listed as close in toughness to imported American hickory, generally regarded as the best timber for axe handles, but it has the disadvantage of being a good deal heavier. It is used to some extent as a mining timber for the support of shafts and tunnels.
Distribution: W.A.

Eucalyptus bosistoana   COAST GREY BOX, GIPPSLAND GREY BOX

Although many of the eucalypts classed as boxes have a scaly fibrous bark over much of the trunk, *E. bosistoana*, the largest of the group, has only a relatively short stocking of rough bark.

The timber is of excellent quality being strong, hard, tough with interlocking grain, and durable. It has been used extensively in heavy construction work such as bridges and wharves, for railway sleepers and for house frames.
Distribution: N.S.W., Vic.

Eucalyptus camaldulensis (E. rostrata)   RIVER RED GUM,
MURRAY RED GUM

River red gum occurs extensively in all mainland States and is the most widely distributed eucalypt in Australia. It is mainly a tree of the drier, inland areas and is particularly common along watercourses, both permanent and seasonal, and on the adjacent alluvial flats. Its bark is smooth, except for a short stocking of rough bark at the base, and is shed in large patches leaving an irregular pattern in shades of cream, blue, grey and dull red. It is an ornamental species, often with a relatively short, massive trunk and a broad crown with irregular branches. Although river red gum is planted to only a limited extent in Australia it is one of the most widely cultivated species overseas where there are approximately 500,000 ha of plantations.

The timber is red, hard, heavy, durable, with an interlocked grain, and a considerable resistance to termites. It has been used extensively in bridges, wharves and other heavy construction, and for railway sleepers, fence posts and stumps, and paving blocks. The sawn timber has a strong tendency to warp during drying and at one time a large amount of warped timber was wasted. However, with better seasoning practices this fault can be much reduced and river red gum is now used also as a flooring timber.

The name *Eucalyptus rostrata*, proposed in 1847, was once the widely accepted name for this species in Australia. However, the species had been grown early in the nineteenth century in the extensive Camalduli Gardens near Naples, and the name *E. camaldulensis*, based on one of the specimens there, was used for the species in 1832. When the existence of this earlier name was realized the name *E. rostrata* had to give way to the one commemorating an Italian garden.

Distribution: All mainland States

Eucalyptus delegatensis

ALPINE ASH,
GUM-TOPPED STRINGYBARK,
TASMANIAN OAK

This tall, straight tree of the southern region of Australia has a distinctive bark, thick and fibrous over roughly the lower half of the trunk, but smooth and white to blue-grey above.

The timber is pale, lightweight, tough and easily worked but not very durable. It is extensively used for furniture making, panelling, plywood and general building purposes. Small quantities have been used for oars and implement handles. A considerable amount of Australian-made newsprint is derived from this species.

Distribution: N.S.W., Vic., Tas.

Eucalyptus diversicolor

KARRI

Karri is among the tallest of Australian trees and is known to reach a height of about 87 m with a butt diameter of about 3 m. It is a smooth-barked eucalypt with a distribution limited to the high rainfall area of the south-western part of Western Australia. The forests are often difficult to penetrate because of the dense understorey of other species. Fortunately, the regeneration rate is high so that although the area of forest is not large, good supplies of timber are available. Karri is second to jarrah in importance as a timber tree in Western Australia. It is grown in plantations as a timber tree in South Africa.

The timber is pale pink to red-brown, hard, heavy and tough with great strength and stiffness and is valued highly for heavy construction work such as bridges and wharves. It is used also in general house construction, for railway wagons and for apple cases. Good plywood can be made from it and there is a possibility of using it for paper pulp. At one time it was used extensively for paving blocks.

Distribution: W.A.

Eucalyptus globulus   TASMANIAN BLUE GUM

Although occupying only a limited range in southern Victoria and eastern Tasmania, *E. globulus* is one of the most widely known eucalypt species, being cultivated in a large number of countries. It is a handsome and distinctive tree with coarsely patterned smooth bark. Leaves on juvenile parts are opposite, roughly heart-shaped and distinctly grey because of the heavy bloom of wax which they carry. This type of foliage persists to the sapling stage where there is a transition to the adult leaves which are alternate, much longer and deep green. The top-shaped fruit has a broad, flat rim.

E. globulus is one of the species planted most extensively overseas. In Australia there are plantations approaching 1000 ha, established mainly for paper pulp production.

The timber is yellow-brown, fairly heavy, with an interlocked grain, and is difficult to season. It is used mainly for poles, heavy construction, house construction and railway sleepers. At one time it was popular for wagon building. Some has been used in boatbuilding, and a report of over a hundred years ago stated, 'The best whale-ships that furrow the South American Seas are those of Hobart Town; the keels of which are made of the *Eucalyptus globulus* '.

Distribution: N.S.W., Vic., Tas.

Eucalyptus gummifera   RED BLOODWOOD

Red bloodwood is one of a group of about thirty eucalypts with several characters in common. The leaves have numerous, fine, parallel veins running out from the midrib and the fruit is urn-shaped, often with a constriction a little below the rim. Most, including red bloodwood, have a rough bark shed in irregularly rectangular flakes, but there are a few species with smooth bark whose other characters justify grouping them with the bloodwoods.

Red bloodwood is found along the coast of New South Wales and extends a little way into Queensland and Victoria. Although its timber is durable it has the serious disadvantage, common to many members of this group, of containing prominent, concentric gum veins. These are the source of the bloodlike

exudate which commonly flows from injured trunks. Because of this defect the logs are sawn to only a limited extent and are used mainly in the round for poles, fence posts, house stumps and fuel. Most other bloodwoods are put to similar uses.
Distribution: Qld, N.S.W., Vic.

Eucalyptus maculata   SPOTTED GUM, SPOTTED IRON GUM

Spotted gum is a distinctive tree with smooth bark shed in irregular flakes to produce a mottled effect in grey-green and salmon. There is commonly a small dimple beneath each flake. (The smooth-barked apple, *Angophora costata*, may sometimes have a trunk resembling that of spotted gum but can be distinguished by its opposite leaves.) It is an important plantation tree in South Africa but Australian forests are usually allowed to regenerate naturally.

The timber has been used in general house construction, railway sleepers and some heavy work such as bridge decking. Because of its rather greasy nature it makes good dance floors. Some has been used for plywood. It is not particularly durable in the ground, and when used for poles the wide pale sapwood has to be treated with preservative. It is one of the most elastic eucalypt timbers and has been used for boatbuilding, tool handles, fishing rods and horizontal bars for gymnasts.

A relatively new use for spotted gum is in the manufacture of laminated snow skis. For this type of construction a core of some lightweight timber such as kauri or hoop pine is sandwiched between layers of a hard-wearing timber. For these outer layers spotted gum has been the most popular, although others such as Sydney blue gum and crow's ash also are suitable.
Distribution: Qld, N.S.W., Vic.

Eucalyptus marginata   JARRAH

Jarrah is Western Australia's most important timber tree, and supplies more hardwood annually than any other species in Australia. The tree is confined to the south-west corner of the State where it often occurs in pure stands; these forests have been suggested as constituting the most valuable hardwood forests in the world. Specimens vary from mallee-like plants to large trees 40 m high. Stringy bark extends to the small branches.

The timber is deep red to red-brown, of medium hardness, with excellent durability both in and out of the ground. It is used for nearly all purposes for which wood is commonly used: for piles and decking in wharves and bridges, for almost all parts of houses, for poles and railway sleepers; its very considerable resistance to fire coupled with its durability in the ground makes it an ideal fencing timber. Although heavy for a furniture timber, its attractive colour and grain and ease of working has led to its extensive use for this purpose also. It peels well and is an important plywood timber. Good carvings have been made from jarrah; it is a shipbuilding timber, and at one time it provided large quantities of wood blocks used for paving streets and roads.

In 1948 a successful wood distillation plant was established in Western Australia using waste timber of *E. marginata* and *E. wandoo*. The timber, either limb wood or blocks of waste wood from sawmilling, was dried then heated for about forty-eight hours in a retort, driving off volatile products and leaving charcoal. This charcoal was used in the smelting of iron ore to produce high quality pig iron. From the distillate was recovered methanol, acetic acid and wood tar. The gases driven off from the wood were used as fuel in the operation.

Distribution: W.A.

Eucalyptus microcorys   TALLOW WOOD

This is a tree of the moister type of eucalypt forest in coastal southern Queensland and northern New South Wales. Its rough bark is of the stringybark type but the tree can usually be distinguished from others of the group by the slightly orange-pink tinge in the bark, by the tendency for the main branches to be horizontal, and by the slender, club-shaped buds.

Tallow wood is one of the best Australian hardwoods. The timber is very strong and durable but fairly easy to work. It has been widely used in general building, in heavy construction, and for poles. The greasy surface of the timber suggested the name tallow wood and has made it probably the favourite timber for dance floors. It is particularly suitable for windowsills. Many of the wood blocks once used for paving Sydney streets were cut from tallow wood.

Distribution: Qld, N.S.W.

Eucalyptus miniata   DARWIN WOOLLYBUTT

As the common name of the species suggests, scaly fibrous bark covers the lower part of the trunk, the upper part and branches being smooth barked. The handsome red or orange flowers have led to this species being fairly widely cultivated.

Although the timber is very hard it is not particularly durable and the logs are often faulty. Nevertheless, in the Northern Territory where there is a shortage of good millable trees, Darwin woollybutt is fairly widely used.

Distribution: Qld, W.A., N.T.

Eucalyptus moluccana   GREY BOX, GUM-TOPPED BOX

Rough, scaly fibrous bark usually covers most of the trunk and, in some cases, extends also to the bases of the main branches which otherwise are smooth and grey. Grey box is a common tree of coastal areas in southern Queensland and northern New South Wales but tends to occupy the drier parts of that region.

The timber is very durable, hard, strong and non-splitting, and is used particularly in heavy construction work such as bridge piles and decking. It is regarded as an excellent fuel.

Distribution: Qld, N.S.W.

Eucalyptus obliqua   MESSMATE STRINGYBARK,
                                  TASMANIAN OAK

Messmate stringybark has the distinction of being the first species of *Eucalyptus* to be named and scientifically described in 1788. The tree is a tall stringybark reaching a height of 75 m, and is found mainly in mountainous country. Many eucalypts have an unevenness in the two sides at the base of the leaf but this characteristic is particularly pronounced in *E. obliqua* and is responsible for the second part of the scientific name.

E. obliqua is one of the most important hardwoods of Australia but, although extending to four States, is of major importance only in Victoria and Tasmania. Along with mountain ash and alpine ash it goes in the timber trade under the name Tasmanian oak. The timber is pale and relatively lightweight, dresses well and splits readily, but its sapwood is susceptible to powder post borer. It is widely used in general building construction,

both indoors and outdoors, and for furniture and joinery. Satisfactory wine casks have been made from it and it is used also as case timber, for preparing wood wool, and for railway sleepers. When used for posts and poles it needs to be treated with preservative as it is otherwise not durable in the ground. Because it is easily split, fence palings and shingles were once made from the timber. It is one of the species in the southern Australian region now used for the preparation of paper pulp.
Distribution: N.S.W., Vic., Tas., S.A.

Eucalyptus paniculata   GREY IRONBARK

Grey ironbark is found along most of the coastal region of New South Wales. As in the several other ironbarks, the bark is hard, deeply furrowed, and dark grey or almost black where it is densely impregnated with kino.

The timber is exceptionally hard, strong and heavy and is remarkably durable. For general building work it has the disadvantage that it is difficult to nail without drilling it first. Its main uses are in heavy construction work such as bridges, wharves and warehouses. Extensive use has been made of it for poles which have been found to last up to forty years in the ground.

Most of the other ironbarks have similar timbers and are used for work of the same type. Queen Street in Brisbane was once paved with ironbark wood blocks. When excavations were being dug for the Brisbane City Hall in 1914 a water main of ironbark laid by Andrew Petrie some time before in 1839 was found to be still in good condition.
Distribution: N.S.W.

Eucalyptus pilularis   BLACKBUTT

Blackbutt is widely distributed along the coast of New South Wales and southern Queensland, and is among the largest of the eucalypts. The tallest specimen in New South Wales is one in the Middle Brother State Forest near Port Macquarie. It is approximately 11 m in girth and 70 m high. Fibrous bark covers most of the trunk but the branches are pale and smooth-barked.

The timber is plentiful and is one of the most important of Australian hardwoods. It is light in colour, usually straight-grained, strong and durable, and is widely used in general house construction. Although not as durable in the ground as some other eucalypts it has been used for fence posts and, because it splits readily, for fence palings. When streets were paved with tarred wood blocks, blackbutt was one of the timbers commonly used.

Distribution: Qld, N.S.W.

Eucalyptus propinqua　　　　　　　　　GREY GUM

Eucalyptus propinqua is one of the smooth-barked eucalypts. When the old bark is shed in midsummer the trunk takes on a handsome salmon-orange colour. Over the months this colour gradually fades so that eventually the trunk is clothed in various shades of leaden grey.

Grey gum is an important timber tree in coastal regions of southern Queensland and northern New South Wales. Although the bark bears no resemblance to that of the ironbarks the timber is of the same general type, being very hard, strong and durable. It is used for heavy construction work, general building, posts and poles, and railway sleepers.

Distribution: Qld, N.S.W.

Eucalyptus regnans　　　　　　　　　MOUNTAIN ASH

Mountain ash is the giant among Australian trees and one of the tallest species in the world. During the latter half of the last century there were several reports of enormous trees growing in Victoria, various heights between 120 and 150 metres being claimed. However, the reports are difficult to substantiate and it is likely that most and possibly all were exaggerated. In one case, a tree claimed by two different observers to be 141 metres and 160 metres respectively was subsequently measured by a Government Surveyor and found to be only 67 metres. While taller trees may have occurred, one of the greatest authenticated heights in Victoria appears to be 99 m for a specimen on a spur of Mt Baw Baw which was carefully measured in about 1880 by a civil engineer and a surveyor. The tallest standing tree is one 98 m high growing in the Styx Valley in Tasmania. So the record for the tallest tree on earth must remain with the United States for a specimen of the giant Californian redwood in the

Humboldt-Redwoods State Park, carefully measured and found to be 112.6 m.

Although reaching a great height, the mountain ash is not particularly long lived. It is thought that the maximum age is about 400 years which makes them youngsters compared with the Big Tree, *Sequoiadendron giganteum*, of California, known to reach 3500 years, and the bristlecone pine, *Pinus aristata*, a small, gnarled tree also of California, still living after 4900 years.

The tree grows rapidly, and twenty years after the widespread destruction of this species in Victoria during the disastrous bushfires of 1939, some regrowth specimens had reached a height of about 40 m.

The timber is surprisingly pale, lightweight and easy to work for a eucalypt. It splits readily, and it is recorded that a man once split 650 five-foot palings in a day. Large quantities are used in house construction, and it is suitable also for joinery, furniture making and plywood. Smaller quantities have gone into case timber, wood wool and match splints. When laminated snow skis were first made in Australia, spotted gum was the favourite timber for the outer, hard-wearing layers; however, with the introduction of plastic soles a wider range of softer timbers could be used, and mountain ash and alpine ash were two of these. Mountain ash is the major Australian timber pulped for papermaking.

In 1907 a plant was established at Warburton in Victoria to process the wood of *E. regnans* which otherwise would have been wasted. This was a destructive distillation plant in which the timber was heated to a high temperature, driving off volatile products and leaving charcoal. Among chemicals recovered from the distilled material were methanol, creosote and acetone. However, the plant was not economically successful and closed in 1925. Distribution: Vic., Tas.

Eucalyptus saligna   SYDNEY BLUE GUM

Sydney blue gum is a species of the wetter type of eucalypt forest often found in association with rainforests. The tall mast-like trunk, white to bluish, is smooth except for a stocking of rough bark at the base. Its timber is a valuable one for general building purposes.

The flooded gum, *E. grandis*, with somewhat similar distribution, also has a magnificent clean trunk. Its timber is not as hard as that of *E. saligna* but it also is used in general building work. Those two species are very similar in general appearance but can be distinguished on opened fruit: in *E. grandis* the triangular valves are incurved, while those of *E. saligna* are spread outwards.

Distribution: Qld, N.S.W.

Eucalyptus tereticornis   FOREST RED GUM, BLUE GUM

Forest red gum is a large eucalypt widely distributed in coastal and subcoastal areas of eastern Australia. It is one of the smooth-barked species with bark shed in irregular sheets of varying size leading to a trunk mottled mainly in blues, greys and creams. The name blue gum is derived from the appearance of the trunk and the name forest red gum from the nature of the timber.

The timber is a valuable, tough, durable one and is used particularly in heavy construction for much the same purposes as the ironbarks, although it is not quite as heavy and strong as those timbers. It is useful for steps because it provides a non-slip surface. A Brisbane boatbuilder has claimed it to be the best timber for stem and stern posts.

Distribution: Qld, N.S.W., Vic.

Eucalyptus tessellaris   CARBEEN, MORETON BAY ASH

Carbeen is an attractive and distinctive eucalypt easily recognized by the appearance of its trunk. The lower part is covered with hard, rough bark, cracked longitudinally and horizontally into small rectangular blocks. The specific part of the botanical name is derived from the Latin word for a small stone block and is applied in allusion to this rough bark. Above, the bark is smooth and varies from pale cream to blue-grey depending on how long it has been exposed. Leaves are very narrow and pendulous and the flowers are produced over only a short period in midsummer. Carbeen's main area of occurrence is in Queensland where it extends from about the New South Wales border to Cape York and up to about 500 km from the coast.

The timber is dark, chocolate-brown, slightly greasy, tough, elastic and heavy. It has the disadvantage of being sometimes marred by gum veins and of lacking durability in contact with the ground. Extensive use has been made of it in road and railway bridgebuilding. It is a good timber for tool handles although too heavy to be ideal for this purpose.

Distribution: Qld, N.S.W.

Eucalyptus tetrodonta   DARWIN STRINGYBARK

Although it is by no means one of the best eucalypts for timber, Darwin stringybark is one of the commonest and largest species in the northern part of the Northern Territory and, consequently, is used extensively for general construction and poles. Distinctive features of the species are the occurrence of flowers in groups of three and the presence of four small teeth at the base of the cap of the bud.

Distribution: Qld, W.A., N.T.

Eucalyptus thozetiana   THOZET'S BOX, THOZET'S IRONBOX

This is a medium to small tree found mainly in inland areas of central and southern Queensland. The rough box-type bark is found only close to the base, the rest of the trunk being smooth with the bark shed in small, irregular flakes to produce a mottled trunk.

The timber is very dark, almost black and has the distinction of being probably the hardest of all eucalypt timbers. It is used in general construction work.

Distribution: Qld

Ficus   FIG

Among the numerous species of fig in Australia many belong to the group known as strangling figs which become established in a pocket of humus near the top of some other tree, usually in a rainforest. The descending roots of the fig gradually enmesh the supporting trunk, leading to its eventual death. On decay of the support the fused roots become the apparent trunk of the fig. Such a trunk is useless for sawing and the only useable timber from the specimen is in the true trunk above the point of establishment.

The timber is pale, lightweight, weak, non-durable, often a

little woolly on dressing, and subject to borers. These limitations have led to its use being restricted mainly to the manufacture of packing cases where these characteristics are not a disadvantage. There has been minor use in brush stocks and toys.

The buttresses of some rainforest figs were used by the Aborigines as shields.

Distribution: Qld, N.S.W., Vic., N.T.

Flindersia australis   CROW'S ASH, TEAK

Crow's ash is a rainforest tree, and in this habitat its bark is its most obvious distinguishing feature — scaly and shed in roughly rounded flakes so that the trunk takes on a mottled appearance. Isolated trees growing on the sites of former rainforests have a particularly characteristic form, almost a domed cylinder, which allows at least a tentative identification from a distant silhouette. The distinctive, pendulous fruits, something like woody spiny cucumbers up to 7 cm long, open in five boat-shaped valves shedding prominently winged seeds. Roughening of the sides of the valves originally in contact with each other helps to distinguish fruits of *F. australis* from other species of Flindersia.

The origin of the name crow's ash is obscure. However, it is reported that crows eat the seeds and this may possibly have led to the use of the common name.

Crow's ash timber is hard, durable, yellow-brown and oily, and its general resemblance to Indian teak is responsible for one of its common names. A claim has been made that it is so hard that it will break an axe unless care is exercised. It is a valuable timber, widely used for general building purposes both indoors and outdoors. Because of its durability and oily finish it is one of the most highly regarded Australian timbers for floors. Ships' decks made from crows ash have given particularly good service. It is durable in the ground and has been used in some places for fence posts. At one time it was used for studs in the gold mine shafts at Gympie in Queensland. It was also regarded as a very good timber for lining wells as it did not discolour the water.

Probably because of the oil it contains the timber is very flammable and it is reported that even a fresh-felled log, once ignited, will burn away completely.

Flindersia ifflaiana, the Cairns hickory or hickory ash, of northern Queensland rainforests has a timber very similar to that of *F. australis*.

Distribution: Qld, N.S.W.

Flindersia brayleyana QUEENSLAND MAPLE, MAPLE SILKWOOD

This northern species of *Flindersia* is confined mainly to the Atherton Tableland. Like other members of the genus it has pinnate leaves and characteristically prickly, woody fruits.

Queensland maple is one of the most highly regarded and widely used cabinet timbers in Australia and, in fact, is classed among the world's best. Yellowish brown to pink in colour with a beautiful and variable figure and attractive sheen, it is also strong, light in weight and easily worked. Its ability to take strain readily has led to its use as a substitute for several high-class timbers of darker colour such as mahogany, rosewood and cedar. Considerable quantities have been used in furniture and in decorative panelling, in buildings, railway carriages and boats. The logs peel well and it makes a good plywood and veneer. The Australian Defence Department has used it for gun stocks and, at one time, it was used in the manufacture of aeroplane propellors; part of Ross Smith's flight from England to Australia in 1919 was made with a propellor of Queensland maple.

Distribution: Qld

Flindersia schottiana (F. pubescens) SILVER ASH, BUMPY ASH, CUDGERIE

Rainforest trees are notoriously difficult to identify when the canopies are twenty metres or more from the ground and interlaced with those of neighbouring trees. However, the irregular swellings or bumps which commonly occur here and there on the trunk of this species give a clue to its identity and provide a good reason for one of its common names. Its large, pinnate leaves have almost stalkless leaflets and in November a profusion of small white flowers makes it stand out conspicuously from other trees. The woody, prickly fruits opening in five valves are characteristic of *Flindersia*.

Silver ash is a highly regarded scrub timber used for a wide variety of purposes. It is very pale, often almost white, and

although plain in appearance unless cut near one of the bumps, its charm lies in an attractive almost silvery sheen. The wood has been used extensively for general indoor work including flooring, and, at a time when many floors were left uncovered, was particularly popular because it was easy to wash and did not stain readily. Good bending qualities led to its use in building boats and carriages, one boatbuilder claiming it to be the best timber for ribs which he had used. It is recommended also for masts and oars, and it has been used for sporting equipment such as cricket stumps, tennis racquet frames, billiard cues and baseball bats.
Distribution: Qld, N.S.W.

Flindersia xanthoxyla (F. oxleyana)   YELLOW-WOOD, YELLOW-WOOD ASH

From *F. schottiana* which also has opposite pinnate leaves, *F. xanthoxyla* differs in having leaflets which are fairly straight and with a short stalk, those of *F. schottiana* being almost stalkless and usually with a distinct curve.

The timber is yellowish, strong, elastic and durable, and dresses well with a high sheen. It has been used for general indoor work and for furniture. Because it is an excellent steam-bending timber it was once used extensively in coachbuilding, particularly for the framework supporting fabric hoods. Some of the timber has gone into boat decking and casks, and, at one time, ammunition boxes for the Australian army were made from this species. It has been recommended for artificial limbs.
Distribution: Qld, N.S.W.

Gmelina leichhardtii   WHITE BEECH, GREY TEAK

White beech is a large rainforest tree with broad, opposite leaves and attractive two-lipped purple and white flowers. The rounded, slightly flattened, mauve-blue fruits about 2.5 cm across are sometimes found in large quantities on the ground beneath a tree.

The timber is a plain one, lightweight, cream to light grey or light brown, somewhat oily and with a resemblance to Indian teak. It is soft but tough, durable and termite resistant. Among Australian timbers white beech is probably the one most highly regarded for carving. When more freely available it was used in general construction work for floorings, verandah rail cappings, chamferboards and weatherboards, and for general indoor work. It has the disadvantage that it will rust iron nails when exposed to the weather. Its lightness, durability and absence of swelling or shrinking with changes in moisture conditions made it an ideal timber for the floats of seaplanes and for boat decking.

G. fasciculiflora of north Queensland rainforests is a similar species with similar timber.

Distribution: Qld, N.S.W.

Grevillea robusta   SILKY OAK

Silky oak is one of Australia's best known and most popular cabinet timbers. Unfortunately, rainforests have been largely exhausted of millable logs and much of the timber sold as silky oak now comes from a north Queensland species, *Cardwellia sublimis*. Although silky oak grows very quickly under cultivation as single trees it does not perform satisfactorily in a plantation, so unless new cultivation techniques are developed timber from *Grevillea robusta* will remain scarce. Its popularity as an ornamental tree has spread beyond Australia and even in Kathmandu the silky oak is one of the most common of the cultivated trees.

The tree is a distinctive one with narrow outline and horizontal branches, in form a little like a pine. Leaves are deeply lobed or 'ferny', and almost white on the underside. Its flowers, all directed upwards, are crowded in pairs along a horizontal axis producing a dense golden brush, each flower with a large drop of nectar resting in its brown throat. The carousing collection of nectar-seeking birds which the tree attracts is a good reason for its cultivation in a home garden.

Silky oak timber is light and easily split. Its most distinctive character is the large size of the medullary rays which, depending on the direction of cut, appear as innumerable little lens-shaped patches or as blotches or broken bands. In the latter view the timber has a distinct sheen and it is not clear now whether the term silky was applied because of this character in the timber or because of the silky undersurface of the leaf. The timber has been used very extensively in cabinetmaking, joinery and panelling. At one time, before the advent of more modern containers, an important use was in the manufacture of tallow casks, butter kegs and milk buckets. For these purposes the timber had to be specially cut so that the contents would not leak through the relatively porous wood rays.

Most members of the family Proteaceae to which the silky oak belongs have timber of the same general type, and a layman would have difficulty in distinguishing many of them from silky oak.

Distribution: Qld, N.S.W.

Grevillea striata   BEEFWOOD

The name beefwood is derived from the reddish appearance of the freshly cut timber which suggests raw beef. Distributed over a considerable area of inland Australia, it is a small tree with a relatively narrow crown. The greyish slender leaves 15-45 cm long and mostly 4-8 mm broad have a striated appearance due to the numerous raised parallel veins. Although the leaves are tough and fibrous they are eaten readily by stock.

Where the species grows in quantity it is regarded as an important fencing timber. Since it splits readily and is durable in the weather it was used for shingles on pioneer houses.

Distribution: Qld, N.S.W., S.A., N.T.

Halfordia kendack   SAFFRON HEART, KEROSENE WOOD,
                                       SOUTHERN GHITTOE

This small to medium-sized tree is found particularly in the sandy rainforests close to the coast in southern Queensland and northern New South Wales. Its simple, alternate leaves are usually broadest a little above the middle point and are well supplied with oil glands which release a distinctive aromatic scent when crushed.

The timber is of only minor importance. However, it has the special characteristics of great toughness, strength and elasticity. Before split cane and, later, fibreglass became generally available, these characteristics made it an ideal timber for fishing rods, and the claim has been made that there is no better timber for this purpose.

The closely related species *H. scleroxyla* is found mainly in northern Queensland. It also has been used for fishing rods and, during World War II, was used for underwater bearings of propeller shafts of some small boats.

Timber of both species is oily and burns readily when green, hence the common name kerosene wood which has been applied to both.

Distribution: Qld, N.S.W.

Harpullia pendula   TULIPWOOD, TULIP LANCEWOOD

A small to medium-sized rainforest tree with pinnate leaves, the most distinctive feature of tulipwood is probably its deeply two-lobed, inflated, leathery fruit, yellow to orange-red in colour, each lobe containing a glossy, jet black seed unless a grub has got at it in the early stages. The tree is ornamental and has been used successfully in street planting in Brisbane.

Since the trunk is often angled or channelled, and in any case is not large the timber is available in only fairly small sizes. However it is striking in appearance, with contrasting yellow and dark brown streaks, in some cases producing a tortoiseshell effect. The main uses of tulipwood have been in cabinet work, table legs and small fancy articles such as billiard cues, paper knives, serviette rings and walking sticks.

Distribution: Qld, N.S.W.

Litsea reticulata   BOLLYGUM, BROWN BOLLYWOOD

Scaly bark, shed in rounded flakes so that the trunk is left with a mottled appearance, gives some guide to the identity of this large rainforest tree, although there are a few other species with similar bark. There is nothing particularly distinctive about the alternate, simple leaves.

The timber is tough and light, pale brown and fairly plain. It is a useful cabinet wood, excellent for carving, very suitable for dinghies and a good plywood timber. As a timber for brush backs it is at or close to the top of the list of suitable species. It was once used extensively as staves for casks.

Distribution: Qld, N.S.W.

Melaleuca   TEA-TREE

A number of Australian broad-leaved paperbark tea-trees at one time went under the name *Melaleuca leucadendron* and it is not now always clear to which particular species of this group older publications referred.

The timber which is mostly available in only small sizes is very tough and durable under moist conditions. It has been used for various purposes such as verandah flooring, rafters (used in the round) and railway sleepers. However the purpose for which the timber was most highly regarded, though a minor one, was the construction of boat knees for which its natural bends were used. Considerable quantities have been used also as stakes in oyster beds.

Distribution: Qld, N.S.W., W.A., N.T.

Melia azedarach   WHITE CEDAR

This deciduous rainforest species is well known as a rapidly growing ornamental tree in cultivation, even in dry western areas well removed from its natural habitat. Its large, bipinnate, ferny leaves are, unfortunately, the food of a hairy caterpillar which, at dusk, can be seen ascending the trunk in large numbers for a night's feeding. It is not uncommon for trees to be completely stripped of foliage. Attractive sprays of lilac flowers are followed by yellow, elliptical fruits which have the reputation of being poisonous to pigs and children.

The timber is soft and light, yellow-brown and with prominent growth rings which give it a fairly fancy appearance. It is used to some extent as a cabinet timber, for decorative panelling and in small ornamental articles.

Distribution: Qld, N.S.W., N.T.

Normanbya normanbyi   BLACK PALM

The black palm of northern Queensland rainforests is one of the feather palms. Its leaflets are cut off obliquely at the ends and are pale on the underside. In palms, the bulk of the trunk is made up of fibrous material of little structural value although logs of the coconut are sometimes sawn lengthwise into beams used in house construction. However, surrounding the fibrous core is a relatively hard outer shell a few centimetres thick. In the black palm this layer is very hard and has ebony-like streaks running through a softer cream-coloured ground tissue. It is used to a small extent for fancy articles such as walking sticks and rulers, and for inlay work where use is made of pieces cut transversely which show a pattern of black spots over a pale background. Aborigines used the wood for spears.

Distribution: Qld

Nothofagus cunninghamii   MYRTLE BEECH

The European beech and its three Australian relatives were once regarded as belonging to the one genus *Fagus* but the Australian species are now placed in the separate genus *Nothofagus*, literally 'bastard beech'.

Myrtle beech is the common representative of the group in the southern part of Australia and is particularly well developed in Tasmanian rainforests where the larger specimens reach a height of 50 m. There is a tendency for the branches to support the foliage in distinct layers. Leaves are toothed, 10-25 mm long. Unlike the European beech, the trees are not deciduous.

The timber varies in colour from grey to pink or brown and is strong, lightweight and of fairly uniform texture. Its main use has been in cabinetmaking, panelling and flooring but it has been used also in manufacture of a wide variety of articles including shoe heels, boot lasts, brushes, bobbins, tool handles, casks and felloes (rims of wheels).

Distribution: Vic., Tas.

Nothofagus moorei   NEGROHEAD BEECH, ANTARCTIC BEECH

The northern representative of the beech family in Australia occurs in Queensland and New South Wales rainforests at elevations in excess of 760 m. In New South Wales the tree generally goes under the name negrohead beech but in Queensland, where it is found only near the tops of a few mountains close to the New South Wales border, Antarctic beech is the name more commonly applied. This name is used because related species once grew on the Antarctic continent when its climate was very different from that experienced today.

Although straight trees reaching a height of 35 m occur, many specimens, particularly in the northern part of its range, have irregular, crooked trunks, often several of them arising from a great knobbly base. A beech forest of such trees, their gnarled butts covered with moss and with mist drifting between the trunks, offers a scene in which the imaginative might well expect to see a gnome or two.

Great ages are sometimes attributed to these trees. It is unlikely that any individual trunk is of exceptional age although probably the bases are considerably older than the trunks.

The pink, tough, durable timber shows considerable resemblance to that of the myrtle beech of Victoria and Tasmania and has been used for lining, floorings, joinery and veneers.
Distribution: Qld, N.S.W.

Orites excelsa   WHITE BEEFWOOD

Orites excelsa is a rainforest tree mainly restricted to elevations above 600 m. Its leaves are whitish on the underside, taper gradually into the leaf stalk and are very variable in form; those on flowering parts are undivided except in some cases for irregularly placed teeth, while those on juvenile and non-flowering branches are commonly deeply incised into three to five large lobes.

The timber is similar to that of silky oak and is usually sold under that name.
Distribution: Qld, N.S.W.

Phyllocladus aspleniifolius   CELERY-TOP PINE

Celery-top pine is restricted to Tasmania where it occurs in rainforests and the lighter types of eucalypt forest. It is very unusual among conifers as it bears true leaves only in the seedling stage; what appear to be leathery, irregularly lobed leaves are really flattened, highly modified branches.

The timber is relatively heavy for a pine. It has fairly prominent, narrow growth rings, works well and is durable even in the ground. It has been used for general indoor work including flooring, cabinet work, railway carriage building and boat-building. Because it shows little expansion or contraction with changes in moisture content and is resistant to some acids it is regarded as one of the best Australian timbers for chemical vats.
Distribution: Tas.

Planchonella australis (Sideroxylon australe)   BLACK APPLE,
                                                    YELLOW BULLETWOOD

A rainforest tree with simple, alternate leaves, the most distinctive feature of the black apple is its purple-black, plum-like fruits containing a few large, shiny brown seeds, each with a prominent scar running the full length along one side.

The timber is yellowish, hard and close grained, and cuts very cleanly. It is highly regarded as a carving timber, particularly for fine work and where sharp outlines are required. Woodcuts for printing have also been prepared from this timber.

Distribution: Qld, N.S.W.

Planchonella pohlmaniana   YELLOW BOXWOOD

The distinctive features which help in the recognition of this rainforest tree are its milky latex and the alternate, blunt leaves broadest a little above the mid point.

In Europe, the box, *Buxus sempervirens*, is the timber traditionally used for high-grade carving work such as chessmen, wood-engravings and rulers. The Australian equivalent, for these purposes, is yellow boxwood, so named for the resemblance of the timber rather than because of botanical relationship. The timber is yellow, very fine grained and firm, cuts cleanly in any direction and is considered at least the equal of the European timber. On a more mundane level it has been used also for bread boards, rolling pins and spoons.

Distribution: Qld, N.S.W.

Podocarpus elatus   BROWN PINE, SHE-PINE

Podocarpus belongs to the same major group as the true pines although from its general appearance and reproductive structure the relationship is not obvious. The dark green rigid leaves are narrow, mostly 5-10 cm long, with the midrib the only vein obvious. Its cone is so highly modified that at maturity it consists of a single round seed seated at the apex of a fleshy structure resembling a large purple grape in appearance but not in flavour.

The timber is browner than that of hoop pine, a little heavier and not quite so strong, hence the appellation 'she', as in she-oak, as a derogatory prefix. Nevertheless, in spite of the scorn of the early settlers, the timber sometimes has an attractive figure (it is, after all, a *she*-pine) and is now well regarded and used in cabinetmaking, general indoor work, and boat planking. It has some degree of resistance to marine borers and has been used to a limited extent for wharf piles.

Distribution: Qld, N.S.W.

Premna lignum-vitae (Vitex lignum-vitae)   LIGNUM VITAE, YELLOW HOLLYWOOD

The typically fluted trunk with pale, fairly smooth bark, distinctly yellow when cut, helps to distinguish this rainforest tree. Its opposite leaves on quadrangular stems have small tufts of hairs on the underside at the junction of main and lateral veins. Although cherry-like in appearance, its fruits will provide a surprise for any one trying to eat them.

Among rainforest timbers this species is remarkably durable, and this feature, linked with its easy splitting, has made it one of the few scrub timbers which can be used for fencing. In appearance, it is a plain timber, yellowish to olive in colour. Some of the interesting uses for which it was once recommended are wooden screws, piano sharps (when stained black), knitting needles, fishing rod butts, and fids (the wooden marlinespikes used to separate strands of rope during splicing).

Distribution: Qld, N.S.W.

Rhodamnia trinervia   BROWN MALLETWOOD, SCRUB STRINGYBARK

Rhodamnia trinervia is a tree of rainforests and the wetter types of eucalypt forest, distinguished by its opposite leaves with three prominent longitudinal veins. This is top of the list of Australian timbers tested for toughness and so is recommended for tool handles and mallet heads. A closely related species, *R. argentea*, with a somewhat silvery undersurface to the leaf has a similar timber.

Distribution: Qld, N.S.W.

Rhodosphaera rhodanthema DEEP YELLOWWOOD, TULIP SATINWOOD

This rainforest tree bears some resemblance to red cedar in its scaly bark and pinnate leaves but its round, shiny brown fruits up to 1.5 cm across clearly distinguish it. The decorative timber is variegated in browns and yellow-browns, and has been used for cabinet work and panelling.

Distribution: Qld, N.S.W.

Santalum lanceolatum QUEENSLAND SANDALWOOD, PLUMWOOD

This is a small, slender tree seldom over 6 m high, with greyish leaves on pendulous branchlets, and edible fruits something like very small purple plums. It grows in dry areas and like other sandalwoods is a root parasite. Swain, in *The Timbers and Forest Products of Queensland*, quotes a resident of Hughenden on the collection of sandalwood: 'On the class of country which it frequents, it is impossible for any vehicle to travel; the timber has to be packed out of the ranges to the flat country by horse, and it often happens that horses cannot be used, and the cutter carries it on his shoulder. The good timber is very scattered, and a few miles have to be travelled before a ton of wood can be gathered.' Swain continues, 'It is harvested by itinerant sandalwood getters, and transported on packhorses to rail or landing perhaps 100 miles away from where it grows. It is thence sent by cutter to Thursday Island for consignment to China.' For this effort the sandalwood getters received between £16 and £40 per ton at Thursday Island. For the year 1919-20, approximately 550 tonnes were exported from Queensland. The species was regarded as producing high quality material which was used for the same sandalwood purposes as *S. spicatum*.

The leaves are reported to have been burnt in fires to repel mosquitoes.

Distribution: All mainland States

Santalum spicatum (Eucarya spicata) SANDALWOOD, AUSTRALIAN SANDALWOOD

Sandalwood is a straggly shrub or small tree of arid regions. One log, harvested in 1925, which was regarded as exceptionally large, was approximately 3 m long and a little under a metre in girth at about its mid point. Camels were often used to bring the timber from inaccessible regions to the coast.

Although sandalwood is available only in small sizes it is particularly valuable because of the volatile oil it contains. This gives the timber an attractive scent which it retains for many years. As well as being used for the extraction of oil (p.34) the wood has been exported to Asia, particularly to China, where it was used in small, delicately carved fancy articles such as fans, beads and boxes, and for the preparation of incense for burning in temples. For the latter purpose sandalwood dust is used, mixed with an adhesive, and applied to thin slivers of bamboo. The greater part of the sandalwood produced in Australia has come from Western Australia whence it was exported as early as 1845. In 1876, at about the peak of the trade, nearly 7000 tonnes were exported, and in the period 1845-1923 a total of approximately 358,000 tonnes was exported. It is believed that, at one time, Western Australia supplied about five-sixths of the Chinese market for sandalwood. Although export from Western Australia continues, supplies are now relatively limited.
Distribution: S.A., W.A., N.T.

Sloanea woollsii   CARRIBIN, GREY CARROBEAN,
                                        YELLOW CARABE EN

Sloanea woollsii is one of the prominently buttressed trees of the rainforest and generally is readily distinguished from other species with this feature by the convex outline of the upper edge of the buttress which may reach up the trunk for a height of 6 m. The timber is light brown, fairly plain with an attractive sheen, and cuts cleanly. It has been used for general indoor work and for case timber, and has been shown to be suitable for the manufacture of match splints.
Distribution: Qld, N.S.W.

Streblus pendulinus   WHALEBONE TREE, AXE-HANDLE WOOD,
(Pseudomorus brunonianus)   GREY HANDLEWOOD

Whalebone tree is a small tree of rainforests, particularly of the narrow fringing rainforests along creek banks. In the adult condition the rather sandpapery leaves are elliptical and drawn out into a long point; leaves on coppice shoots or seedlings may be quite different in form, being either much smaller and holly-like or much longer and more slender with a pair of prominent teeth at the base. The species has some resemblance to *Aphananthe philippinensis* which grows in similar situations and whose timber has been marketed under the same common name of grey handlewood. It may be distinguished from *Aphananthe* by the presence of a small conical sheath at the branch apex and by a milky latex exuding from the injured bark.

Because of its relatively small size, the species is of only limited value as a timber tree. However, the cream-coloured wood is tough and elastic, not readily split, and consequently has found its main use in the manufacture of tool handles and mallets and in some sporting equipment such as baseball bats and croquet mallets. Aborigines used it for boomerangs.
Distribution: Qld, N.S.W.

Syncarpia glomulifera (S. laurifolia)   TURPENTINE

Turpentine is an essential oil found in the resinous exudate of certain pine trees, and is extracted from pine wood. The Australian tree which bears the name turpentine has nothing to do with this substance and seems to have been so named because of a resinous exudate which exudes when the inner bark is injured. Maiden, in his *Forest Flora of New South Wales* has an interesting note on the use of the name turpentine for this tree: 'Turpentine timber has scarcely any odour, but I have known of perfectly well-authenticated instances in which men, insisting that turpentine timber is so called because of an odour of turpentine, were obliged by accommodating timber-getters who sprinkled their logs with turpentine prior to inspection.'

Syncarpia glomulifera is a large tree up to approximately 45 m high with flaky-fibrous bark, found in eucalypt forests, often particularly well developed in the transitional region between eucalypt forest and rainforest. Leaves, dark glossy green on top and pale on the underside, tend to be in groups along the twigs. The flowers, with numerous white stamens, are fused into a head and are followed by woody fruits, similarly fused, one at the apex of the group and six around the circumference.

Turpentine is a good, durable, general purpose, termite-resistant hardwood, which is used in general construction, particularly for heavy purposes such as beams, wharf decking and heavy poles. Probably the tree's main claim to fame is that it heads the list of Australian timbers resistant to marine borers. The shipworm or cobra causes enormous damage to wooden boats and wharves both in Australia and overseas. It enters by a small hole and proceeds to eat its way through the timber, sometimes reaching a length of about two metres. The original inhabitants of Australia appreciated the shipworm as an edible delicacy, as fishermen in parts of the Malayan region still do; they set out stakes of suitable timber to serve as a culture medium for these highly modified molluscs which are later harvested and eaten. Modern Australians find no such attraction in these shipworms which can destroy a boat's one-inch planking in less than two months. Although not wholly immune to attack, its very considerable resistance, coupled with its strength, has made turpentine the favourite timber for wharf piles. It is also used for underwater boat planking. The resistance to borers is due largely to small deposits of silica which occur in the timber and blunt the animal's cutting organs just as they do the sawmiller's saw.

Turpentine is claimed to be one of the world's most resistant timbers to damage by fire. Maiden has an interesting note also on this characteristic, reporting that surprise had been expressed that in a large fire in Sydney the building had not been gutted; it turned out that for the wooden girders and joists, for which ironbark had been specified, the contractor had substituted turpentine.

Distribution: Qld, N.S.W.

Syncarpia hillii   RED SATINAY, FRASER ISLAND TURPENTINE

Fraser Island's sandy valleys are the stronghold of this magnificent tree which grows to 40 m high. The bark is fibrous, and both the leaves and fruits rather larger than those of *S. glomulifera*.

The timber is strawberry coloured with an attractive ripple-like figure, and polishes well. There are the added advantages of termite resistance, considerable fire resistance, and durability; it has been reported that a log cut and left in the bush for forty years milled satisfactorily. It is used in general building for both indoor and outdoor purposes and for cabinet work where a fairly heavy timber is not a disadvantage. Fraser Island turpentine was used in the construction of the Suez Canal.

Distribution: Qld

Syzygium francisii (Eugenia francisii)   GIANT WATER GUM,
ROSE SATINASH

This species, known to reach a height of 42 m, is possibly the largest of the numerous species, once grouped in the genus *Eugenia*, which occur in the rainforest of eastern Australia. It was named after W. D. Francis, pioneer botanist of rainforests and author of the widely known *Australian Rain-forest Trees*. The opposite leaves, 4-8 cm long, are often drawn out to a long, blunt point and are distinctly paler on the lower than on the upper side. Its fruit is blue-purple, rounded and somewhat flattened, and about 13 mm in diameter.

The timber is pinkish, plain, tough and rather too heavy for cabinet work. However, it is used for the interior parts of houses, including floorings, for case timber and for small tool handles. At one time it was steam bent for the making of heavy wheelbarrows for concrete work.

Distribution: Qld, N.S.W.

Toona australis (Cedrela toona)   RED CEDAR

Red cedar is one of the large trees of Australian rainforests, reported to reach a height of about 60 m and a trunk diameter of approximately 3 m, although trees of such size would be exceptional.

The bark is prominently cracked, both longitudinally and horizontally, giving it a tessellated appearance which makes red cedar fairly easy to recognize by its trunk. Among rainforest plants it is one of the few deciduous species, a character which contributed to its heavy exploitation. The new pinnate leaves produced in spring are pinkish, so the trees stand out clearly in the dark green canopy and thus could be easily spotted from a considerable distance by the cedar-getters. The long sprays of small white flowers are followed by dry fruits up to 2.5 cm long, opening in five valves to release the winged seeds held in five grooves in a central, angular column. These dried, opened fruits are attractive structures, flower-like in appearance, and are sometimes used in dried floral arrangements.

Red cedar bears no close botanical relationship to the true cedars such as the cedar of Lebanon, although there is some resemblance in the timbers. However, both the red cedar and the cedar of Lebanon are alike in having been grossly over-exploited; the cedars of Lebanon were plundered 3000 years ago by Solomon and others of the area, so that today hardly any cedars grow on the sites of the original forests in Lebanon; in Australia, the cedar-cutters often extracted from the forests only the red cedar which was used in a most profligate manner, whole buildings sometimes being constructed mainly of cedar.

Red cedar was first cut in the vicinity of Sydney but as the supplies there became exhausted the cedar-cutters gradually worked their way up the coast, finally, by 1842, to the Big Scrub of northern New South Wales, a vast rainforest now represented by only a few small remnants. In this area, cutting was at first restricted to the vicinity of streams so that the logs could be floated down to the coast. Much of the early exploration of rainforests resulted from the activity of these cedar-cutters, a hardy group said to be very hospitable but not universally held in high esteem; it was claimed that '. . . vice of the most abominable kind was practised among those cedar hordes, to the total annihilation of every correct principle'.

In the early days of the Moreton Bay settlement, convicts were set to cutting red cedar, which soon became exhausted in the readily accessible areas. Dr Dunmore Lang, who was so active in promoting immigration to Australia, wrote in 1847, 'On most of the rivers that fall into Moreton Bay, the cedar has long since been cut away . . . and large quantities of that timber were actually piled up, and left to rot on the beach at Dunwich.'

Red cedar is now a rare timber. Although specimens cultivated in home gardens and on farm properties often show rapid growth it seems unlikely that supplies of the timber will be augmented from cultivated trees; the plants are attacked by the larva of the red cedar twig-borer which is usually more troublesome under plantation conditions than it is with isolated trees.

The timber is an exceptionally durable one, and logs may lie in the rainforest for many years suffering only superficial decay. There is one record of a log described as almost perfectly sound when it was rediscovered after having been cut about thirty years earlier. The pale sapwood, however, is prone to attack by borers.

No Australian cabinet timber is better known or generally more highly regarded than red cedar and its identification as the timber in a piece of furniture is generally accepted immediately as a guarantee of quality.

Red cedar timber typically has a handsome, dark red colour although some specimens are pink or even yellowish; it has a tendency to darken with age. Some pieces have an attractive figure and these have been used very successfully in veneers. It is light, soft, very easy to work, bends well, is extremely durable, and takes an excellent polish. Apart from the general purposes to which it was put in the early days of plenty, it has been used mainly for furniture and interior fittings. Considerable quantities have gone into railway carriage construction in eastern Australia. Minor uses have included cigar boxes and the planking for small boats. Cedar sawdust used for smoking ham was said to impart a 'particularly nice flavour'.

Distribution: Qld, N.S.W.

Tristania conferta   BRUSH BOX, BRISBANE BOX, SCRUB BOX

Tristania conferta, known under half a dozen different common names all containing the word 'box', varies from a forest giant in marginal rainforest areas to stunted trees only a few metres high in harsher situations. In coastal Queensland its growth is usually too vigorous for it to be a suitable home garden or street tree, but in Sydney, Melbourne and Perth it forms a moderate-sized tree with compact crown and has been successful in footpath planting.

Bark on the lower part of the trunk is rough and scaly fibrous but the upper trunk and branches have an attractive, smooth, salmon-coloured bark. The distinctive flowers have the stamens united in five claw-like bundles.

Apart from its tendency to blunt saws and to shrink and warp on drying, brush box is an excellent hardwood, reasonably resistant to marine borers and termites. It is used as a general building timber, particularly for floorings and weatherboards. On ageing it becomes extremely hard and is a particularly good timber for bridge and wharf decking. For the wooden tram rails once laid extensively in Australia for hauling timber, brush box was regarded as ideal, becoming polished and very hard with use. Small quantities are used for making mallets and chisel handles. Distribution: Qld, N.S.W.

Tristania suaveolens   SWAMP MAHOGANY, SWAMP BOX

Swamp mahogany has flowers of the same general type as *T. conferta*, but is readily distinguished by the rough, scaly-fibrous bark which extends to the small branches, and by the crooked nature of its branches. Although reaching a height of 25 m it is, in general, a much smaller tree than *T. conferta*.

The hardwood timber is dark red-brown to chocolate brown, not particularly strong, and has a strong tendency to warp and shrink on drying. Sapwood is rapidly destroyed by borers. It is used for general building purposes but its main claim to fame is its considerable resistance to marine borers, ranking next to *Syncarpia glomulifera* among Australian timbers. However, not being particularly strong, it is not generally used for those parts of wharves subject to the greatest strain. As a fuel, it is poor, burning reluctantly and producing large quantities of soot. Distribution: Qld, N.S.W.

Zanthoxylum brachyacanthum   THORNY YELLOW-WOOD,
                                        SATINWOOD

Thorny yellow-wood is not an economically important tree but is so distinctive that it deserves a mention. It is a small rainforest tree with pinnate leaves and densely prickly stems, the robust prickles often found even on the trunk. The wood is a surprisingly bright yellow colour, and although it is not available in large sizes or quantity its striking appearance makes it suitable for fancy articles and inlay work. Distribution: Qld, N.S.W.

7

Honey and Pollen

ALTHOUGH the Aborigines collected honey stored by native bees they did not engage in beekeeping, and it was not until 1822 that the honey bee was first brought to Australia. This species now forms the basis of an important industry, producing annually about 20 million kg of honey, making Australia one of the four leading honey-producing countries of the world.

Honey is a concentrated solution of various sugars derived from nectar collected and processed by bees. Nectar is produced by glands usually at the base of a flower. Although not obvious in most flowers, in some it is produced in such large quantities that a glistening drop can be seen resting in the throat of the flower. There is so much nectar present in grass trees and silky oaks that anyone standing under a shaken inflorescence will receive an uncomfortable, sticky shower. Bees may also collect some sugary solution from nectar glands not associated with the flower, or from honeydew excreted by various insects living on plants; however, these sources are of little importance in Australia.

The amount of sugars in nectar varies a great deal, both between different species and in the one species at different times of the day. However, a concentration of 25-30% sugars is fairly common. This relatively weak solution is gathered by the worker bees and deposited in the hive where the water content is rapidly reduced by a system of fanning in which the bees drive air into and out of the hive. When evaporation has reduced the water content to usually less than 20% the honey is sealed in the hexagonal cells of the wax combs. Various authorities set standards of between 18.5% and 21% as the maximum permissible water content of marketable honey.

The sugars secreted by nectar glands are glucose, fructose and sucrose or cane sugar, the nectar composition varying from species to species. In honey, however, the proportion of sucrose is usually very low, often no more than 2%, because an enzyme produced by the bee splits most of the sucrose into the simpler glucose and fructose. To guard against adulteration of honey with sucrose, a standard of no more than 5% sucrose is set for most honeys, although special provision is made for honey from some species known to contain naturally a percentage of sucrose in excess of this figure. Most Australian honeys pass the 5% test but samples from a small number of species including *Xanthorrhoea, Banksia menziesii* and *Eucalyptus globoidea* contain more.

Although to some people a honey is at its peak when candied, liquid honeys are preferred for the export trade. The tendency for a honey to candy or granulate is, in general, greatest in those with a high proportion of glucose.

In addition to the sugars and water in honey there are various other constituents such as pigments, acids, essential oils and esters that are responsible for the distinctive colour, texture and flavour of individual honeys. The colour of a honey is not unchanging, and there is a tendency for it to darken on ageing or if heated. In general, Australian honeys are darker than overseas honeys which places them at a disadvantage in the export trade, since honey importers prefer the lighter coloured products with which they are familiar.

Not all nectar produces a marketable honey. Some has too poor a flavour for use as a table honey but can be used in manufactured products; some is so unpalatable that it is unfit for human consumption, and is usually left in the hive for the use of the bees. There are even honeys poisonous to man although, fortunately, cases of human poisoning are rare. The earliest recorded incident of this type occurred in about 400 B.C. Xenophon led an army of 10,000 Greek mercenaries against the Persians, and on the retreat from this campaign his men when camped on the shores of the Black Sea ate honey probably derived from *Rhododendron ponticum*. The results were spectacular: '. . . all of the soldiers who ate of the combs lost their senses, vomited, and were affected with purging, and none of them were able to stand upright. Those who had eaten little were like men intoxicated; those who had eaten much were like madmen, and some like persons at the point of death.' Such honey poisoning is fairly well known in the region of the Black Sea and Caspian Sea. Poisonings have occurred in New Zealand but fortunately no cases have been reported in Australia from commercial honey.

However, native-bee honey derived from the mangrove *Rhizophora* is believed to be poisonous, and there is a recorded case of two men suffering severe internal pains after eating native-bee honey from hives in the vicinity of a *Rhizophora* swamp. It was noted at the time that the Aborigines avoided cutting out hives in such localities. Nevertheless, *Rhizophora* has not been proved to be the source of this poisonous honey.

As important to the bees as nectar is pollen, which is the source of protein and other nutrients particularly for the developing bees. An active colony may collect more than 30 kg of pollen in a season.

Flowers of a very large number of species are visited by bees. Some of these plants may produce useful quantities of nectar or pollen for a hive in their vicinity but are of only minor importance on a broad scale. For example, Iceland poppies in a garden are worked very actively by bees but are of no real significance to beekeepers. Plants important to apiarists fall into three groups; native plants, weeds, and crop plants. In this chapter only a selection of the native plants and weeds are considered, and there are species which have been omitted although they may be of importance in limited areas.

Acacia   WATTLE

Wattles produce an abundance of small lemon to golden flowers arranged in fluffy heads or fingers. The flowers produce no nectar but they do supply an abundance of pollen, which, in the case of some species, is important in the brood-rearing season. With over 700 species in Australia, wattles have an even more extensive range than the eucalypts, being found from rainforests to parts of the interior too harsh to support gum trees. Some species can be found flowering at almost any time of the year but the main burst of flowering is in spring when brood-rearing occurs.
Distribution: Some species in all States.

Angophora costata   RUSTY GUM, CABBAGE GUM,
                                       SMOOTH-BARKED APPLE

Rusty gum is a tree of eucalypt forests, generally on poor sandy or stony country. On general appearance it is easy to confuse it with *Eucalyptus maculata* (spotted gum) but the two can be readily distinguished on the arrangement of the leaves, opposite in rusty gum and alternate in spotted gum. The flowers of *Angophora* have the same general appearance as *Eucalyptus* flowers but small white petals are present on the open flower, not thrown off as a cap or operculum as in *Eucalyptus*. Trees are smooth barked, and at about Christmas time the old bark is shed exposing the bright salmon-pink or orange new bark which makes the tree very striking and attractive. Over the months the colour gradually fades to grey.

Vigorous flowering occurs only once every few years and at these times the species is a valuable source of pollen. It yields a fairly pale honey of minor importance.
Distribution: Qld, N.S.W.

Angophora floribunda (A. intermedia)   ROUGH-BARKED APPLE

Rough-barked apple is found mainly in subcoastal districts of Queensland and New South Wales, growing particularly on alluvial flats. It is a species with flaky bark and narrow leaves approaching those of *A. costata* in appearance. The flowers, which are borne in greatest profusion in the drier years are an important pollen source. However, the honey is strongly flavoured and is generally left in the hive.
Distribution: Qld, N.S.W.

Angophora subvelutina   BROAD-LEAVED APPLE

Broad-leaved apple has a fairly short trunk, spreading crown and very crooked branching, not the sort of tree to excite a timber man, but one with character and considerable aesthetic appeal. However, its tendency to shed branches unexpectedly reduces its attraction at a camp site. The bark is rough and flaky and leaves are opposite, often more or less heart shaped. Broad-leaved apples are trees of eucalypt forests and are particularly common on alluvial flats.

Bees work the flowers for pollen and nectar in midsummer. It is an important source of pollen but the honey is of poor quality. Distribution: Qld, N.S.W.

Arctotheca calendula (Cryptostemma calendulaceum)   CAPE WEED

Cape weed was an early introduction from South Africa that has become widely established in Australia, particularly in southern regions. While it is eaten by stock, it is a troublesome weed because the plants often crowd out more desirable species. It is an annual herb with prostrate stems; leaves are cottony on the underside and deeply incised almost to the midrib. The yellow flowers, somewhat calendula-like as the name suggests, make a spectacular display when seen in the mass.

Cape weed is a very valuable pollen producer when it occurs in quantity. The honey has a poor flavour and is not gathered to a large extent. Distribution: All States

Argemone ochroleuca   MEXICAN POPPY

The Mexican poppy is an introduced weed widely naturalized in Australia and particularly common on the alluvial borders of streams. Its grey leaves are irregularly indented with the lobes ending in needle-like spines; the pale yellow flowers are of the typical poppy type. Poppies have little nectar but produce an abundance of pollen; grains falling from the disturbed anthers fall into the cup formed by the petals and so are not lost to the bees. In some areas the plant is a valuable source of pollen, important in brood-rearing. Those who have grown Iceland poppies know how eagerly bees tear at the petals of an opening bud trying to reach the new supply of anthers. Knowledge that poppies are a source of opium has prompted the suggestion that bees visiting poppies become drug addicts and that their eagerness at opening buds is the result of their frantic need for the first shot of the day. The fact that the pollen contains no opium spoils a good story. Distribution: Qld, N.S.W., Vic.

Baccharis halimifolia   GROUNDSEL BUSH

This immigrant from South America was present in coastal

Queensland for many years without causing undue trouble before it 'exploded' in 1937 and became a serious pest, forming dense shrubby stands up to 3 m high and crowding out valuable pasture plants. However, the infestation was not totally without value since the flowers produced in large numbers in small cream heads are a valuable source of pollen during March and April when many other species have finished flowering.

Distribution: Qld, N.S.W.

Banksia integrifolia   BOTTLEBRUSH, WHITE HONEYSUCKLE

Banksia integrifolia is mainly a small tree of coastal sand dunes where it is often one of the earliest trees to colonize the sand. In this habitat the leaves, white on the underside, have mainly smooth margins. The species occurs also to a limited extent away from the coastal dunes and such specimens often have leaves with distinctly toothed margins. Its cream flowers are grouped densely in a rigid bottlebrush.

The flowers supply good quantities of pollen and nectar and although the honey is of poor quality the species is useful in supporting hives during autumn and early winter when flowering, in general, is sparse.

Distribution: Qld, N.S.W., Vic.

Boronia rosmarinifolia   FOREST BORONIA

Forest boronia is a rather sparse, small shrub of coastal and subcoastal southern Queensland and northern New South Wales. The simple, slender leaves are in opposite pairs and the lolly-pink flowers with four petals are borne singly in the leaf axils. Although its nectar is of minor importance the plant is a major source of pollen in spring.

Distribution: Qld, N.S.W.

Casuarina   SHE-OAK

Species of *Casuarina* have very reduced male and female flowers without petals and in some cases flowers of different sex are borne on different trees. *C. littoralis* (black she-oak) is one of these and here the male flowers are borne so densely that the whole tree commonly takes on a rusty appearance at flowering and constitutes a reasonably important pollen source. Other species of the genus are of varying importance.

Distribution: Some species in all States

Centaurea solstitialis   ST BARNABY'S THISTLE

This weed of European origin flowers in its native land in midsummer at about the time of St Barnabas's Day, 11 June. In Australia it is a common weed in wheatfields. There is a basal rosette of leaves and an erect branched, ridged stem bearing leaves which are deeply incised in the lower part, often much smaller and entire in the upper parts. Soft cottony hairs cover much of the plant. The yellow thistle-like heads of flowers have robust, needle-sharp prickles on the outside.

The nectar yields a pale, high quality honey which candies readily.

Distribution: All States

Echium plantagineum   PATERSON'S CURSE, SALVATION JANE

E. plantagineum is a European immigrant which has found conditions very much to its liking in parts of southern Australia where in spring it forms glorious lilac-blue sheets over pasture and agricultural land. In areas where it is a troublesome weed it is known as Paterson's curse commemorating a family which introduced it as an ornamental near Albury. But where it has formed a useful emergency stock food it has received the more complimentary name of salvation Jane. At some periods it is a useful source of a reasonable quality light-coloured honey.

Distribution: Qld, N.S.W., Vic., Tas., S.A., N.T.

Eucalyptus   GUM TREE

Because it occurs so widely and has so many species, *Eucalyptus* is an important genus for honey production. However the species vary greatly in their usefulness to the beekeeper, some being major sources of nectar while others are valued mainly for their pollen, while many others again are of little or no interest at all.

The following species are of considerable importance as nectar sources: *E. accedens, E. caleyi, E. calophylla, E. camaldulensis, E. diversifolia, E. drepanophylla, E. redunca, E. sideroxylon.*

Eucalyptus melliodora   YELLOW BOX, YELLOW JACKET

Yellow box is one of the group of eucalypts sometimes called half-barks which have a rough bark extending well up the trunk and sometimes to the main branches. A distinctive feature of this species is the bright yellow colour of the inner bark.

Yellow box is a major source of honey and is generally regarded as the best among the eucalypts, producing a pale product with very little tendency to candy.

A claim has been made that the original Black Stump, so celebrated as an Australian geographical landmark, was a yellow box tree in the Merriwagga district of the northern Riverina. However, this is only one of several claims made to the distinction.

Distribution: Qld, N.S.W., Vic.

Eucryphia lucida (E. billardieri)   LEATHERWOOD

Leatherwood, restricted to Tasmanian rainforests, varies from a shrub to a tree up to 30 m high. The opposite, blunt leaves 25-45 mm long are pale on the underside and the leaf buds are covered with yellow specks of gummy material. Sepals are shed from the flower bud as a cap or operculum and the four white petals and numerous stamens then expand to form a most attractive flower up to 4 cm across with a slight resemblance to a small single rose. This is one of the most important nectar plants in Tasmania, and Tasmanian leatherwood honey is justly famous for its fine and distinctive flavour.

Distribution: Tas.

*Heliotropium amplexicaule   BLUE HELIOTROPE

This South American species is well established as an attractive weed in parts of coastal and subcoastal Queensland and New South Wales. In fact, were it not a weed probably it would be cultivated to some extent as an ornamental. It is a hairy, prostrate plant with purple-blue flowers arranged in distinctive terminal coils which gradually unroll as the buds mature. Where it is common it forms a useful source of pollen. The honey is at first pale and palatable but on keeping it darkens and deteriorates in flavour so is used mainly in manufacturing.

Distribution: Qld, N.S.W.

Jacksonia scoparia   DOGWOOD, BROOMBUSH

Over wide areas of coastal Queensland and New South Wales, dogwood is a common constituent of eucalypt forests, particularly those on fairly poor soil. It is found mainly as a shrub but sometimes becomes a small tree with deeply furrowed bark. The 'foliage' is made up of slender, green angular branchlets, often pendulous, and true leaves are found usually only in juvenile plants. In spring it is a handsome sight with its masses of small yellow pea flowers. Bees work actively over the flowers which are a valuable source of pollen.

The common name, dogwood, is derived from the unpleasant odour which the timber gives off when burnt.

Distribution: Qld, N.S.W.

Leptospermum flavescens   TEA-TREE, WILD MAY

Leptospermum flavescens has a widespread distribution along the coastal and subcoastal areas of eastern Australia and in Tasmania, occurring particularly on fairly poor soil. It is a densely twiggy shrub with small leaves containing oil glands. Its rapid growth and the attractive, white flowers with some resemblance in form to the well-known Geraldton wax have made it a popular garden subject, and several forms with particularly attractive flowers have entered into cultivation.

The plants are a useful source of pollen but the honey jellies in the comb and usually is not extracted.

Distribution: Qld, N.S.W., Vic., Tas.

Melaleuca lanceolata (M. pubescens)   WESTERN TEA-TREE,
                                                             MOONAH

Melaleuca lanceolata bears little obvious resemblance to its relative, *M. quinquenervia*, of coastal swamps. It is a species of relatively dry country with rough, non-papery bark and small, crowded, narrow leaves not over 2 mm broad. It produces a honey of poor quality but is a valuable pollen source.

Distribution: All mainland States

Melaleuca quinquenervia   PAPERBARK TEA-TREE

This tea-tree is a common and well-known species in coastal swampy country from north Queensland to Sydney. It often grows in almost pure stands, the slender, densely placed trunks covered with whitish, papery bark producing a forest of most distinctive appearance. When well developed, trees in such forests may reach a height of about 25 m but isolated specimens are much lower, often irregular and gnarled. The rigid leaves, mostly 1-2 cm wide, taper evenly to both ends and have 5-7 longitudinal veins. White or pale cream sweetly scented flowers with long stamens are borne in dense bottlebrushes, mainly during autumn.

The honey is light to dark amber, depending on the district from which the nectar was gathered. It is strongly flavoured and candies readily, and although not regarded as a high-grade product, tea-tree honey is popular among many people. The flowers are also an important source of pollen.

Distribution: Qld, N.S.W.

Opuntia stricta (O. inermis)   PRICKLY PEAR

At one time when this terrible weed covered large areas of Queensland and New South Wales a minor benefit from the plant was the honey derived from the large yellow flowers. It was fairly pale, with an almond flavour, and was generally used in blends.

Distribution: Qld, N.S.W., Vic., S.A.

Pultenaea villosa   HAIRY BUSH-PEA

This is one of the species which heralds the spring burst of wild flower blooming. When covered with the masses of small yellow flowers it is a conspicuous part of the wildflower flora of much of the coastal regions of southern Queensland and New South Wales. It produces good quantities of pollen and is valued by beekeepers in coastal districts.

Distribution: Qld, N.S.W., Vic.

Rapistrum rugosum   TURNIP WEED, GIANT MUSTARD

This widespread weed, common in some wheatfields, originates in Europe. It has a basal rosette of lobed leaves and an erect branched stem often a metre or more high with widely scattered leaves. Yellow, four-petalled flowers are borne on the long, leafless final parts of the branches. The fruit is distinctive with a narrow sterile basal part and a rounded, furrowed, upper part containing a single seed.

This is an important source of pollen in some areas but only small quantities of a rather strong honey are produced from it. Various other introduced mustards also produce useful quantities of pollen.

Distribution: All States

Rubus proceras   BLACKBERRY

Blackberries are often serious pests in Australia, forming dense thickets almost impenetrable because of the vicious prickles arming the stems. In cooler parts of Australia this plant is of some value as a nectar source which provides a pale honey of mild flavour. In Tasmania it is one of the three most important nectar species.

Distribution: Qld, N.S.W., Vic., Tas., S.A.

Salvia reflexa   MINTWEED

Mintweed is an annual herb mostly not over 45 cm high, with angular stems, small blue flowers, and a strong mint odour in crushed leaves. It is a North American species widely naturalized in Australia, particularly on heavy soils in subcoastal areas. The plant is poisonous and has caused some stock losses, mainly among hungry animals. However, on the credit side is its value to beekeepers. It is a valuable pollen source and although only small quantities of honey are produced from it this is of high quality.

Distribution: Qld, N.S.W., Vic., S.A.

Tribulus terrestris   CALTROPS, CAT-HEAD

Caltrops is a herb of mainly dry country which grows very rapidly after rain. It has a usually deeply penetrating taproot and opposite pinnate leaves on long, prostrate stems. The attractive, bright yellow flowers are followed by fruits splitting into five segments which always lie so that one of the robust prickles is directed upwards ready to puncture a foot or inner tube. It is to these fruits that the plant owes its most used common name. A caltrop was a ball-like structure with projecting iron spikes so arranged that one always pointed upwards. During the Middle

Ages these were strewn in the path of an advancing army and were particularly effective in impeding cavalry advances.

Caltrops is a valuable pollen plant in some areas. Pollen which falls from the stamens is often caught in the saucer formed by the petals and so is not lost to the bees. Useful quantities of nectar also are produced but the pale honey is usually blended with others.

Distribution: All mainland States

Tristania conferta   BRUSH BOX, BRISBANE BOX, SCRUB BOX

Tristania conferta is a common constituent of many eucalypt forests of coastal Queensland and New South Wales, and varies from a giant of rainforest margins to small mallee-like specimens. A strong tendency for the broad leaves to be in groups along the twigs and the white flowers with five prominent bundles of stamens makes the tree distinctive.

Honey from this species is of good quality, very pale, and candies readily. It is used particularly in blending with honeys of stronger flavour and deeper colour.

T. suaveolens, the swamp mahogany, distinguished by its scaly fibrous bark extending to the final branches, yields a similar honey.

Distribution: Qld, N.S.W., N.T.

Xanthorrhoea   GRASS TREE, BLACK BOY, YACCA

The grass trees with their pole-like spike of densely placed small white flowers topping a crown of slender, arching leaves are a conspicuous part of the flora wherever they occur. A large drop of nectar can usually be seen in the throat of each flower and these were collected for food by the Aborigines. However, although the nectar is so obvious the plants are not major sources of nectar and pollen for apiarists, and the honey produced from *Xanthorrhoea* is of poor quality.

Distribution: Some species in all States

8

Grazing and Browsing

'I s'pose the flats is pretty green up there in Ironbark.'

A. B. Paterson

PASTURE PLANTS

AUSTRALIAN pasture plants have evolved in association with marsupials, and not all stand up well to the relatively heavy grazing of domestic animals. There has therefore been a strong tendency to improve pastures by the introduction of exotic species, many of which respond better than native plants to the application of fertilizer and have various other advantages. Nevertheless, native species are still of very considerable importance, particularly in drier parts of the country, and some of the most important of these are included here.

Astrebla lappacea   CURLY MITCHELL GRASS

Travellers who drive through the central west of Queensland from Charleville through Blackall, Longreach and Winton to Cloncurry will cover more than 3000 kilometres of country, almost all of which will be black soil plains whose vegetation is dominated by species of *Astrebla*, the Mitchell grasses. This community extends discontinuously across the Northern Territory into Western Australia, and southward into the north-western part of New South Wales. In Queensland it is the vast areas of the Mitchell grass plains that comprise the main sheep-raising country.

There are four species of *Astrebla* of value for grazing, with *A. lappacea* the most important in Queensland, and *A. pectinata* (barley Mitchell) in the Northern Territory and Western Australia. The grasses are perennial summer-rainfall species mainly in the 250-500 mm rainfall zone. They grow in dense tussocks and the dense crown development and hardiness enable them to resist drought and heavy grazing. Between the tussocks the ground may be bare in dry weather, but is sometimes covered with annual grasses such as Flinders grass, *Iseilema membranaceum*, and herbs such as native legumes. Seed-heads of *Astrebla* are spike-like, similar in form to wheat.

Distribution: Qld, N.S.W., S.A., W.A., N.T.

Atriplex nummularia   OLD MAN SALTBUSH

Old man saltbush is an arid-land shrub growing to about 3 m high with rounded, blue-grey leaves covered with small scales. There are distinct male and female flowers, rather inconspicuous, borne on different plants. On the female plant the small fruits are enclosed by two toothed, scale-like structures pressed closely together.

The plant is an excellent drought fodder of high nutritive value and with a pronounced salty taste. In some areas it has been heavily overgrazed and is now scarce.

Distribution: All mainland States

Atriplex vesicaria   BLADDER SALTBUSH

One of the commonest of the saltbushes, *Atriplex vesicaria* is found widely in the inland, from the Mallee of Victoria, through the mulga areas of South Australia to the saltbush shrublands where it is frequently the dominant species on shallower soils. A low erect shrub to about 60 cm tall, it has white, rounded or oblong leaves; its conspicuous feature is the fruit with large inflated appendages which give rise to the common name.

Following rains the spaces between saltbush shrubs are occupied by ephemeral grasses and other small plants; these are normally preferred by stock, but during long dry periods the saltbushes and similar shrubby species provide an invaluable fodder for survival. In the drier saltbush areas stocking may be as low as one sheep to 15 ha. Some cattle are grazed on these areas in the northern part of South Australia.

Distribution: All mainland States

Danthonia   WALLABY GRASS, WHITE-TOP

Danthonias are tussocky, fine-leaved, perennial grasses, often only about 30 cm tall. Tufts of white hairs on the flowering spikelets make them attractive grasses, especially when the mass of feathery tops catches the light and presents a silvery appearance.

Wallaby grasses are the characteristic species of the temperate grasslands and woodlands, and are particularly important on the tablelands and slopes of south-eastern Australia. These grasses have been described as probably the most important economic grasses of New South Wales, and by Victorian scientists as probably supporting the bulk of the sheep population of their State. Their wide distribution is an advantage, but so too is their palatability to stock and their ability to withstand grazing. There are several species of importance; being closely related they are often difficult to distinguish from one another.

Distribution: Some species in all States

Dichanthium sericeum QUEENSLAND BLUE GRASS

Widespread over the drier woodland areas in north-eastern Australia, this perennial grass is one of a group known collectively as blue grasses, belonging to *Dichanthium* and *Bothriochloa*. The blue grass downs provide very good grazing and are regarded as superior to areas of bunch spear grass; however, being on fertile soils, a considerable area of these native grazing lands has been converted to agriculture. Queensland's Darling Downs are typical of this community.

D. sericeum is a tufted perennial grass, with silky-hairy spikelets borne on a cluster of two to four spikes; each grain has a long, erect awn. When not in flower or seed, the grass can often be recognized by the tuft of long white hairs at the nodes on the stem.

The species extends well beyond its name State, and is fairly common as far as the Riverina. It is frost-sensitive but recovers well with warm weather.

Distribution: All mainland States

Eragrostis eriopoda WOOLLY BUTT, NEVER FAIL

Woolly butt is typical of the grasses of the semi-arid areas of inland Australia. It is extremely well adapted to withstand dry summer conditions: its numerous deep roots carry a casing of sand, while the base of the stem is protected by felted hairs and sheathing leaves; the leaves are somewhat narrow and sparse. Drought-resisting characters usually make a grass unpalatable, and woolly butt is neither succulent nor abundant as a feed; however it is important as a drought fodder, as it will 'never fail' to produce some feed in hot dry conditions. Communities dominated by this grass often have a carrying capacity of only about one sheep to four hectares.

Eragrostis is a large genus whose species are commonly known as love grasses. A number of species occur in semi-arid areas but there are others in a wide variety of communities, mainly on poor soils. Usually they are sparsely foliaged, with small-seeded spikelets overlapping one another in the seed head. On the whole they are poor fodder.

Distribution: Qld, N.S.W., S.A., W.A., N.T.

Heteropogon contortus   BUNCH SPEAR GRASS,
                                           BLACK SPEAR GRASS

Bunch spear grass takes its common name from the black clusters of seeds hanging from the stems. Each grain has a long awn like a twisted tail up to 10 cm in length; these awns tangle together at maturity and the grains are shed often in a bundle. The end away from the awn is sharply pointed and very hard, and these 'spears' cause much damage to stock by penetrating the softer parts of the skin and causing inflammation and infection.

The grass is a tall, coarse species, growing up to 1.5 m high. By the time the seeds are produced the plant is too coarse and unpalatable to be eaten by stock. Young growth, however, is a valuable cattle feed, and the grass is so widespread in tropical Australia and the subtropical east coast areas that it is a very important fodder species. These areas are regularly burnt early in the summer to provide fresh growth which comes on well following storm rains.

Distribution: Qld, N.S.W., W.A., N.T.

Iseilema membranaceum   FLINDERS GRASS

Flinders grass is an annual grass of the Mitchell grass downs, very frequently occurring between the tussocks of *Astrebla*. It is generally similar in appearance to kangaroo grass, *Themeda australis*, but is smaller in size and less whiskery.

The combination of Mitchell and Flinders grasses provides valuable grazing in the northern semi-arid areas. Flinders grass has an excellent reputation for palatability and nutrition, and is well known for its fattening qualities. It makes a good hay.

Red Flinders grass, *I. vaginiflorum*, is a similar species of value as a forage grass, widespread in the drier grasslands.

Distribution: Qld, N.S.W., S.A., W.A., N.T.

Maireana sedifolia (Kochia sedifolia)   PEARL BLUEBUSH

The family Chenopodiaceae includes a number of succulent-leaved plants with very small flowers which are particularly adapted to unfavourable conditions; *Suaeda* and *Salicornia* are common inhabitants of coastal salt pans. In the inland arid zones there are large areas of shrubland characterized by members of this family: the saltbushes, which are species of *Atriplex, Rhagodia* and *Enchylaena*; the bassias; and the bluebushes, species of *Maireana*.

Pearl bluebush is a robust shrub to about 1 m tall, freely branched with small thick club-shaped leaves which appear a blue-grey colour because of their cover by dense cottony hairs. A papery wing extending horizontally from each fruit gives it a flower-like appearance.

This is one of the commonest species of *Maireana*. It is present as an understorey in parts of the Mallee, under mulga, and as a dominant in the arid shrublands. A deeply rooted plant, it has been shown to be more drought-tolerant than the bladder saltbush. As in the case of the latter species, stock prefer the short-lived grasses and other plants that spring up in good seasons but the bluebush is palatable enough to be a valuable drought fodder; it is often cropped very severely but recovers well if protected.

Distribution: All mainland States

Panicum decompositum   NATIVE MILLET

Major Mitchell, the famous explorer of inland Australia whose glowing reports of the country encouraged many settlers to come to 'Australia Felix', was very enthusiastic about areas of native millet along the Narran River in north-western New South Wales. He wrote of riding through miles of the grass which reached to the saddle-girths, and reported, 'I had never seen such rich natural pasturage in any other part of New South Wales.'

The species is one of the panic grasses which are best developed in the warmer parts of Australia. It is frost sensitive and dies back during winter, but develops rapidly from its perennial rootstock following the early summer rains. A large, rather soft grass, it has freely branched seed-heads with very numerous small seeds; the entire head frequently breaks off at maturity and is bowled along by the wind.

Native millet is of value only in good seasons as it dies back during droughts. Mitchell had seen the country under ideal conditions, so his reports unfortunately gave false encouragement to some prospective settlers.

The grass makes good hay and ensilage.

Distribution: All States

Stipa   SPEAR GRASS

Along with *Danthonia*, the spear grasses are characteristic grass species of southern temperate Australia. In the short-grass woodlands and grasslands *Stipa* is often the dominant genus, different species being prominent in different communities.

Spear grass takes its name from the form of the grain which has a hard sharp point, often with a little tuft of hairs projecting backwards from the tip, and a shaft formed by a long twisted awn. Some species, especially the common *S. setacea*, are known as corkscrew grass because of the action of the awn which twists and turns with changes in moisture conditions. This screwing action in nature may force the seed into the ground and plant it, but unfortunately it has the same action on sheep; the spear may penetrate the skin and work its way even into the heart or lungs. F. M. Bailey wrote in 1909, 'At one time it was no uncommon thing to see the seeds thick on a roast of mutton when on the table. Such a joint before being cooked would have the appearance of being sprinkled with caraway seeds.'

The value of the spear grasses lies in their drought resistance. Species found in desert areas are virtually useless for fodder as they are too harsh, but some in marginal areas, for example Balcarra grass, *S. nitida*, occurring in the sugarwood communities, have forage value. None of the species is as palatable as *Danthonia,* and in general the mature growth is of no value. However young growth is nutritious; as the seeds germinate quickly after rain and species of *Stipa* are about the first grasses to appear in the early spring when feed is limited, they are of importance.

Amongst the principal species are: *S. scabra,* rough spear grass, which is one of the dominants in the drier parts of the Monaro region; *S. variabilis,* one of the dominants in the temperate woodlands; and *S. aristiglumis,* plains grass, a taller species more common in northern New South Wales.

Distribution: Some species in all States

Themeda australis   KANGAROO GRASS

Before European settlement, *Themeda australis* was the dominant grass over a large proportion of Australia. A perennial species which shows most of its growth in summer, it is still very widespread occurring from the tropical wet-summer forests of northern Australia to the temperate woodlands of Victoria and Tasmania.

Kangaroo grass is an erect, tufted perennial; when mature it has a yellow or reddish colour, with short, broad, whiskery clusters of spikelets produced at intervals along the flowering stem.

This species is readily eaten by stock but is very susceptible to grazing, and has virtually disappeared from a number of areas where it was formerly present, and even dominant. It has mostly gone from the temperate woodlands of southern Australia, including the south-west of Western Australia and much of the grazing land of Victoria and New South Wales. In these areas it has been replaced by a series of native and introduced grasses, especially by *Danthonia* and *Stipa;* in coastal Queensland it has been succeeded to a considerable extent by *Heteropogon contortus.* The species has survived grazing better in the northern summer rainfall areas and is still an important fodder in such places.

Distribution: All States

FODDER SHRUBS AND TREES

Grasses and herbs form the main fodder of introduced grazing animals but there are numerous trees and shrubs which are also eaten; in some cases this happens even where grasses and herbs are available, in others it occurs mainly during drought, when the trees are lopped or felled to bring the leaves within reach of the starving animals. In this short account no attempt is made to list all the species eaten, and those discussed are, in the main, common widespread ones of most importance as drought fodder, together with a selection of less important species.

Acacia aneura   MULGA

Mulga is an Aboriginal name for this widespread small tree of inland areas, regarded as the most important fodder tree in Australia. The greyish phyllodes vary from almost cylindrical to flattened and up to about 13 mm broad, and the flowers are borne in spikes. Stock readily eat foliage they can reach and, during drought, large quantities have been felled, pushed with bulldozers or lopped to provide food for starving sheep. Fortunately, the trees recover from lopping if this has not been too severe, and regeneration from seed is satisfactory if the young plants are protected from heavy grazing and fire.
Distribution: Qld, N.S.W., S.A.

Acacia pendula   MYALL, WEEPING MYALL

Although not spectacular in flower, the weeping myall with its silver-grey phyllodes on pendulous, willow-like branches is one of the most attractive of the wattles. Sheep and cattle eat it readily and often dispose of nearly all seedlings so that in some inland areas where it once grew in quantity it is now relatively rare.

Over thirty other acacias are used to varying extents as stock fodder.
Distribution: Qld, N.S.W.

Alphitonia excelsa   RED ASH

Red ash is a common coastal tree of eastern Australia, usually found in the moister types of eucalypt forest but extending also to subcoastal districts. Its pale, smooth bark, generally encrusted with thin lichens, and the almost white undersurface of the leaf make it an easily recognizable tree. In spite of containing considerable quantities of saponin, the leaves are readily eaten by stock, and the plant has been a useful drought fodder in some areas.

Distribution: Qld, N.S.W.

Atalaya hemiglauca WHITEWOOD

Whitewood is a common small tree in many arid areas of the tropical inland. It has dull greyish, usually pinnate leaves with two to six leaflets borne on pendulous final twigs. The tree makes a handsome sight when covered with masses of small white flowers. Fruits are two- or three-lobed, each lobe with a membranous wing.

Cattle, sheep and horses eat the leaves readily, and the trees have been felled for fodder during drought. However, there is evidence that suckers are poisonous, and the fruits have been shown to be poisonous to horses.

Distribution: Qld, N.S.W., S.A., W.A., N.T.

Avicennia marina GREY MANGROVE

The grey mangrove is one of the commonest and most widespread mangroves on the east coast of Australia, reaching a height of about 12 m and easily recognized by its 'cobbler's peg' roots emerging from the mud. Cattle find the shiny leaves palatable, and in some areas keep the plants grazed to a low, shrub-like form.

Distribution: All mainland States

Lysiphyllum carronii (Bauhinia carronii) BAUHINIA

Leaves of bauhinias are divided into two lobes, hinged along the midrib, giving them a butterfly-like form. *L. carronii* is a deciduous tree of inland regions bearing reddish flowers and broad, flat pods. Both leaves and pods are eaten by sheep and cattle and are regarded as of moderate nutritional value. *L. cunninghamii* and *L. hookeri*, the latter with white flowers, are also eaten to some extent.

Distribution: Qld, N.S.W.

Brachychiton populneum KURRAJONG

Kurrajong is a small to medium-sized tree widespread in subcoastal and inland areas of eastern Australia. It shows considerable resemblance to its relative, the bottle tree, but lacks the bottle tree's enormously inflated trunk. It has the reputation of being one of the best fodder trees in Australia, although analysis shows that it is poor in protein. Under good conditions it is a rapidly growing species and trees usually recover well from lopping.

Distribution: Qld, N.S.W., Vic., S.A.

Brachychiton rupestre   BOTTLE TREE,
                                          NARROW-LEAVED BOTTLE TREE

There is no mistaking the remarkably swollen trunk of the bottle tree of subcoastal and inland areas. Its wood is very soft and contains large quantities of mucilaginous material. During drought the plant has proved a valuable fodder; trees are felled and the soft wood put through a chaff cutter before feeding, or cattle are simply left to eat out the logs after removal of part of the bark. Bottle tree has occasionally caused deaths in cattle through nitrate poisoning.

Distribution: Qld

Capparis lasiantha   NIPAN, SPLIT JACK

Species of *Capparis* have alternate leaves usually with a pair of curved spines at the leaf base. In some species the spines disappear or become much reduced in the adult plant. The flowers are handsome with white, membraneous petals and numerous long white stamens, but unfortunately are short-lived and after they have been open for often less than twenty-four hours the petals and stamens will fall at a touch.

C. *lasiantha* grows as a very spiny, much-branched shrub or as a climber over trees. Its leaves often have a yellowish tinge. Man finds the pulp of the yellow fruits pleasant to eat, and stock apparently find the foliage palatable.

Other species of *Capparis* which stock eat are C. *canescens* (wild orange), C. *loranthifolia* (narrow-leaf bumbil), C. *mitchellae* (bumbil), C. *spinosa* var. *nummularia* (Flinders rose) and C. *umbonata* (wild orange).

Distribution: Qld, N.S.W., S.A.

Carissa ovata CURRANT BUSH

Currant bush occupies a wide range of habitats from coastal creek banks and rainforest margins inland to the 500 mm rainfall belt. It is a low, dense shrub with opposite leaves often almost as broad as long, and pairs of robust simple or forked spines which must detract from its appeal to a browsing animal. Nevertheless, in the drier parts of its range it is a useful fodder.

The closely related conker berry, *C. lanceolata*, with more slender leaves is similarly browsed.

Distribution: *C. ovata* — Qld, N.S.W.
C. lanceolata — Qld, W.A., N.T.

Casuarina SHE-OAK

Species of *Casuarina* with their tough, slender, green branchlets carrying whorls of minute scale leaves do not give the appearance of being attractive fodder trees. *C. cristata* (belah), *C. cunninghamiana* (river oak) and *C. luehmannii* (bull oak), have been used as emergency fodder but the material is very fibrous and generally regarded as of poor quality.

Distribution: *C. cristata* — Qld, N.S.W., Vic., S.A., W.A.
C. cunninghamiana — Qld, N.S.W.
C. luehmannii — Qld, N.S.W., Vic., S.A.

Dodonaea angustissima SLENDER HOP BUSH

The hop bushes are readily recognized by the prominent, papery wings on the fruits. *D. angustissima* is a shrub with narrow, viscid leaves, found usually in arid areas where it has been a valuable drought fodder. *D. lobulata* is another member of this genus eaten by stock.

Distribution: All mainland States

Ehretia saligna PEACH BUSH, COONTA

The slender leaves, about 8 cm long, taper to a blunt point and are bright green and pendulous. This shrub or small tree is found in brigalow and gidgee country and is browsed by stock, sometimes being cut as a drought fodder.

Distribution: Qld, W.A., N.T.

Eremophila longifolia   WEEPING EMU BUSH, BERRIGAN

The name *Eremophila*, derived from the Greek words *eremos*—a desert, and *philo*—to love, is an appropriate one for this large genus of shrubs and small trees widespread in the arid regions of the continent.

One of the most widely distributed is *E. longifolia*, 3-6 m high, with slender, pendulous, dull leaves 5-15 cm long, tapering gradually to a slender curved tip. The tubular, dull red flowers are covered with fine hairs. It is a widespread species and is regarded as a useful fodder plant. One of the common names is applied because emus eat the ellipsoid, dark purple fruit.

Other species which have been used as fodder are *E. bignoniiflora* (gooramurra), *E. glabra* (black fuchsia), *E. latrobei* (native fuchsia), *E. maculata* (fuchsia bush), *E. mitchellii* (budda), *E. oppositifolia* (mountain sandalwood) and *E. polyclada* (lignum fuchsia).

Distribution: All mainland States

Eucalyptus   GUM TREE

Eucalypts are not an important source of drought fodder. Perhaps the one most commonly eaten is *E. albens* (white box) found mainly on the western slopes of New South Wales. *E. largiflorens* (black box), found mainly in the western plains of New South Wales, seems to be more popular with stock than most species and it is reported that sheep will sometimes eat its leaves even when other food is available. Leaves of *E. ochrophloia* (napunyah) are reported to be eaten readily. In the southern region of Australia *E. gunnii* (cider gum) is reported to be sweet and to be eaten by sheep and cattle.

Other fodder species, generally regarded as being of poor quality, are *E. camaldulensis* (river red gum), *E. cladocalyx* (sugar gum), *E. gummifera* (red bloodwood), *E. melliodora* (yellow box), *E. microtheca* (coolibah), *E. papuana* (ghost gum), *E. pilligaensis* (ribbon box), *E. populnea* (poplar gum), *E. tessellaris* (carbeen) and *E. thozetiana* (Thozet's box).

Ficus   FIG

There are numerous species of fig native to Australia. Man can use the conical shoot as an emergency food, and grazing animals,

△ *Heteropogon contortus* (bunch spear grass) p. 168

▽ *Heliotropium amplexicaule* (blue heliotrope) p. 160

Opuntia inermis (prickly pear) p. 162 △

Asclepias fruticosa (balloon cotton) p. 183 ▽

able to accept much more fibrous material, readily eat the mature leaves on farms in coastal districts. It is common to see specimens of Moreton Bay fig, *F. macrophylla*, trimmed on the lower side to the maximum reach of cattle. However, figs are plants of the moister, coastal belt and are seldom present in sufficient quantity to be of importance as emergency stock feed.
Distribution: Qld, N.S.W., Vic., N.T.

Flindersia maculosa   LEOPARDWOOD

Most species of *Flindersia* are rainforest trees but *F. maculosa* is a plant of dry inland areas. It is an attractive slender tree generally not over 7 m high with drooping branchlets and bark shed in irregular flakes leaving an attractively mottled trunk. In its early stage the plant is a tangle of slender branches but eventually a main shoot arises near the centre and is protected for a time from browsing by the surrounding tangle. Finally the shrubby mass disappears.

Both sheep and cattle eat the leaves and twigs readily. It is regarded as a good stock food.
Distribution: Qld, N.S.W.

Geijera parviflora   WILGA

Wilga is a well-known and widely distributed shrub or small tree of inland areas. Its slender, pendulous, leathery leaves, 7-15 cm long, taper gradually to a blunt or fine point. When crushed, the leaves give off a strong aromatic odour as the numerous oil glands are burst. Groups of small white flowers are borne at the ends of branches.

The leaves of shrubs which branch from near the base are commonly not acceptable to stock but those on plants which form a single trunk are usually eaten readily.
Distribution: Qld, N.S.W., Vic., S.A.

Pittosporum phylliraeoides   MEEMEEI, WEEPING PITTOSPORUM

This is an attractive small tree, mainly of inland areas, which does well in cultivation even on the coast. It has a narrow outline and pendulous, willowy branches with rather leathery, slender leaves. The yellow fruits, often borne in great abundance, open widely to reveal a group of red seeds held together by a sticky

substance. Both leaves and fruits are very bitter but the tree has been cut for stock feed in times of drought.
Distribution: All mainland States

Santalum lanceolatum   QUEENSLAND SANDALWOOD, PLUMWOOD

Queensland sandalwood is a sparsely foliaged small tree of inland areas bearing succulent, opposite, grey, pendulous leaves. Stock find it very palatable and eat it readily. It has a reasonably high protein content. The quandong, *S. acuminatum*, also is readily eaten.
Distribution: All mainland States

Terminalia volucris   ROSEWOOD

This tropical, dry-country tree which bears the name rosewood is in no way related to rainforest species with the same common name. *T. volucris* is a small tree with oblong leaves crowded near the ends of twigs, and fruits with two prominent wings. Stock graze the plant readily and sometimes keep it to shrub-like form.
Distribution: Qld, W.A., N.T.

Ventilago viminalis   VINE TREE, SUPPLEJACK

In inland areas the vine tree is one of the easiest trees to recognize with its pendulous willowy branches, slender leaves and peculiar trunk which is often made up of two or more intertwined stems. In some areas, vine tree is regarded as the best fodder tree available. Fortunately it shoots well after lopping.
Distribution: Qld, N.S.W., S.A., N.T.

9

Fibres, Ropes and Canes

'Stringy-bark will light your fire,
Green-hide will never fail yer.
Stringy-bark and green-hide,
The mainstay of Australia.'

Old bush song

FIBRES, along with the foods, timbers and medicines provided by plants, have played an important part in man's progress to civilization. Although animal hides no doubt provided his first protective covering, clothing made from plant fibres gradually replaced hides in many areas and, in fact, have been used for this purpose since prehistoric times. Even today when synthetic materials have become so competitive vegetable fibres such as cotton and flax are still of enormous importance.

Almost as important has been the use of fibres for cordage enabling men to fish, trap, hunt with bows and arrows, carry goods conveniently and attach one structure to another. Rather less important has been the use of fibres in stuffing, caulking and sweeping.

In a botanical sense, a fibre is a single, long, thick-walled cell. However, many fibres, at least those in bark and leaves, occur firmly attached to each other in bundles, and it is the whole bundle which is generally termed the fibre in the commercial sense.

Since the white man arrived in Australia the barks of several native plants have been investigated as possible sources of commercial fibre for cordage, textiles or paper. Although some have been shown to be suitable on an experimental basis none has been exploited on a commercial scale and it is unlikely that any will be used for these purposes in the future. The two native sources which have been exploited by the white man are the *Posidonia* fibres in marine deposits in South Australia and the wood fibres used for paper manufacture.

The Aborigines did not use plant fibres for clothing other than in a minor, decorative way but they did have important uses for the great variety of fibre plants available to them. Plant fibres provided the bulk of the material for the twine used for various bags, fishing lines, harpoon ropes and nets, both the relatively small nets used for fishing and the more massive ones constructed to trap emus and kangaroos.

In a few cases, thin strips of bark would be used without preparation to make a rough rope but usually it was the fibres of the inner bark that were used. Commonly, these were separated from the outer hard bark after soaking in water. This method of extracting fibres is practised world-wide and is known as retting. The process involves subjecting the fibrous part of the plant to moist conditions which may involve complete submersion or exposure to dew; under these conditions, bacteria attack the material cementing the cells together, so allowing the fibres to separate more readily from the useless, softer tissues. After an appropriate time which varies from a few days to a few weeks depending on the plant material and other conditions, the fibres are removed from the rest of the tissues, a process which often involves beating or scraping. Once extracted and cleaned, the fibre was made into twine by the Aborigines usually by rolling the fibres on the thigh and plying two strands together. In making bags and nets a great variety of netting patterns were used. Several of these have been described and figured by W. E. Roth.

In some cases a part of a fibrous plant may be used as it is, rather than having the fibres extracted from it. For example, some flexible stems may be used directly as a rough twine, or a cane or leaf may be used in weaving baskets or nets. Fibrous material for thatching is also generally used whole. Such fibrous materials are grouped together with extracted fibres in this chapter.

One important use for fibres is in papermaking. A type of paper known as papyrus was made in ancient Egypt over 4000 years ago by beating and laminating the pithy stems of a sedge. However, paper as we know the material was first prepared in

China in the second century A.D. Primitive paper is made by separating the fibres of some suitable bark by retting and beating, suspending the fibres in water, then scooping out a layer on a fabric screen. After the matted layer of fibres has dried in the sun a sheet of paper can be peeled off. In parts of South-east Asia, paper is still being made by this method, mainly for craft items such as paper umbrellas. Modern manufacturing processes use the fibres from wood, and although many technical improvements have been made, the principle of primitive papermaking remains the same.

Abutilon albescens   LANTERN BUSH

The genus *Abutilon* belongs to the same family as *Hibiscus*; its yellow flowers have much the same appearance as *Hibiscus* flowers except that they lack the extra calyx-like structure found outside the calyx in *Hibiscus*. *Abutilon albescens* is a decorative small shrub with bright orange-yellow flowers often about 5 cm across, found mainly on coastal dune country. The green bark strips readily from the stem as very strong strands. In Malaysia the bark fibre has been used locally for cordage but is not a commercial fibre. Several other species of *Abutilon* occur in Australia and it is likely that these yield a fibre similar to that of *A. albescens*. One of them, *A. octocarpum*, found mainly in dry country of northern Australia, was used by the Aborigines to make nets for trapping game.
Distribution: Qld, N.T.

Acacia   WATTLE

The white man found *Acacia* bark to be a rich source of tannin (p. 51) but the Aboriginal interest in the material was mainly as a fibre source. The following species are recorded as having been used for this purpose: *A. flavescens, A. latifolia, A. leptocarpa* and *A. lysiphloea*.
Distribution: Some species in all States

Acrostichum   MANGROVE FERN

Ferns are usually thought of as delicate plants of shaded moist positions; *Acrostichum* differs from this image in having erect fronds with tough leathery leaflets, and in growing in swampy areas usually at the rear of a mangrove forest and subject to occasional flooding at high tides. There are two Australian species, both also occurring commonly in the coastal areas of southern Asia. *A. aureum*, which in Australia is found only along north Queensland shores, is the larger with fronds sometimes up to 4 m tall; those of *A. speciosum*, which occurs from the north of Western Australia to near the Queensland—New South Wales border, are less than 2 m high. In both species the uppermost leaflets are fertile, and are covered on their undersurfaces with a velvety layer of spore-cases.

Leaves of *Acrostichum* have been used in some south-east Asian countries and Pacific islands for thatch. The fronds are dried and threaded on light rods, then placed overlapping one another. This material is said to be more expensive but more durable than straw for the same purpose, and has a further advantage that if it catches fire it burns so fast that the blaze is out before the rest of the building catches.

Distribution: Qld, W.A., N.T.

Aristida pruinosa   WIRE GRASS

A widespread grass of the dry inland, *Aristida pruinosa* is one of the wire grasses or three-awned spear grasses, so called because the grain is surrounded by a bract with three long, minutely barbed projections, the awns, which aid in seed dispersal; the lower end of the grain is sharply pointed and can cause discomfort and injury to animals including man.

Perennial in habit, this species grows in thick tufts up to about a metre high. In the Hooker Creek area of central Australia, the Aborigines have used it to build a shelter from the desert winds: the grass is cut in bunches near the base, laid on the ground and trodden to mat it together; the upper ends are then plaited together in handfuls and the stem ends are splayed out producing a tunnel-like shelter 70-80 cm in height, about 2 m long and with a spread of about 60 cm. With the shortage of bark and timber generally in such desert fringe areas, such a shelter made good use of the plant material at hand.

Distribution: Qld, W.A., N.T.

Aristida utilis   HAT GRASS

Hat grass is one of the three-awned spear grasses, a group well known for the troublesome way their fruits penetrate socks. This species is notable mainly for the use of its stems in making hats at Cooktown in the early part of this century.
Distribution: Qld, N.T.

Asclepias curassavica   RED-HEAD COTTON-BUSH

If this species were not a weed it would probably be cultivated for its striking red and yellow flower clusters. The plant is an erect perennial, sometimes behaving as an annual, with slender opposite leaves, exuding a copious milky latex when injured. The slender, pointed egg-shaped fruits split on one side to reveal neatly packed dark seeds with silky plumes which are readily spread by the wind. In the Philippines, these seed hairs were used as a stuffing for pillows. Bark fibre has been used in India to a minor extent.
Distribution: Qld, N.S.W., Vic.

Asclepias fruticosa   BALLOON COTTON, SWAN PLANT,
                                    BLADDER COTTON-BUSH

The two balloon cottons are most distinctive plants with their softly spiny, balloon-like green fruits splitting to release numerous black seeds with silky plumes. Fruits of *A. fruticosa* are somewhat pointed while those of the closely related *A. physocarpa* are almost globose. The erect stems, up to a couple of metres high, are about the right thickness for basket work and were used for this purpose in Australia about 120 years ago. However, even at that time they were being replaced by lawyer vine imported from India.
Distribution: Qld, N.S.W., Vic., S.A., W.A.

Boehmeria nivea   RAMIE, RHEA, CHINA GRASS

A hairy shrub of the nettle family, ramie is a well-known fibre plant in Asian countries, especially southern China. It is not widespread in Australia but has been found, apparently native, in north Queensland scrubs, where it was given the name 'jalcan jalcan' by the Aborigines. The shrub is 1-2 m tall with alternate toothed leaves hairy white beneath, and short clusters of small flowers of different sexes.

Ramie fibres have many useful attributes; they are the longest of any commercial fibre, up to 30 cm, and are eight times as strong as cotton, four times as strong as linen. They are white, lustrous, very durable, and resistant to moulds and water. However there are a number of disadvantages which reduce their usefulness: the fibres are so durable they outlast any dye, so must be used undyed; they are somewhat hairy, inflexible and inelastic; in the stem they are gummed together by material which is difficult to remove. The fibres cannot be retted by normal soaking methods but must be separated by pounding and scraping, thus adding greatly to the labour costs of production.

The fibre has many local uses in eastern Asia; its strength and durability makes it highly suitable for ropes, fishing nets, hats, fire hoses, sailcloth, and mothproof fabrics. It is sometimes woven to make grass cloth which can be used for fine-quality tablecloths. At times it is blended with other natural or synthetic fibres to make lustrous crease-resistant textiles. Ramie will be familiar to people who go camping as the fibre used for gas mantles; it was used during World War II in the making of gas masks.

There is no record of exploitation of Australian plants of this species.

Distribution: Qld

Boehmeria platyphylla   QUEENSLAND RAMIE

Like the better known ramie, this species of *Boehmeria* was listed by the Queensland Colonial Botanist, F. M. Bailey, as a useful fibre plant, but no use seems to have been made of it in Australia.

B. platyphylla is a soft-wooded shrub with large, opposite, toothed leaves with three main veins; the small flowers are produced in spikes.

The species extends through South-east Asia to India where it has been used locally for ropes and fishing lines.

Distribution: Qld

Bombax ceiba (B. malabaricum)   SILK-COTTON TREE

This is a distinctive tropical tree with a clearly defined central trunk and the horizontal branches more or less in whorls. Stout prickles occur on the stem. The handsome large flowers up to

13 cm across have bright red or orange petals and numerous stamens.

Pendulous, elongate, woody pods 10-19 cm long contain numerous seeds embedded in a dense mass of silky hairs arising from the fruit wall. This silky material, sometimes known as Indian kapok, is similar to true kapok and although often regarded as a little inferior to it is usually used in India for filling lifejackets, mattresses, cushions and quilts.

The wood is soft and not particularly durable but is easily worked and probably for this reason was used by the Aborigines for dugout canoes and the shallow wooden vessels commonly known as coolamons.

Distribution: Qld, N.T.

Brachychiton populneum   KURRAJONG

Like its relative the bottle tree, the kurrajong has a straight, rounded trunk and is gradually tapered rather than bottle-like. The leaves, borne on long slender stalks, are variable in form, some entire and drawn out into a long point, others deeply three-lobed. Its bell-shaped flowers, dull red and yellowish, are not particularly conspicuous.

The inner bark is very fibrous and can be removed in attractive, lace-like strips. This was an important source of fibre for the Aborigines who used it to make fishing lines, dilly bags and nets. Bottle tree, *B. rupestre*, yielded a similar fibre. Strips of this inner bark and wood shavings of kurrajong were used to a limited extent in making 'straw' hats. The flame tree, *B. acerifolium*, was used for similar purposes.

Distribution: Qld, N.S.W., Vic., S.A.

*Cocos nucifera   COCONUT

In Australia the coconut is of only minor importance but in many tropical countries has been the staff of life, providing food, drink, clothing, shelter and fuel.

The spongy husk of the nut contains a mass of fibres which have been widely processed in Asia by prolonged soaking in salt water, followed by beating to separate the fibres. This fibrous material, known as coir, is used mainly as a stuffing material, and for the manufacture of mats and coarse ropes.

Although there are other palms whose leaves make better thatch, coconut leaves have been used for this purpose in some places. Leaves have been woven into mats used without preparation or as food wrappers. The stiff midribs of leaflets are bound together to form a broom still widely used in some tropical countries. Baskets may be woven from these midribs. A decorative, but now minor, use for young leaves is in making 'grass' skirts.

Distribution: Qld, W.A., N.T.

Calamus   LAWYER VINE

Anyone with a reasonable acquaintance with rainforests will be familiar with lawyer vine as the climber which in some places can make passage through the forest almost impossible. In the rainforests of northern Queensland there are several species of this large group of climbing palms but in southern Queensland and northern New South Wales there is only one, *Calamus muelleri*. As well as having the leaves liberally armed with needle-like prickles the plant has slender lateral branches a metre or more long armed on all sides with closely set, very sharp hooks. It is these branches which provide the main support of the plant stems as they thrust towards the canopy. Only slight contact with the hooks is necessary for the skin to become uncomfortably anchored, and as one thorn is carefully removed another one is likely to take its place. It is the difficulty of escaping from this plant, when once entangled in it, that has given rise to the common name uncomplimentary to one of the professions.

Since *Calamus* stems often take a circuitous route from the forest floor to the top of the canopy where they scramble over the uppermost branches, their total length is often considerably greater than that of the tallest trees in the rainforest. In fact, outside Australia, *Calamus* has been reported up to 180 m long which gives it the record for the longest known plant.

Once the prickly leaf bases are stripped away the hard, lustrous surface of the stem is revealed. These strong fibrous stems, commonly known as rattans, are of considerable economic importance. They may be used without further treatment, they may be split or they may be skinned leaving a more flexible product but one with considerably less strength and with a dull surface. Western society knows *Calamus* mainly in the form of cane furniture and basketware; the Malacca cane so popular for walking sticks also is derived from a stout South-east Asian species. However, in less developed countries where the plants are readily available they have been put to many other uses such as making strong cables for hauling logs and boats, rigging for boats, suspension bridges, mats, fish traps and for tying together the framework of houses.

Cane used in Australia has mostly been imported from South-east Asia but during World War II when these supplies were unavailable, *Calamus* was collected from New South Wales and Queensland rainforests. In earlier days in Australia lengths of cane 66 feet long were often used as chain measures in surveying.

The Aborigines also found several uses for lawyer vine. In northern Queensland, canes were used for making the frames of fish nets. Those in the Princess Charlotte Bay area used a length of cane for extracting honey; one end was frayed to form a rough brush and was then pushed through a hole in a tree trunk into the bees' nest and twisted until a sufficient mass of honey and wax was attached to the brush. A cane with frayed end was used also to detect the presence of an eel in a submerged hollow log; after the cane had been poked about in the log the end was examined for any slimy deposit which would indicate that an eel was sheltering there.

To detect the presence of an animal in a hole in the ground or in a hollow tree a lawyer cane tipped with native beeswax was pushed in; if any fur was picked up by the beeswax, further action could be taken with reasonable certainty of obtaining results. A more exciting Aboriginal use was in capturing the saltwater crocodile. One member of the party would dive into the pool, slip a noose of lawyer vine over the animal's head, the other members of the party then attempting to pull the snared reptile out of the water.

Lawyer vine, along with other vines, was used as a support during climbing. For this purpose the cane was greased and stored in the shade. In northern Australia, Aborigines used the leaves as a thatch.

Distribution: Qld, N.S.W.

Cissus antarctica　　　　　　　NATIVE GRAPE, KANGAROO VINE

Amongst the climbers of the rainforest, the various species of native grape can be recognized easily if one looks for the tendrils, which are always produced on the side of the stem opposite the leaf, rather than in the leaf axle as in many climbing plants. *Cissus antarctica* has shiny toothed leaves, with rust-coloured, hairy young shoots; it produces short branched clusters of black berries.

This vine was used in climbing trees by Aborigines of coastal New South Wales. They cut a long length of vine which was passed around both the trunk of the tree and the waist of the climber.

Distribution: Qld, N.S.W.

Commersonia bartramia　　　　　　　BROWN KURRAJONG

Brown kurrajong is a tree of moist coastal districts occurring commonly where rainforest has been cleared. Its branches tend to be arranged in horizontal tiers and, when covered with masses of small white flowers about Christmas time, it is a most distinctive tree unlikely to be confused with any other.

Fibrous bark from this species was used in South-east Asia for ropemaking and by the Aborigines for fish and kangaroo nets. It is reported that there is great difficulty in removing the mucilaginous material from among the fibres and that, on drying, this material makes the fibres brittle.

Distribution: Qld, N.S.W.

Crotalaria cunninghamii　　　　　　　GREEN BIRD-FLOWER

This attractive shrub of the dry sandhills of the interior has greenish yellow flowers similar to those of the bird-flower, *Crotalaria laburnifolia*, which is a popular garden native. Each flower has the striking form of a flying bird, its yellow body and raised wings striped with green, the head and neck formed by the velvety light grey of the calyx attached to the stem by the beak-like stalk. The stems and leaves are uniformly grey with a close felting of hairs over the surface.

Like a number of other crotalarias, this species is a good source of bark fibre which was used by the Aborigines of central

Australia for plaited ropes. An unusual purpose to which they have been put is described by Dr Donald Thomson; the fibre was woven to make sandals, a most useful article of wear in rough rocky desert areas. Bark was stripped from the branches and used fresh in relatively broad strands; the shoemaker looped the strand around his big toe and tied it behind his body, using two lengths joined if necessary; this maintained the tension while strands were woven back and forth between the two sides of the loop to make the sole. When this was completed the sandal was worn with the broader end forwards and the two strands passed between the big toe and the next to tie behind the ankle in an article of footwear similar to the popular modern thong.

Distribution: Qld, N.S.W., S.A., W.A., N.T.

Crotalaria juncea   SUNN HEMP

Crotalaria juncea is one of the rattle pods, so named for the rattling noise which the numerous loose seeds make on shaking the dry pod. It is a tall annual, 2-3 m high with simple leaves mostly 3-7 cm long and yellow, pea-like flowers in small groups. No use seems to have been made of it in Australia, but in India it has been an important fibre crop plant. The harvested stems are first soaked to allow retting before the bark fibres are stripped. Main use of the fibres is in cordage, matting and sacking. During World War II sunn hemp was used extensively in the manufacture of camouflage netting.

Distribution: Qld, N.T.

Cyperus   SEDGE

The outer part of the stems of many sedges are tough and fibrous and in various parts of the world the fibres have been used for cordage or, in some cases, the stems used directly as a rough string or for matting.

C. vaginatus is one of possibly several species of *Cyperus* whose stem fibres were used by the Aborigines for cordage and fishing nets. *C. haspan* and *C. javanicus* were used by Aborigines for weaving. *C. exaltatus* has been used for matting in India but no use has been recorded for it in Australia.

Distribution: Some species in all States

Dendrocnide excelsa   GIANT STINGING TREE

The giant stinging tree of subtropical rainforests is one of the most easily remembered trees of the scrub, both for its broad, hairy leaves, sometimes 30 cm across on young plants, and for the extremely painful sting which the hairs inflict on the slightest contact.

The bark was a popular source of fibre for Aboriginal fishing lines and nets. Root bark was preferred to stem bark and its method of preparation was simple even if fairly laborious: the bark was chewed until the fibres were sufficiently separated to be twisted into cord. This chewed bark was used also as a mop for extracting honey from native bees' nests.

In southern Queensland the inner bark of the giant stinging tree was beaten out while green to make a rather rough cloth used as a baby's blanket. The well-known tapa cloth of Polynesia was prepared in a similar way from the bark of the paper mulberry. Inner bark of the shining-leaved stinging tree, *Dendrocnide photiniphylla*, also was used by the Aborigines as a fibre source. Distribution: Qld, N.S.W.

Dianella laevis   FLAX LILY

The species of *Dianella* are perennial, non-bulbous members of the lily family. Their strap-like leaves are distinctly keeled, at least in the lower part, and are very tough and fibrous, justifying the name flax lily. The attractive blue flowers make some species worthwhile garden subjects.

Leaves split readily between the parallel, longitudinal veins, and it is a simple matter to strip off strands each containing three or four veins and to plait them into a cord of reasonable strength. The Aborigines used the leaves of *D. laevis* for making baskets and may well have used other species of the genus also, although no records of this have survived. Distribution: All States

Dicranopteris linearis   CORAL FERN

A widespread tropical fern, *Dicranopteris linearis* is one of a group often called, for some unknown reason, coral ferns. It has subterranean stems with long straggly erect fronds branching dichotomously and tangling to form thickets up to 2 m tall. Individual fronds may reach considerable lengths as they are capable of unlimited growth. The strong wiry stalks and stiff leaflets up to 3.5 cm long can form a very effective barrier to walkers.

The stalks of the fern are very strong but supple and can be woven. In South-east Asia they have been used to weave fish-traps, baskets, chairseats and even internal partitions for houses. Caps made from this material were so durable they were said to be handed down from one generation to another. The strands of conducting tissue inside the stalks are particularly strong and can be drawn out of a split stalk; these black strands can be used alone for weaving or mixed for decorative effect with the brown stalks. Stalks have also been made into ropes.

Older stalks are very hard and can be sharpened for use as pens; these were widely used in earlier times in Malaysia and India, and there was even a minor export trade in them to India from Malaysia where the fern grew more vigorously.

Distribution: Qld, N.S.W., W.A., N.T.

Doryanthes excelsa   GYMEA LILY, SPEAR LILY

This spectacular plant produces a large cluster of sword-like leaves up to 1.5 m long, and a tall flowering axis 3-5 m high with a cluster of red flowers at the apex. The leaves contain a strong fibre, and this was extracted and made into rope which was exhibited at the Great Exhibition in London in 1851. However, whether the fibre was ever used by the settlers other than on an experimental basis is not known. It would be likely that the Aborigines made use of such an easily obtained fibre but there appears to be no record of their doing so.

A second species, *D. palmeri*, of southern Queensland and northern New South Wales, has a flowering axis with flowers borne over a greater length than in *D. excelsa*. It has similar fibrous leaves.

Distribution: N.S.W.

Eleocharis dulcis   TALL SPIKE-RUSH, WATER CHESTNUT

Eleocharis dulcis is a sedge often forming dense stands up to a metre high in shallow water. The leafless, cylindrical stems, up to 1 cm thick, have diaphragms at intervals along the central hollow. Insignificant flowers are formed in the terminal, scaly part of the stem.

Aborigines in northern Queensland used whole stems for weaving mats. Emu feathers were sometimes worked into the mat and such blankets were said to be very warm for sleeping under on cold nights. Split stems were used for dilly bags. In South-east Asia also the stems have been used for rush matting.
Distribution: Qld, N.S.W.

Eucalyptus   GUM TREE (STRINGYBARK)

The stringybarks are a group of eucalypts with a persistent, strongly fibrous bark which can be removed in sheets, flattened and dried under pressure, then used as roofing material which will last up to twenty years. This bark was a very important building material in the early days of white settlement in Australia, and 'the old bark hut' is now part of the country's folk history. As well as going on the roof some slabs of bark went on the floor as reasonably effective door mats.

However, the Aborigines had used this bark before; the white man may well have learnt its value from the Aborigines who used species of stringybark for making canoes. Bark of *E. agglomerata* (blue-leaved stringybark) was used as torches for spear-fishing at night.

The characteristic fibrous bark can often be pulled from the trunk in long strips. Weathering renders fibres of the outer bark relatively weak and brittle but the inner bark provides much stronger material which the Aborigines used for making fishing lines, nets and baskets. The white settlers also used the fibrous strands for making durable ropes. Large quantities of fibrous bark are available as a result of the jarrah timber industry; in the early 1920s rough rope was made successfully from this bark on an experimental scale and it was hoped that ropemaking might become a useful subsidiary industry. However, the enterprise does not seem to have proceeded beyond the experimental stage.

It has been shown that coarse paper could be made from the bark fibres of some of the stringybarks but, again, the process was not commercially viable.

However, some of the stringybarks have at least a reasonable

△ *Macaranga tanarius* (tunkullum) p. 201

▽ *Hibiscus tiliaceus* (cotton tree) p. 196

Avicennia marina (grey mangrove) pp. 111, 173, 236 △

Durandea jenkinsii p. 235 ▽

potential for modern use. The bark of the white stringybark, *E. globoidea*, widespread along the coasts of New South Wales and Victoria, and of the blue-leaved stringybark which is confined to New South Wales, have been investigated by the CSIRO, and found to yield a fibre suitable as a substitute for the imported sisal and coconut fibre usually used as strengthening material in fibrous plaster sheets. As is the case with most fibres, before they can be used the softer tissues must be removed and the fibre bundles partly separated. This is accomplished by steeping the bark in water for about a month after which the material is washed and mechanically teased.

Distribution: Some species in all States

      E. agglomerata — N.S.W.

      E. globoidea — N.S.W., Vic., Tas., S.A.

      E. marginata (jarrah) — W.A.

Eupomatia laurina   NATIVE GUAVA

Native guava is a glossy leaved rainforest shrub or small tree with white flowers which appear to have the usual order of petals and stamens reversed. Actually what appear to be petals are broad, sterile stamens. The strong perfume of the flowers is heavy, somewhat fruity and very distinctive — pleasant to some but oppressive to others.

In New South Wales, the plant provided raw materials for Aboriginal fishing lines. Narrow pieces of the bark were stripped, dried, then soaked in a tanning solution made by steeping bark of *Persoonia laurina* in water. Alternatively the sap of *Eucalyptus gummifera* was used as a preserving material. Until the advent of synthetic materials, professional fishermen in Australia similarly soaked their nets in a tanning solution to improve their resistance to decay.

Distribution: Qld, N.S.W., Vic.

Ficus   FIG

The inner bark of figs contains strong fibres, and in South-east Asia has been used in ropemaking. Several species are known to have been used by Aborigines in Australia as a source of cordage for dilly bags and fish nets. In the Brisbane district root bark of the well-known Moreton Bay fig, *Ficus macrophylla*, was used.

At least half a dozen other species have been recorded as sources of fibre for Aborigines and possibly almost any species would be suitable.

In northern Queensland the inner bark of *F. ehretioides* and *F. pleurocarpa* were used to make a bark blanket similar to the Polynesian tapa cloth. A complete cylinder of bark was removed from the trunk by making a vertical and two horizontal cuts and pounding the bark to loosen it. With a piece of broken candle-nut shell a cut was made in the outer layer across the sheet near one end. From this cut the outer bark was gradually pulled from the inner and discarded. The sheet of inner bark, roughly 100 x 50 cm, was then placed, inner side up, over an anvil consisting of a low buttress root and beaten along the grain with the narrow side of a piece of wood something like a cricket bat. This resulted in the bark becoming softer, thinner and greater in area. It was doubled on itself three times, each time with more beating. All this took five to six hours after which opening up and drying completed the process.

Distribution: Qld, N.S.W., Vic., N.T.

Flagellaria indica   SUPPLEJACK

One of the most distinctive of the rainforest climbers, supplejack has the appearance of a climbing reed with long stems and alternate leaves ending in 'watch-spring' tendrils by which the plant grasps its way over tall scrub trees.

Tom Petrie gives a clear account of the Aborigines' use of the vine for climbing: 'A length was cut about twelve feet long, and after the outer bark was peeled off with the teeth it would become quite supple, and a loop was made at one end . . . this vine was put round the tree, the loop would be held in the left hand and the other in the right, then with his right foot placed against the trunk, and his body thrown backwards the native would commence to ascend by a succession of springs. At every spring the vine was jerked upwards, and so with wonderful rapidity the ascent was accomplished.'

Other observers of the Aborigines described variations on this method of tree-climbing. Sometimes the length of stem, after being stripped of its outer layer, was knotted to form a large loop used to climb trees and to sit in while chopping out bees' nests.

The supple canes had other uses as well. They were woven into fish traps and nets over a wide area of Australia, and they provided the cord for tying together the bunched ends of bark canoes, at least in the Moreton Bay district. On some of the Torres Strait islands the canes have been used in house building and fence making.

Flagellaria indica is a widespread species in southern and eastern Asia, and has been used through most of its range for purposes such as basket-weaving, tying, and stitching roof materials.
Distribution: Qld, N.S.W., N.T.

Geitonoplesium cymosum   SCRAMBLING LILY

The scrambling lily is a slender, wiry twiner with alternate, parallel-veined leaves, found in most eucalypt forests and sparse rainforests. It climbs its support in a clockwise direction, ascending from right to left, one of the few Australian species to climb in this direction. The green-tipped white buds open widely and are followed by round, black berries.

In Papua New Guinea the strong, wiry stems are used as a rough rope in house-building.
Distribution: Qld, N.S.W., Vic.

Gymnostachys anceps   SETTLERS' TWINE

This plant is a member of the arum lily family although there is little superficial resemblance to the garden plant. *Gymnostachys* has long, grassy leaves and a dark flowering spike with only an inconspicuous bract in place of the large white petal-like structure of the arum lily. The plant occurs as scattered individuals mainly in the wetter types of eucalypt forest.

F. M. Bailey, the Colonial Botanist of Queensland, reported, 'Probably this produces one of the strongest fibres known'. Leaves were used by the settlers as a ready-made twine for sewing up bags and tying the legs of pigs. Before use, the leaves were drawn through a fire which probably had the effect of making them more pliant. Mr A. Meston who led the government scientific expedition to the summit of Mt Bellenden-Ker in 1889 commented on this plant in the characteristically expressive style of his report on the expedition: 'Among the fibrous plants is one called "Boorgay" by the blacks, a ground plant with radiating long narrow leaves extending, to three feet in length. The leaves are about two inches wide tapering to a point; one of them would suspend 100 lb. The blacks use the leaves as rope, twist a couple into a band, and carry surprising loads, the weight all bearing on the band passed round the forehead; of course only the skull of a myall or an alderman will submit to such a formidable strain. The botanical name is *Gymnostachys anceps*, a title about as tough as the plant.'

Distribution: Qld, N.S.W.

Hibiscus tiliaceus COTTON TREE

Hibiscus is very well known as a popular garden shrub in tropical and subtropical parts of Australia. There are also numerous native species, some with large and showy flowers which justify their cultivation. The genus is well known for the fibre yielded by its inner bark, and several species have been utilized by the Aborigines and by inhabitants of South-east Asia.

Hibiscus tiliaceus is probably the most widely distributed species, very common along seashores of the tropical Indo-Pacific region, where it forms a broad-crowned small tree often collapsing sideways to form a tangle of branches close to the ground. Its yellow flowers with dark purple centre are smaller than those of the common garden hibiscus. The Aborigines soaked the bark until the fibre could be separated from the outer useless material, then used it to manufacture dilly bags, fishing lines and nets, and the ropes for dugong and turtle harpoons. The fibre has been used extensively for rope and twine in the Pacific and South-east Asia; even ropes by which elephants drag timber have been made from it. The method of fibre preparation in South-east Asia was to dry the bark for a couple of days after which the fibre could be separated from the outer bark.

Other Australian species of *Hibiscus* used as sources of fibre by the Aborigines were *H. heterophyllus, H. huegelii, H. meraukensis* and *H. panduriformis*.

Distribution: Qld, N.S.W., N.T.

Imperata cylindrica var. *major* BLADY GRASS

Blady grass, known as kunai grass in Papua New Guinea, is a

common and unwelcome grass in many parts of Australia. It is a stiff, erect grass appearing particularly after repeated firing, and is so tough and fibrous that stock will not eat it except in the very early stage. Its rapidly growing underground stems lead to clumps of the grass rapidly increasing their area. A type of beer has been made from these stems in Malaysia.

Since at least as early as 1881 there have been investigations, mainly in South-east Asia, into the possibility of using *Imperata* leaves as a source of fibres for paper pulp. In Queensland also there were suggestions at one time that this grass should be used for papermaking and a yield of four tons per acre was recorded. In fact a strong type of wrapping paper can be made from *Imperata* pulp but the proposed Australian enterprise seems to be economically unattractive.

In India, the fibres of the stem have been used to make ropes, bags and baskets, while in northern Queensland, Aborigines soaked dried leaves in water and split them into suitable widths for weaving into dilly-bags. They also thatched their huts with the grass.

The fibres which make blady grass such poor, tough fodder contribute to its value as a thatching material. In south-east Asia it has been used for this purpose although there are other thatching materials such as nipa palm and bamboo which are more highly regarded. Blady grass was reported as thatch in New South Wales in 1827, and was probably used much earlier. In *Tom Petrie's Reminiscences of Early Queensland* its use is reported in Brisbane: 'Just at the corner of Elizabeth and Albert Streets, where a public house now stands, there used to be a large building erected for holding and thrashing the maize grown by the prisoners. This barn was built of tea-tree logs notched into one another, the roof was thatched with blady grass, and it had a wooden floor.'

A fruiting stand of blady grass can present a very attractive appearance as the stiff, erect silvery white fruiting plumes catch the light when gently moved by a breeze. The silky hairs of these plumes have been used in India and Malaysia for stuffing pillows but there seems to be no record of similar use in Australia.

Distribution: All mainland States

Kennedya prostrata   RUNNING POSTMAN

Running postman is a widely spreading prostrate vine with trifoliate leaves and handsome red pea flowers reminiscent of Sturt's desert pea although not quite so spectacular. The slender, tough stems were used by Aborigines in New South Wales as a ready-made twine.

Distribution: Qld, N.S.W., Vic., Tas., S.A., W.A.

Kingia australis   GRASS TREE

Kingia is similar in general appearance to the more widely distributed *Xanthorrhoea* but its flowering cluster is drumstick-like rather than an elongate spike as in *Xanthorrhoea*.

Within the armour of leaf bases on the trunk is a fibrous ring of tissue 3-7 cm thick surrounding a central, lightweight core. Fibres extracted from the fibrous ring are very tough and pliable, and in the 1920s provided the raw material for an industry manufacturing brushes and brooms, particularly heavy brooms of the type used for street sweeping. Investigations were made at about the same time into the possibility of using *Kingia* leaves as match splints, and the lightweight core for insulating material and lifebelts.

Distribution: W.A.

Lavatera plebeia   AUSTRALIAN HOLLYHOCK

Australian hollyhock is a tall, more or less herbaceous plant 1-3 m high which may be either an annual or a short-lived perennial. Its toothed leaves up to 15 cm broad are divided into five to seven lobes and bear small, star-shaped hairs. The veined flowers up to 7 cm across vary from white to pale pink or lilac, and are similar to those of *Hibiscus*. The species is widely distributed, mainly in inland areas, and particularly on sites subject to flooding.

Like nearly all members of the *Hibiscus* family the bark of *Lavatera* contains strong fibres and was used by the Aborigines for fishing lines and dilly bags. Paper has been made from the bark on an experimental basis but has no economic future.

Distribution: All States

Linum marginale   NATIVE FLAX

Linen is the material made from the bark fibre of the cultivated flax plant, *Linum usitatissimum*, whose seeds supply linseed oil.

Native flax, which belongs to the same genus, is a slender, erect plant 30-60 cm high with clusters of most attractive veined blue flowers. A very strong fibre occurs in the thin bark. The Aboriginal method of preparing the fibre was to soak a bundle of the stems in water for several days after which the bark was stripped off, beaten and teased, then dried in the sun. Twine was made by rolling the moistened fibres on the thigh, and was used for fishing lines and nets.

Distribution: All mainland States

Livistona australis   CABBAGE PALM

Livistona australis is the most widely distributed palm in Australia, occurring from Victoria to Queensland, mainly in the wetter types of eucalypt forest where the tallest specimens may reach a height of nearly 30 m. Its common name derives from the fact that in the early days of settlement the fleshy growing point provided a cabbage-like vegetable for the settlers.

The large, fan-shaped leaves are tough and fibrous and were used by the Aborigines for making bags, baskets, fishing nets and fishing lines. At least in northern Queensland, the part used was the outer layer stripped from young, unopened leaves. The leaves of *L. benthami* from Cape York were used by the Aborigines for thatching.

Over a hundred years ago it was recorded that 'the unexpanded fronds, prepared by immersion in boiling water and dried, are used in the manufacture of durable hats, highly valued by the colonists'. The leaves were split into strips about a centimetre wide with an implement consisting of approximately ten metal cutting teeth set into one end of a piece of wood. After the strips had been plaited the braids were sewn together to form the hat.

Distribution: Qld, N.S.W., Vic.

Lomandra longifolia   MAT-RUSH

Along creek banks *Lomandra longifolia* grows in dense tussocks up to a metre tall, although in eucalypt forests the plants are usually much smaller. Inconspicuous cream flowers give off a delightful perfume.

The strap-shaped leaves are extremely tough and were used by the Aborigines for making baskets. Leaves were first split into strips of suitable width and then softened by drawing through hot ashes. Another Aboriginal use was as a ligature in cases of illness. Settlers in the Port Macquarie district used the leaves for tying up grape vines.

Distribution: Qld, N.S.W., Vic., Tas., S.A.

Luffa cylindrica var. *peramara*   LOOFAH

Fruits of *L. cylindrica* are permeated by a network of fibrous strands which persist after the fleshy parts have rotted away and constitute the loofah sponge, once widely used in personal washing but now rarely seen in Australia.

This Australian variety is similar in general features to the one exploited commercially. It is a tendril climber of the pumpkin family with deeply five-lobed leaves and fruits about 7 cm long, said to be extremely bitter and to cause severe throat irritation.

Green fruits were used by the Aborigines as a fish poison.

Distribution: Qld

Lygodium microphyllum   CLIMBING MAIDENHAIR FERN

There are a number of ferns which grow up the trunks of rainforest trees, clasping the bark with numerous specialized roots. *Lygodium* is unusual in climbing by its leaves; the stem is underground, producing compound leaves with numerous leaflets on a wiry black rachis or stalk. It is the rachis of the leaf which turns and tangles, sometimes forming a dense curtain of fern, up to 6 m or more high, draped over a supporting tree along a rainforest margin or in a coastal tea-tree swamp.

The long rachis is tough and shiny, and has been put to use in Asian countries. Twisted together, stalks make a rough cord which can be used for such purposes as binding sheaves of rice; they are sufficiently valued to have been offered for sale in local markets. The black stalks have also been plaited and made into baskets which, in parts of Malaysia, have been used particularly on ceremonial occasions.

Distribution: Qld, N.S.W., W.A., N.T.

Macaranga tanarius   TUMKULLUM

Macaranga tanarius is a very common small tree of coastal tropical and subtropical regions of eastern Australia. It is easily recognized by its large leaves with the leaf stalk inserted some distance from the margin, and by the clusters of green fruits with soft spines. It is one of the species in which it is possible to strip off long lengths of fibrous bark so it is not surprising that it was used by the Aborigines for its fibre. Its preparation was described in 1901 by W. E. Roth, Protector of Aborigines: 'A fairly smooth switch is cut down, and stripped of its bark envelope. The strip is next sharply broken at an angle, the process enabling the immediately-underlying "fibre" to be separated from its pigmentary covering, which is removed and cast aside. The shreds of fibre, in quantity as may be required, are washed and rinsed for a few minutes "to make the milk come out" — the water turning cloudy — and then dried in the sun. When fully desiccated, each shred is finally split with the nails until the desired fineness is obtained; each comes out ultimately to a length of 8 to 10 in. and more.'
Distribution: Qld, N.S.W., N.T.

Macrozamia   ZAMIA PALM

Species of *Macrozamia* have tuberous or short trunk-like stems and tough pinnate leaves. Although like palms in appearance they belong to a quite different group of plants.

On the bases of young leaves there are soft brown hairs. Those from *M. communis* in New South Wales were called pulu because of their resemblance to true pulu, which was the hairy material from the young fronds of a Hawaiian tree fern. That material was once used extensively in upholstery and cushions and, earlier, was employed in Hawaii in a type of embalming, the pulu being used to fill the spaces left by the removal of organs. During the early days of settlement in New South Wales the pulu from *M. communis* was collected to a limited extent and used for the more conventional of the two stuffing processes noted above. In Queensland, the hairs from *M. miquelii* were used for stuffing under the name of banga, the term applied by the Rockhampton

Aborigines to this species; in Western Australia the material from
M. fraseri was similarly used.

Distribution: Some species in all mainland States

Malaisia scandens   BURNEY VINE

Burney vine is rainforest twiner of nondescript appearance which
excites little attention unless one brushes against one of the many
long, almost leafless branches. These branches are well supplied
with short but very robust, backward-directed hairs which can
quickly rasp off a surface layer of skin leaving a burn-like graze.
The distinctive fruits are like minute, orange-red acorns.

   The inner bark of this vine was a useful source of excellent fibre
for the Aborigines. In *Tom Petrie's Reminiscences* the method of
preparation in the Brisbane area is described. Lengths of the vine
were beaten with sticks until the bark could be pulled off easily
with the teeth. After soaking in water for a few days the inner and
outer bark could be separated, the outer discarded and the inner
split into strands with the thumbnail. When dry, the strands were
twisted on the thigh into string. This string was used for dilly
bags, fish nets and for the strong nets made to catch dugongs.
Lengths of burney vine stem were used to strengthen the sides of
bark canoes.

Distribution: Qld, N.S.W., N.T.

Melaleuca   PAPERBARK TEA-TREE

Within the genus *Melaleuca* there are numerous species which
have a bark made up mainly of cork cells arranged in thin papery
layers. These separate readily from each other as the bark ages,
and progressively flake off at the surface as papery fragments.
However, running longitudinally through the bark there are also
fibres which add greatly to the strength of the material.

   In the past, considerable use has been made of this type of bark
by both the Aborigines and the white man although at the
present time almost the only use for this bark in Australia is for
lining hanging baskets.

   In early times the bark was used also as insulation in cold
stores, as a packing material and for caulking boats. More
recently, in the 1950s and 1960s, a small industry operated in
Queensland and New South Wales stripping *Melaleuca* bark

and processing it for use as a filler in mattresses and pillows and as insulation material. Since cork is a waterproof material, the pillows and mattresses containing pulverized melaleuca bark could be boiled or steam-sterilized. Over 400 tonnes of bark were used annually in this way.

The Aborigines used the bark of these species in several different ways. Knife sheaths were made from it, rough huts were thatched with strips of bark, and a kind of girdle made from paperbark was used for carrying a baby on its mother's hip. In cases of fracture of a limb, the affected part was wrapped in tea-tree bark, outside in, and fastened in place with twine. Women in the Princess Charlotte Bay area made ring pads of the bark for placing on the head when heavy weights were carried.

Sheets of bark made useful blankets in cold weather. Although the Aborigines normally went barefoot, in parts of the Northern Territory rough sandals made from tea-tree bark were used to protect the feet from sharp stones or hot sand.

A sheet of tea-tree bark was the equivalent of the modern disposable raincoat.

Distribution: Some species in all States

Nypa fruticans   NIPA

Nipa is a peculiar palm, often classed as a mangrove since it grows in tidally inundated mud. Its prostrate stem produces large pinnate leaves often about 6 m high and, where it grows in sufficient quantity, these leaves are generally the most favoured material used for thatching. It is a common plant in parts of Papua and South-east Asia and large quantities of leaves are cut there. In Australia it occurs in only very limited areas of the tropics and does not seem to have been exploited here for this purpose.

An interesting use for the plant in South-east Asia at one time was in the manufacture of cigarette papers. Young, unopened leaves were cut and the cuticle or thin outer membrane was removed before drying.

Distribution: Qld, N.T.

Pandanus   SCREW PALM

In southern Queensland and northern New South Wales *Pandanus* is confined to coastal habitats. The low spreading trees with stout prop roots from the lower trunk and the crown of keeled, sword-like leaves at each branch apex form a distinctive feature of many ocean headlands.

In northern Queensland and the tropical Indo-Pacific region, numerous species occur and occupy a much wider range of habitats. Beyond Australia, the leaves of certain species are often woven into mats, mainly for sleeping but also for sails, baskets and bags. Leaves for this purpose are usually passed through a fire to make them more flexible, then the prickly midrib and margins are removed and the leaf split into strips of suitable width for plaiting. Leaves have also been used without preparation as wrappers in cooking and for thatching. In some places cordage and bags have been made from fibrous strands extracted from the leaf although these are not of good quality. In Papua New Guinea ropes are made from fibrous strands extracted from both aerial prop roots and stems. Aboriginal use is recorded from northern Queensland where the leaves were used for dilly bags, sieve bags, mat-cloaks and armlets.

Crude paintbrushes have been made in India from lengths of the prop roots by beating out one end to form a bristly tuft. Both paintbrushes and scrubbing brushes have been made from the fruits by scraping away the sweet, fleshy material from between the fibres of the lower end of the fruit.

Distribution: Qld, N.S.W., W.A., N.T.

Panicum trachyrhachis   COOLIBAH GRASS

This tufted, perennial grass, up to 2 m high, is widespread in northern Australia. Its leaves yield a fibre used by the Aborigines for making twine. The method of extraction was described as follows: 'The fibre is peeled from the undersurface of the leaf, by breaking it in the middle across with a sudden jerk while held between the fingers, and drawing the threads away.'

Distribution: Qld, W.A., N.T.

Phragmites australis (P. communis)   COMMON REED

This tall grass, often 2-3 m high, is generally found at the margins of streams, lakes and swamps. It is almost cosmopolitan in distribution.

The Australian Aborigines used the stems for making bags and baskets, while in India the plant was used for matting and was plaited into sandals. It has made serviceable thatching material in various parts of the world, including Australia. The explorer E. J. Eyre had accommodation for himself, servant and visitors made from *Phragmites*. In South Australia, soldiers were housed in huts made from this grass until stone barracks could be erected.

In Papua, robust stems are used for arrows which are tipped with hardwood or have a piece of heavy wood inserted near the tip to improve the flight behaviour. Aborigines used the stems similarly for the hafts of reed spears.

Pens were made from the stem in both Egypt and India. The fibres extracted from the stem have been shown to be suitable for making good quality paper but the plant seems to have been little used for this purpose. Musical reeds have been made from the stem but these are mostly manufactured from another grass, *Arundo donax*.

Distribution: All States

Pimelea   RICE FLOWER

The numerous species of *Pimelea* vary from herbs to small shrubs. Their flowers, which are white, pink or yellow, have two stamens and four petal-like sepals. Commonly, they are arranged in heads although in some species they are in axillary clusters. The bark strips very readily from the stems as long, very strong, fibrous strands which can be used directly as an emergency string. Aborigines used this bark for preparing cordage.

Distribution: Some species in all States

Posidonia australis   FIBRE-BALL PLANT

Posidonia australis is one of the sea grasses widely distributed in the southern part of Australia, growing on sandy floors from low water mark to a depth of about 10 m. Prostrate stems give rise to short erect branches bearing ribbon-like leaves 6-15 mm broad. Numerous strong fibres, the remains of leaf bases, clothe the stems. South Australian Aborigines used the fibres for making their baskets.

In some places the fibres have been aggregated by water movement into compact balls which are rolled around beaches by the waves. The fibrous material is very resistant to decay; and in parts of Spencer Gulf and St Vincent Gulf it has accumulated in extensive beds, up to a couple of metres thick, and extending out from the shore for up to 8 km. It has been estimated that the deposits cover about 62,000 ha and contain over four million tonnes of fibre. Beginning in 1902 there have been several attempts, with varying degrees of success, at exploiting these vast deposits. However, the separation, at reasonable cost, of 1 part by weight of fibre from about 380 parts of sand, has been a problem. The most successful method of extraction was by suction dredge, after which the material was washed in sea water to remove sand, rolled to expel excess water, washed with fresh water, then rolled again and dried with hot air. The main uses of the material were as insulation and as a stuffing material. Some was mixed with low grade wool in coarse textiles. No exploitation has occurred since World War I.

Distribution: N.S.W., Vic., Tas., S.A., W.A.

Rhipogonum album   WHITE SUPPLEJACK

White supplejack is a common rainforest climber of fairly variable nature. Some stems carry numerous stout prickles, others are quite smooth, while the leathery leaves may be arranged alternately or in groups of two or three. The very tough stems were used by the Aborigines of New South Wales for making crayfish traps.

Distribution: Qld, N.S.W.

Rulingia dasyphylla (R. pannosa)   KERRAWANG

Kerrawang is a shrub, usually a metre or two high, with small whitish flowers and serrated leaves 3-10 cm long with depressions on the upper surface marking the position of the veins. The undersurface is velvety with star-shaped hairs. Its inner bark is very fibrous and was used by the Aborigines for cordage.

Distribution: Qld, N.S.W., Vic.

Schoenus melanostachys   BLACK BOG-RUSH

The generic name of this plant is derived from the Latin *schoenus* meaning a rope of bulrushes or skein of silk, in recognition of the use of some species in ropemaking.

Schoenus melanostachys is one of the sedges, perhaps not much more attractive than the common name it bears; it is widely distributed in swampy country along the east coast of Australia. Its slender, cylindrical stems, mostly 60-100 cm high and 1-2 mm thick are leafless except for some dark brown sheathing leaves at the base and in the flowering part at the end of the stem. Individual flowering branchlets are like small spindles, 5-10 mm long, of overlapping brown-black scales; these are arranged loosely on the upper 5-10 cm of the plant. Stems are recorded as being used for dilly bags by Aborigines of Stradbroke Island and the Logan River in southern Queensland, and their use was probably more widespread than this.

Distribution: Qld, N.S.W., Vic.

Scirpus validus (S. lacustris)   RIVER CLUB-RUSH

Along the edges of slow-moving streams and swamps *Scirpus validus* is one of the common large sedges. It forms dense, grey-green stands of gradually tapering leafless stems 1-2 m high, bearing a loose cluster of brown, cone-like flowering branches at the apex.

Over a hundred years ago there was a proposal in Australia to manufacture a type of pith helmet from this sedge but the industry failed to eventuate.

Distribution: All States

Sesbania benthamiana (S. aculeata)   SESBANIA PEA, PEA-BUSH

Sesbania pea is an annual, herbaceous plant which can quickly reach a height of a metre or two even in unpromising roadside sites. It bears pinnate leaves 15-30 cm long with numerous small leaflets, and dull yellowish pea-flowers on branches much shorter than the leaves.

A good fibre was once obtained experimentally from the bark by bruising the stems and soaking them in water but its collection never became a commercial proposition. The dried stems were used by the Aborigines as drills for making fire and for tipping reed spears.

Distribution: Qld, N.S.W., N.T.

Sida rhombifolia   SIDA-RETUSA, PADDY'S LUCERNE

This very common weed of the warmer parts of Australia occurs naturally in a number of countries and has been introduced to others so that it is now found almost all over the world. It is a tough fibrous plant, becoming slightly woody, and as home gardeners know, is deeply rooted and hard to pull from the ground. Leaves vary greatly in shape, being sometimes narrow and pointed, at other times broadly angular; they are grey beneath and usually bluntly toothed. The pale yellow flowers 1-1.5 cm diameter are similar to *Hibiscus* in form, and are produced singly or in pairs on relatively long stalks; the calyx, which persists around the fruits, has ten ribs.

In the latter half of the last century considerable hopes were held that this widespread pest could be utilized for its bark fibre which is similar to that of jute and has been used to some extent in other countries, where it has even been cultivated. Samples of the fibre which were prepared and sent overseas were found suitable for use in place of jute but to be acceptable to the manufacturers had to be available in large quantities. Wild plants were not suitable for economic harvesting and probably other crops provided a higher return so a *Sida* industry never developed in Australia.

Distribution: Qld, N.S.W., Vic., S.A., N.T.

Spinifex hirsutus   COASTAL SPINIFEX

Spinifex hirsutus is a familiar grass of sand dunes along wide stretches of the Australian coastline. On newly deposited sand it is often the first plant to appear; its long prostrate stems, with sparse tufts of hairy grey leaves at intervals, spread rapidly over the surface and help to stabilize it.

The glossy, yellowish stems are very tough and fibrous and were used by the Aborigines for making sieve bags and dilly bags. Its softly spiky seed head is readily bowled along the beach in a breeze and served as a toy for Aboriginal children.

Distribution: Qld, N.S.W., Vic., S.A., W.A.

Sterculia quadrifida   PEANUT TREE

The peanut tree is a rainforest species with insignificant flowers, but makes up for this deficiency by its spectacular fruits which split along one side and open widely to reveal a brilliant, orange-red interior with elliptical black seeds along each edge — discoloured teeth in a widely gaping mouth.

Like the bottle tree and kurrajong to which it is closely related, the peanut tree has bark with a strong fibre. In the Atherton district of northern Queensland the Aborigines used it in the preparation of twine at least 6 mm thick from which they made kangaroo nets.

Distribution: Qld, N.S.W., N.T.

Telopea speciosissima   WARATAH

Probably one of the best known and most handsome wildflowers in Australia is the waratah. Now carefully protected for its spectacular, rigid domes of red flowers, its young branches were used in the early days of settlement for basket-making.

Distribution: N.S.W.

Thespesia populnea   PORTIA TREE, INDIAN TULIP TREE

Along tropical shores of the Indo-Pacific region *Thespesia populnea* is one of the commonest small trees. It has considerable resemblance to *Hibiscus tiliaceus* (cotton tree) but its heart-shaped leaves lack hairs on the underside and the stigma of the large flowers is undivided, that of *Hibiscus* being divided into five distinct lobes.

The inner bark yields a good fibre which was used in South-east Asia for cordage and fishing lines, and for caulking boats. It would be surprising if the Aborigines had not used this fibre as they did that of *Hibiscus tiliaceus* but no record seems to have survived of their doing so.

The timber in Australia is available only in quantities and sizes too small to be of economic interest, but in some areas it has been popular for boatbuilding because of its great durability in water.

Distribution: Qld, N.T.

Typha   BULRUSH

Bulrushes, with their distinctive dark brown rod-like masses of minute fruits disintegrating at maturity into clouds of fluff, are characteristic marsh plants found in most parts of the world. In

Australia, three species occur and these are not particularly easy to distinguish from each other. Although the genus has been little used in this country, it has been widely exploited overseas. Leaves have been used for thatching, for making mats, trays and ropes, and as a caulking material. The fluff from the female part of the flowering spike has made useful stuffing for pillows and mattresses, and this use is recorded for South Australia. About one hundred years ago the captain of an Italian ship visiting Australia offered to the Royal Humane Society in Melbourne a sample of the mattresses used on his ship. These were stuffed with bulrush floss and served, in emergency, also as effective liferafts. The suggestion was made at the time that *Typha latifolia*, from which the floss was obtained, should be introduced to Australia to supply stuffing for maritime mattresses. However, the native species yielded very similar material and, in any case, nothing seems to have come of this suggestion for exploitation of the plants in Australia. Bulrush floss has been used overseas also as a binding material in mortar and as an emergency absorptive material in surgery.

Aborigines of the Murray-Darling river system found a double use for bulrushes. After the underground stems had been baked and skinned they were thoroughly chewed to extract the considerable quantities of starch which formed a useful food. What remained was a mass of white fibre which was rolled on the thigh into twine.

Distribution: Some species in all States

Urena lobata   PINK BURR

Urena lobata is a small shrub bearing roughly rounded hairy leaves with three to five lobes and ornamental pink flowers resembling very small hibiscus flowers. However, its burr-like fruits which readily become attached to clothes detract from its attractiveness.

The bark yields a good, cream-coloured, soft fibre approaching jute in quality and used mainly in India and some other tropical countries for rope, hessian and sacks. Mostly it is wild plants that have been used although there has been limited cultivation in some areas. While common on tropical Australian coasts it is not recorded as having been used by the Aborigines.

Distribution: Qld, N.T.

Urtica   STINGING NETTLE

Before flax was introduced into northern Europe the fibre commonly used in the Scandinavian and Germanic countries was obtained from nettles. Of the two principal species used, the lesser nettle, *Urtica urens*, has become naturalized in Australia and is widespread in the south.

Nettle fibre is similar to linen, but generally regarded as inferior; it can be prepared in the same way by steeping the dried stems in water, separating the fibres and spinning them into a yarn which can be used for cordage and cloth of all types, from damask and brocade to sailcloth and sacking. Although we tend to think of nettles as an antiquated fibre source, they are still used, and even cultivated for use, in some parts of northern Europe. Wild nettles on the whole have poorer fibre content than cultivated plants as they are usually shorter and more branched; nettles growing in a damp ditch have been recommended.

During World War I when Germany and Austria found it impossible to obtain sufficient supplies of cotton, they turned to nettles as a substitute, and thousands of tonnes were harvested, mainly from wild plants. The fibre, often blended with cotton, or in some cases with ramie, was used for products ranging from underclothes and shirts to tarpaulins.

There seems to be no record of the use of our native nettle, *U. incisa*, as a fibre plant. This is probably another case of it being too late on the scene, as the plants are strongly fibrous.

Distribution: *U. urens* — All States
              U. incisa — Qld, N.S.W., Vic., Tas., S.A.

Wikstroemia indica   TIE BUSH

This species occurs mainly close to the seashore where it forms a shrub with elliptical leaves and small yellow-green flowers, quite undistinctive except for its bright red ellipsoid fruits about 5 mm long. However, the scent of crushed leaves is distinctive, and although difficult to describe is certainly not pleasant.

The species belongs to the same family as *Pimelea* and, as in members of that genus, the bark can be easily stripped from the stem in long fibrous strands. In India the bark fibres have been used for ropemaking, and at one time the bark was exported from the Philippines to Japan for the manufacture of strong paper such as that used for bank notes.

Distribution: Qld, N.S.W., W.A., N.T.

Zostera   GRASS-WRACK, EEL GRASS

Zostera is one of the sea grasses, growing mainly in estuaries at or a little below low-water mark. Its narrow, strap-shaped leaves have large internal air spaces so that the dried material is very light and makes reasonable stuffing material for mattresses, preferably after weathering for a period sufficient to shed its fairly strong marine odour. *Zostera* has been used for this purpose both overseas and in Australia but the identity of the species used in Australia is now uncertain.

Distribution: All States

OTHER SOURCES OF FIBRES AND CANES

Abroma fastuosa	*Juncus effusus*
Agathis robusta	*Lepironia articulata*
Alloteropsis semialata	*Melochia corchorifolia*
Alphitonia excelsa	*Normanbya normanbyi*
Apluda mutica	*Phaleria blumei* var. *latifolia*
Barringtonia racemosa	*Pipturus argenteus*
Brachychiton diversifolium	*Planchonia careya*
Chrysopogon pallidus	*Poa australis*
Cissampelos pareira	*Pongamia pinnata*
Cissus adnata	*Psoralea archeri*
Cochlospermum gillivraei	*Psoralea patens*
Coix lachryma-jobi	*Ptychosperma elegans*
Cordia myxa	*Scirpodendron ghaeri*
Curculigo ensifolia	*Scirpus mucronatus*
Derris trifoliata	*Sida cordifolia*
Digitaria brownii	*Sporobolus indicus*
Eleocharis fistulosa	*Stenochlaena palustris*
Eleusine indica	*Sterculia caudata*
Fimbristylis dichotoma	*Trema orientalis*
Grewia spp.	*Triumfetta pilosa*
Haemodorum coccineum	*Vandasia retusa*

10

Ornament and Adornment

'Their ornaments were few: necklaces prettyly enough made
of shells, bracelets wore round the upper part of their arms,
. . . a peice of Bark tied over their forehead . . .'

Joseph Banks

BARK PAINTINGS

ABORIGINAL PAINTINGS were done on a variety of surfaces,
including wooden weapons and utensils, bark, and rock surfaces.
One of the 'canvases' used in Arnhem Land was the bark of the
Darwin stringybark, *Eucalyptus tetrodonta,* (p. 133).

The paints used were ochre, mixed sometimes with water, but
often with the juice from the fleshy stems of some of the native
orchids growing in the trees. Two species known to have been
used were *Cymbidium canaliculatum* and *Dendrobium dicuphum.* The
juice, starchy and sticky, helps the ochre adhere to the surface.

On the Bloomfield River in north Queensland, Aborigines
used the seed-oil of the candle-nut, *Aleurites moluccana,* (p. 39) to
fix the ochre for spear-painting. In other northern areas, a resin
obtained from *Leptospermum fabricia* was used; chips of the bark
were warmed and rubbed over the surface to be painted, after
which the pigment was warmed and rubbed in to give a
permanent coloration.

Eucalyptus papuana   GHOST GUM, LIMEWOOD

In the paintings of Albert Namatjira and other Arunta artists the
characteristic eucalypt seen is the ghost gum, a smooth,
white-barked species growing as a small tree, often stunted and
gnarled in the dry areas. It is widespread throughout tropical
Australia, and is one of the few eucalypts extending beyond this
country; as its name suggests it occurs in Papua.

The very white bark of the ghost gum is covered with a fine white powdery layer which comes off on the hand; this is responsible for the less common name of limewood. it was this powder which was used by the Aborigines of the Northern Territory on their headbands, giving a brilliant white which produced a striking effect.

Distribution: Qld, W.A., N.T.

CEREMONIAL DECORATION

As adornment for ceremonies and corroborees the Aborigines generally used clay, ochre and feathers, often with blood as the medium for sticking the downy feathers to the skin. However a few items involved the use of plants. Several writers have described the conical helmets worn by tribes in central Australia; these were formed from twigs of *Cassia eremophila* or *Hakea* that were tied at the apex with hair string, a plume of emu feathers often being placed in the top. The downy white or coloured trimmings seen on the helmet and on the skin were either down feathers of birds or a cottony fluff of long hairs from *Portulaca filifolia,* a hairy species of pigweed. This fluff is white, and was used either in its natural state or coloured red or yellow with ochre; it was stuck on with blood, in different patterns, sometimes over the whole face except for circles around the eyes, and continued over the helmet to create a striking mask effect.

A milder form of decoration has been to use wattle flowers stuck on the body with honey. Along the Tully River in north Queensland, a sticky exudation from the bark of *Alstonia scholaris* (p.106) was spread over the body as a glue to attach downy feathers to the skin. Old man's beard lichen was used for head-dresses for corroborees in some areas.

In some coastal areas of north Queensland and in the Torres Strait Islands, halved empty seed-coats of the matchbox bean, *Entada phaseoloides,* (p. 93) were strung together to make leg-rattles worn by women in dancing.

Pisolithus tinctorius   HORSE-DUNG PUFFBALL

Tom Petrie has described a puffball which was used by the Aborigines of the Moreton Bay district for purposes of decoration. A large puffball found growing often at the base of ants' nests was rubbed over the body to powder it with the yellowish spore mass. From his description it seems clear the fungus was *Pisolithus tinctorius,* a honeycomb-like puffball found in many countries.

Distribution: All States

Podaxis pistillaris   TERMITE PUFFBALL

Podaxis pistillaris is a widespread fungus in Australia, showing considerable variation in form. In some coastal areas it grows typically on termite mounds and may be up to 50 cm tall, while in the inland it is usually found growing in soil and does not exceed 15 cm. It is a stalked puffball with an elongate shape so that the whole has the shape of a club. When it is mature the entire outer layer of the swollen end of the club either flakes off or may be lifted, to expose a purple-brown powdery mass of spores. This puffball was used as a sort of powder-puff by central Australian Aborigines, who spread the spore powder over their faces for decoration.

Distribution: Qld, N.S.W., S.A., W.A., N.T.

Pycnoporus   SNAKE'S BREAD

Amongst the wood-rotting fungi, this genus stands out; a brilliant orange-red, the bracket-shaped fruiting bodies keep their colour for a long time even when dry. It is a very common species on fallen logs in eucalypt forest.

It is not surprising that this fungus was used for personal adornment; Roth records that the Aboriginal women of Keppel Island off the Queensland coast used pieces of it to make a headband.

This genus is very popular for use in dried arrangements, being effective for colour contrast with driftwood and similar materials. There are two common species, both of the same bright colour.

Distribution: All States

SEEDS FOR BEADS

In general, seeds for jewellery and other decorative purposes need to be not only attractive in appearance but to have a hard coat which ensures some durability of the finished product. As well as necklaces, they can obviously be used for earrings and other jewellery items. It is well worth considering making your own set of distinctive dress buttons from quandong, coral tree, or another of the natives; if this is to be done it would be wise to test the chosen material for the possibility of staining the garment on washing.

We have prepared a variety of necklaces from seeds, and have found it necessary to avoid very large ones which are often heavy. *Milletia australis*, a native wistaria, is near the limit; the seeds are handsome, orange-brown, smooth discs about 2.5 cm diam., 1 cm thick; a moderate length of necklace weighs about 170 g. Some seeds may be found too prickly; a string of *Elaeocarpus grandis* seeds is uncomfortable if worn with a coat pressing on it, but otherwise entirely satisfactory.

Abrus precatorius   JEQUIRITY, CRAB'S EYES, INDIAN LIQUORICE

Clusters of greyish twisted pods with brilliant red and black seeds serve to identify this highly ornamental native twiner. The seeds are also extremely hard and durable, making them suitable for ornamental purposes. They have been widely used for necklaces, rosaries and decorative bead work. Aborigines used them as necklace beads, and also as decorative additions to some of their implements. Care should be used in handling the seeds as they are highly poisonous; one that is broken or pierced for threading would be dangerous if swallowed.

Since ancient times seeds of *Abrus precatorius* have been used in east Asian countries as a unit of weight for goldsmiths and jewellers; they are believed to have been used in a system of weights in that area before the tribes around the Mediterranean devised their system based on grains of barley and wheat. The seeds show considerable uniformity of size, although they are not identical; their durability and conspicuous colour would have been very helpful. Later the unit of weight was standardized at 1.75 grains troy, the approximate weight of the seed.

In Malaysia and India the seeds, ground and mixed to a paste with water, were used to mix with solder in making jewellery. It is thought that it acted as a temporary cement.

Distribution: Qld, W.A., N.T.

Adenanthera pavonina   CORAL WOOD

The most striking feature of *Adenanthera pavonina* is the shiny red lens-shaped seeds produced in a long twisted pod. These seeds have been used in Asia for numerous ornamental purposes: they can be strung for rosaries and necklaces, and hollowed-out seeds are used to make the small novelties containing three, ten or a hundred tiny ivory elephants. Each seed is about one centimetre in diameter.

A. *pavonina* seeds were for centuries used as weights by Asian goldsmiths in conjunction with *Abrus precatorius* described above. Standard seeds of the tree are twice the weight of the standard *Abrus* seed. The common Malay name 'saga' is used for both plants; its origin has been traced to the Arabic word for goldsmith. Not only are the seeds used for weights but, as with A. *precatorius*, they can be ground to a powder and used by the goldsmith in a cement for soldering jewellery.

The related A. *abrosperma* with red and black seeds somewhat resembling large *Abrus* seeds was used by northern Aborigines in decoration.
Distribution: Qld

Caesalpinia scortechinii   FLAT BLUE-BEAN

This scrambling shrub of rainforest margins is one of those known as wait-a-while because of the recurved prickles on the leaf rachis; the twice-pinnate leaves are about 30 cm long. Yellow five-petalled flowers in sprays are followed by flattened circular pods with a firm membraneous wing along one side; each pod contains a single greenish disc-shaped seed which has been used ornamentally.
Distribution: Qld, N.S.W.

*Coix lachryma-jobi   JOB'S TEARS

Seeds of this ornamental tropical grass are known, although perhaps not by name, to many tourists to South-east Asia who buy locally made necklaces. The seed-coats are glossy, white, grey or caramel coloured, and very hard due to their high silica content; many are the traditional tear-shape, but there is also a variety with cylindrical seeds.

Job's tears have been used for centuries for decorative purposes; they are strung for rosaries, necklaces and bead curtains. In parts of Indonesia it was believed that wearing a string of these hard seeds helped to give a child strong teeth. The seeds are easy to thread as removal from their stalk leaves a hole lengthwise through the centre.

Although not native to Australia, the grass has been planted as an ornamental, and has escaped to become naturalized in some areas. It is interesting to notice that the seeds are now being used to make souvenir necklaces for sale at some Northern Territory Aboriginal settlements.

Distribution: Qld, N.S.W., W.A.

Elaeocarpus grandis   QUANDONG, BLUE QUANDONG, WHITE QUANDONG

This handsome large tree, one of the tallest of the rainforest, may often be recognized by having a few red leaves standing out amongst its foliage. Its round fruits, which may litter the forest floor beneath, are a beautiful sky blue. Each contains a woody stone somewhat like that of the sweet quandong, but more deeply pitted. The stone similarity is responsible for the shared common name, although the species are not closely related.

We have found it better, when gathering stones to make a necklace, to pick up freshly fallen fruits with the stone still enclosed in its blue skin. If these are left to soak in a bucket of water for three or four weeks the thin layer of flesh rots off, and a fairly uniformly coloured set of wooden beads in good condition is obtained. These can be drilled for stringing with little difficulty.

Distribution: Qld, N.S.W.

Erythrina vespertilio   BAT'S-WING CORAL TREE, GREY CORKWOOD

When ripe, the pods of the bat's-wing coral tree split open and curl back to release bright orange-red bean-like seeds about 1 cm long, with a black spot at the point of attachment. The seeds are hard and durable, so much so that it is generally necessary to file the seed coat when planting them to assist germination.

Their attractive appearance was appreciated by the Aborigines, who used the seeds to make necklaces; each one was pierced with a fire-stick and hundreds were threaded on a hair string to make a long rope which was worn around the neck, across the chest, under each arm and across the back. These necklaces formed an article of trade from the north of the continent where the coral tree is fairly common.

It is probably easier to form the hole in the bean with a drill, but a heated needle could be substituted for the fire-stick.
Distribution: Qld, N.S.W., S.A., W.A., N.T.

Gyrocarpus americanus (NO COMMON NAME KNOWN)

Gyrocarpus is a tall tree widespread throughout the tropics, including northern Australia. The leaves, which are deciduous, are often deeply three-lobed in young plants, more or less heart-shaped in older trees. Very small flowers are followed by fruits each with two long paddle-shaped wings which cause the fruit to spin as it falls from the tree. The fruit contains a single bony stone used in India for making rosaries and necklaces.
Distribution: Qld, N.T.

Melia azedarach WHITE CEDAR

This graceful native tree is popular as a cultivated ornamental. Its lilac-coloured flowers are followed by abundant yellow rounded-ellipsoid fruits. The flesh of the fruit, which is poisonous, encloses a roughened, bony, ellipsoidal stone. These are used in India as beads for necklaces and rosaries, and are attractive although perhaps less decorative than those of the quandongs.
Distribution: Qld, N.S.W., N.T.

Santalum acuminatum QUANDONG, SWEET QUANDONG

The fleshy red fruits of the quandong contain a round woody stone, interestingly pitted. These stones, painted appropriate colours, were used in Australia as the marbles for Chinese checkers at one time. Left unpainted, they make attractive beads for stringing as necklaces.

In colonial times, the stones of the quandong were sometimes mounted in silver or gold for such items of jewellery as ladies' bracelets, shirt-pins and 'stud-buttons for gentlemen'.
Distribution: All mainland States

PRESSED FLOWERS

Most people have at some stage pressed a few flowers in a book, and later probably have found their specimen looking squashed rather than pressed; faded, and perhaps falling apart. However with a little care it is possible to press plant material so that it retains its colour and attractive appearance. Some plants are not worth attempting unless the collector wishes to have them for a special purpose such as a scientific collection. Plants with fleshy leaves or flowers, for example, usually partly decay and fall apart before they are dry; this can be prevented by dipping them in boiling water or formalin solution for a minute before pressing, but this treatment causes loss of the colour and attractive appearance.

The spray of leaves or flowers should be pressed as soon as possible after collection; use unglazed paper such as newspaper. Arrange the specimen with the flower displayed to advantage, if necessary trimming some leaves so the piece is not too thick. A moderate weight, such as a couple of books, is placed on top. Pressing the plants in an old telephone book with a volume of an encyclopaedia on top works well. The main thing to remember is to change the pressing paper frequently, each day for a week, then every second day for about another week, depending on the plant; when drying is complete the specimen should be quite stiff.

Pressed flowers such as these can be used to make attractive greeting cards — possibly using native plants from the home garden. Flowers and leaf sprays are usually too fragile to use as bookmarks although they can easily be kept in a book; however, a single large *Eucalyptus* leaf, pressed and dried, makes a working bookmark that is very distinctively Australian.

Another attractive leaf preparation is the skeleton leaf. In rainforests and other moist areas we frequently see fallen leaves, the soft parts of which have rotted away leaving the framework of more resistant veins. Similar skeletons can be prepared from fresh leaves. Well-shaped leaves are chosen, boiled gently in a 10% solution of potassium hydroxide for about twenty minutes, then rinsed under a tap; finally the soft parts can be gently removed with a brush. Potassium hydroxide is caustic potash and must be handled with caution, care being taken not to get it on the skin; the vessel used for boiling must be enamel or pyrex, not metal. Twenty minutes is a rough estimate of the time; some leaves will take longer, some less, and the exact time for any is found only by experimenting. The appearance of the skeleton is sometimes improved by soaking it in household bleach after brushing. Robust skeleton leaves make good bookmarks, or specimens may be mounted on black paper if desired for display.

MATCHBOXES

Nowadays we do not carry wax matches which can be struck on any rough surface to give a light, but in the days when these were used a number of ingeniously contrived matchboxes were available. In the Australian colonies these were sometimes made from large seeds. *Entada phaseoloides,* the matchbox bean (p.93), owes its common name to this; the seeds are large, flat and brown (much like a chocolate-coated biscuit at a quick glance) and were split and fitted with a hinge and clasp to make a container.

Another species whose seeds were used was the largest of the native cycads, *Lepidozamia peroffskyana* (formerly *Macrozamia denisonii*). This palm-like forest tree of Queensland and northern New South Wales bears cones with large scarlet egg-shaped seeds up to 6 cm long; the seeds have a hard coat, and when emptied of their starchy contents can be hinged and clasped to make an attractive small box.

INKS

Coprinus comatus   INK CAP

Ink caps are very easy fungi to identify, especially if older specimens are found. On becoming past their prime, the caps of these tall, dark-spored, gilled fungi collapse, starting from the margin; they liquefy to a watery black fluid which can be used as a writing ink although it is less permanent than India ink.

C. comatus is a large, shaggy ink cap, common overseas as well as in eastern Australia. Reaching 30 cm or so in height it is sometimes found in large numbers on disturbed ground, especially on enriched soil such as rubbish dumps. This species is known to have been used at least two hundred years ago in France for making ink. Other species of *Coprinus* can be used similarly.

Distribution: Qld, N.S.W., Vic., S.A.

Phytolacca octandra   INKWEED, DYEBERRY

A weed found in many parts of Australia, inkweed is particularly common in rainforest clearings of the eastern States. It is a large herb whose succulent stems often have a red or purple coloration. The spikes of small white flowers are followed by conspicuous flattened juicy berries up to 2 cm across; these fruits are red when unripe, turning black on ripening, and if crushed release copious amounts of red juice.

Although one of the names used for the plant is dyeberry, and the juice stains skin and clothes of those who brush against the fruits, the colour is impermanent so of no value for dyeing cloth. The juice can be easily obtained in sufficient quantity to use as ink and is of interest to use with a quill or sharpened fern stalk, although the writing tends to fade.

Inkweed is closely related to the American pokeweed, well-known in herbal medicine; the pokeweed has been introduced to Australia but is uncommon.

Distribution: All mainland States

Solanum nigrum   BLACK NIGHTSHADE

This common introduced plant is often wrongly referred to as deadly nightshade. It is a semi-shrubby weed whose small white flowers with yellow centres are followed by a heavy crop of juicy purple-black berries about 6 mm in diameter; the berries are very popular with birds.

The purple juice of the berries has been used as writing ink in the past in Sicily. We have not heard of its use for this purpose in Australia.

Distribution: All States

11

Other Uses

CANOES

IN MANY PARTS of Australia the Aborigines used bark canoes for water transport. Use of these was restricted mainly to inland rivers and sheltered coastal waters. Around the northern coastline stouter craft were paddled and sailed; these vessels showed strong affinities with the more elaborate vessels of the islanders of Indonesia and New Guinea.

Calophyllum tomentosum   POON SPAR TREE

Several species of trees were used to provide bark for canoes along the coast of north Queensland. One of these was *Calophyllum tomentosum*, a straight tall tree of the coastal rainforests with firm shiny leaves and four-petalled flowers a little more than a centimetre across.

A large sheet of bark was stripped from the trunk; this species had the advantage that it could be stripped at any season. After heating to make the bark pliable, the sheet was folded lengthwise and clamped together at one end with a spreader holding out the sides; the prow was shaped and sewn together with split lawyer vine and caulked with paperbark. The stern of the canoe was joined in the same way, but spread wider than the bow. Along the gunwhales a strengthening length of lawyer vine or supplejack was oversewn with split cane; the inside of the canoe was lined with crosswise pieces of bark held in place with lengths of cane. It took about a day to make a craft of this kind, which was very durable if kept in the shade when not in use. The paddle used to propel the canoe was generally a piece of bark or a shell. Distribution: Qld

Erythrina variegata   CORAL TREE

The handsome coral tree, popular as an ornamental especially in
street plantings, is a tropical species very common in southern
Asia and northern Australia. Being leafless when in flower makes
the brilliant scarlet bunches of long pea-flowers even more
conspicuous.

Timber of the coral tree is very soft and of no use for most
conventional purposes, but it is suitable for dugout canoes and
has been the preferred material for them in parts of the north of
Australia. It is thought that the Aborigines first obtained the
idea from the visiting trepang (bêche-de-mer) fishermen from
Macassar, but quickly developed their own canoes. The log is
hollowed out with axes to leave a shell 2-3 cm thick on the sides,
8 cm thick on the bottom. Outriggers, masts and *Pandanus* sails
were all added in some areas following contacts with New
Guinean and Indonesian islanders.

This wood has been used in India also for canoes, rafts, floats
and catamarans.

Distribution: Qld, N.T.

Eucalyptus camaldulensis (E. rostrata)   RIVER RED GUM

The broad, comparatively calm waters of the lower Murray River
were ideal for bark canoes, and in this area they were widely used.
River red gum was the preferred source of the bark; the trees were
plentiful and large and had a good thick bark which made
excellent canoes. Dugouts were not used in this region, possibly
because there were no suitable trees for their preparation. A
young German traveller in 1851 found this out the hard way: he
was journeying down the lower reaches of the Murray River and
decided to make a dugout canoe; the only trees large enough to
make a canoe were the river red gums, which were very heavy and
unwieldy, and he found it took days to hollow a trunk out
sufficiently to make a canoe; the resulting craft, as well as
amazing the local Aborigines, was a failure as it was very heavy
and floated too low in the water; it had to be abandoned after 130
exciting kilometres.

To prepare the bark canoe, a suitable sheet of bark on a curved
trunk was chosen, marked out, then carefully cut around;

removal was possible only in spring and summer, as at that time there is a fragile layer between bark and wood which can be fairly easily ruptured. Removal of the bark was done cautiously with flat flexible sticks used to ease the layer off a little at a time; a rope was tied around the trunk to prevent the bark from crashing prematurely to the ground and breaking. When separated, the sheet of bark was lowered carefully and was then shaped by various means, often weighting the bottom with stones and using heat to make the bark more pliable; it was fixed in the desired shape either in a prepared hole in the ground, or supported by props with stays inside to hold the shape. The thinner end from the upper part of the trunk was bent up to become the prow, while the thicker layer of bark at the rear was stopped up with clay to prevent leaks; the inside was washed with a thin layer of clay to protect it from the sun.

These canoes were made in various lengths to carry different numbers of people, approximately one metre per passenger, so for a family of six a six-metre canoe was about the right size. The craft were propelled using heavy fishing spears which acted as paddles in deeper water, and like poles in punts in shallower places.

Along the lower reaches of the Murray there are still a number of beautiful huge old river red gums carrying the large scars left by removal of the bark.

Distribution: All mainland States

Eucalyptus obliqua   MESSMATE STRINGYBARK

Another type of craft, the tied canoe, was made in south-eastern Australia from sheets of bark of *Eucalyptus obliqua*. After the bark was removed from the tree, the rough stringy layer was trimmed off. Heat was applied by a small fire and the sheet of bark, when sufficiently pliable, was turned inside out; the ends were bunched up and tied with cord made from bark fibre. These tied canoes were improved by using spreaders of thin timber to maintain the right width, and sometimes by adding wooden ribs.

Distribution: Qld, N.S.W., Vic., Tas., S.A.

Eucalyptus tetrodonta   DARWIN STRINGYBARK

Darwin Stringybark is today one of the most useful timber trees over considerable areas of northern Australia. At least until recent times the tree also played a significant part in the life of the Aborigines of the area. Spears and canoe paddles were made from the wood, and hollow branches were used for drone tubes and drums.

The bark was particularly important and was used for covering shelters, for small troughs and for canoes. In 1922 these canoes were still being made in some areas, and N. B. Tindale witnessed the process and described the preparation of the bark as follows: 'Two rings are cut at a distance of twelve or fifteen feet apart, and joined with a single longitudinal cut. The bark is then hammered with stones until it becomes detached from the tree. This is only possible during the wet season. The long sheet of bark naturally forms a cylinder. It is held over a fire and thoroughly heated, the dry, ragged outer bark being partially burnt off. When sufficiently hot the bark is laid inner side downward, on smooth ground, and kept flat with rocks, logs, or heaps of sand. After several days the outer loose ragged bark is peeled off, and the sheet is ready for canoe-making. The bark is never turned inside-out in use.'

Distribution: Qld, W.A., N.T.

Ficus   FIG

Ficus racemosa, a cluster fig, is a northern species which produces its fruits in branched clusters from the main trunk and large branches, rather than on leafy branchlets. A soft-wooded species, as are all the figs, it was used for dugout canoes by the Aborigines around the Gulf of Carpentaria.

A different type of canoe was made from the bark of one of the native species of *Ficus* in central Queensland. This was a sewn canoe made from three oval pieces of bark, one for the floor of the craft and one for each side. The pieces were shaped in a hole in the ground, fire as usual being used to make them more pliable, and the three pieces were sewn together with a thread commonly made from the bark of the fig root. Saplings were sewn in place to strengthen the rim of the canoe, and the ever-useful paperbark was used to caulk the cracks.

Distribution: Qld, N.S.W., Vic., N.T.

Melaleuca   TEA-TREE

Several species of soft-wooded trees were used for dugout canoes by the Aborigines along the shores of the Gulf of Carpentaria; one of the trees frequently used was the paperbarked tea-tree. Norman Tindale of the South Australian Museum has recorded detailed observations on the canoes and how they were made. Seagoing canoes were elaborately fashioned and large, up to about 8 m long and able to seat up to twelve persons; they had a well-shaped prow tapering to a knife-edge at the waterline. Projections left on the inner surface of the sides supported cross-pieces which acted both as strengtheners and as seats; these seats were made more comfortable with cushion-like pads of paperbark. This bark was also useful for caulking cracks and leaks.

The waterproof quality of the bark was useful in simpler craft. Bundles of bark were used as crude rafts for transporting children and goods across streams too deep for wading. At other times small rafts of dry sticks bound with string were covered with tea-tree bark for the same purpose.

Distribution: Some species in all States

Tristania suaveolens   SWAMP MAHOGANY

Swamp mahogany is a tree with the general appearance of a broad-leaved stringybark eucalypt, but with flowers having five petals and five bundles of stamens. It is typically found in low-lying country and withstands some flooding, but is by no means uncommon on higher ground.

Bark of this tree was used by the Aborigines of Moreton Bay to make tied canoes. Tom Petrie has given a good description of the process. Firstly the scaly outer layers were picked off while still on the tree, the bark was removed in a long cylinder, up to about 6 m long in some cases, in a manner similar to that for the Darwin stringybark. Then, 'A piece of vine was tied around each end to prevent it flattening out, and in the hollow dry leaves and small sticks were put and set fire to. While the fire was burning the bark was rolled about, and so it got equally heated all over . . . When the fire had burnt out, but while the bark was still hot, it was loosened free of the vines tying it, and then both ends were bent up and tied in a bunch with string made for the purpose from "yurol" (*Flagellaria indica*). Through each of these folded up ends a wooden skewer was run, and more string bound round kept all firm.' The rims of the canoe were strengthened with strands of wattle or burney vine sewn on with more *Flagellaria*. Both ends of these canoes were the same. These craft were used in salt water as well as fresh, and the stoutest of them were used for catching turtles.

Distribution: Qld, N.S.W., N.T.

WATER-CARRIERS AND OTHER VESSELS

For carrying water, honey and some sloppy foods, the Aborigines used a variety of leak-proof containers. A number of these were made in just the same way as the bark canoes, but on a small scale. Thus there were carriers made with the ends bunched up and tied, while others had the ends sewn. The plants used were in many cases the same; the bark of different eucalypts, *Tristania suaveolens* and *Calophyllum tomentosum* were used in the areas where they occurred. Paperbark from *Melaleuca* was widely used; it also made a commonly found wrapping material for carrying and protecting small objects.

Coolamons are wooden troughs made in the same general way as dugout canoes. The coral tree, *Erythrina*, being soft wooded, was frequently used. Some were made of eucalypt wood, which required more work in the preparation; a curved branch was chosen and cut, the hollow being made by charring and gouging. These vessels were used for a wide variety of purposes, and varied in size and shape according to that purpose, which might be carrying food, water or the baby, or preparing food. If used for water a few twigs placed on the surface helped to prevent spillage.

With present-day metal tools available, making these containers would be a much easier task.

Archontophoenix cunninghamii   PICCABEEN, BANGALOW PALM

The handsome feather palm of subtropical rainforests has different common names in New South Wales and Queensland. South of the border it is known as the Bangalow palm; we have given priority here to the Queensland name because it is derived from an Aboriginal use for the tree.

Tall slender trunks carry a cluster of graceful pinnate leaves, each with a large sheathing base which clasps the stem and helps to protect the growing point at the top. When the leaf is shed, this sheath falls with it; the whole fallen leaf makes an excellent vehicle for giving small children a sleigh-ride along a forest path; it can make a useful rain cape during a sudden shower. The Aborigines of the Moreton Bay region used the sheaths to make a pikki, or vessel, and it is from this that the name pikkibean or piccabeen was derived. In Tom Petrie's *Reminiscences of Early Queensland* there is a description of the method of manufacture: 'Both ends were tied up, and had a small skewer run through them, then a long stick passing down the centre lengthwise formed the handle. The skewers and handle were kept in place by string.'

In northern Queensland, leaf-sheaths of two other palms, *Normanbya normanbyi* (black palm) and *Archontophoenix alexandrae* (Alexandra palm), were used to make scoop-shaped carriers; one end only was tied up and used as the handle, the base of the sheath forming the mouth of the scoop.

Distribution: Qld, N.S.W.

Durvillea potatorum (Sarcophycus potatorum)   BULL KELP

Bull kelp is a massive seaweed growing near low-water level and below on wave-beaten rocky shores of southern Australia. There is a large, disc-like attachment organ, a stout stalk sometimes nearly the thickness of a forearm, and a broad leathery blade dividing into numerous whip-like segments. Large specimens may reach approximately 4 m in length.

There is a record of the Aborigines of Tasmania using 'portions of its great leaves, folded in the form of a pouch, for the purpose of keeping fresh water'. More recently, bull kelp has been used, along with *Macrocystis*, as a source of alginate (p.246). However, it has the disadvantage that it must be gathered manually while *Macrocystis* harvesting can be mechanized.

Distribution: N.S.W., Vic., Tas., S.A.

Erythrina vespertilio   BAT'S-WING CORAL TREE

Several exotic species of *Erythrina* with brilliant red or orange-red flowers are popular trees in cultivation. The native *E. vespertilio* has less spectacular orange-pink to brick-red flowers and distinctive leaflets which suggest the outline of a bat in flight. The bark is corky and, as in other erythrinas, the branches are liberally supplied with stout prickles.

Today the timber of this species is almost worthless. It is available only in small sizes, and although light and tough it is rather soft, non-durable and subject to borer attack. However for the Aborigines such a light, tough and easily worked timber was ideal for shields and the wooden troughs used for carrying food and water. Tom Petrie has given an account of the manufacture of these shields; to form the handle, the wood on either side was loosened then burnt out with coals, the operation being repeated until the holes met beneath the handle. Both the shields and the food troughs were covered with the wax of native bees. Shields were traded to areas where the bat's-wing coral tree did not grow.
Distribution: Qld, N.S.W., S.A., W.A., N.T.

Eucalyptus   GUM TREE

The irregularities on the trunk of a gum tree add greatly to the charm of its appearance. Some of the smooth-skinned bumps or burls provided bark carrying vessels for the Aborigines. In spring and summer they could be relatively easily removed by cutting around through the bark, hammering all over the surface with a stone, and carefully easing off the bowl with flat sticks. If necessary the inside was further smoothed and trimmed by charring and scraping, and a string handle could be attached through two holes drilled near the edge on opposite sides. Such containers were used for various purposes such as carrying honey.

Knobs of this kind on fallen timber are sometimes used as hanging baskets for plants. On a dead tree, if it is at the right stage of decay, the bowl will be found with the inside conveniently hollow.
Distribution: Some species in all States

*Lagenaria siceraria   BOTTLE GOURD, CALABASH GOURD

This vine, thought to be of Old World origin, has spread to most tropical countries. It is found naturalized in eastern districts of Australia. The plants have considerable resemblance to pumpkin vines with their long-stalked, five-lobed leaves and strong tendrils. They are found either climbing over other plants or sprawling along the ground. Flowers are white with sexes produced separately, although both may be on the same plant.

The fruit are large gourds with a very hard outer layer. Those seen in Australia are typically 40 cm or so long and shaped like a flask, with a narrow neck at the stem end and a swollen flower end. Overseas there is considerably more variety: gourds grow up to 180 cm long and anything from a sausage to a globe or a dumbell in shape. It is possible to manipulate the shape by binding the young developing fruit. Although some forms are cultivated in tropical countries as vegetables, those found in Australia are generally very bitter and are regarded as poisonous.

The hard outer layer of the gourd is impervious to water; this has led to their use since ancient times as containers for water and other liquids. They are known to have been used by the ancient Egyptians and by the Chinese two thousand years ago. The gourds had considerable advantages over pottery; they were light to carry and withstood rough handling reasonably well. Rumpf, a German naturalist writing in the seventeenth century, gave an account of the use of the gourds in Sulawesi (Celebes) for drawing toddy from palm trees; he added that 'they take and retain for a long time the smell and taste of the liquor put into them, and must only be used again for the same kind of liquor'. They were also carried by the Aborigines of the north as water containers for canoe trips to islands where there was no water; grass stoppers were used.

To prepare the fruit for use as a calabash, it is left to ripen on the vine, then cut open at the required point; the flesh is allowed to decay then emptied and cleaned out with ashes, and the vessel smoke dried. Shells of different shapes have been used as bowls, ladles, pipes, and small or large boxes. We have seen the shell carved in a decorative pattern with a light inside somewhat like a permanent Hallowe'en pumpkin. Hats have been made in the Philippines from the half-shell of a large fruit. In Papua New Guinea a hollowed gourd is used as a lime-pot to carry the lime chewed with betelnut, or as a container for oil or salt.

Although the gourds have had such widespread traditional use for storage of liquors, it was recorded by Maiden that some

sailors were fatally poisoned by beer that had been left standing
in one of the 'bottles'. A possible explanation may be that the
flesh had not been properly cleaned out of the shell.

Bottle gourds can be used in making remarkably varied
musical instruments. The Indian snake-charmer's pipe with its
characteristic bulge is basically one of these gourds; in northern
Thailand an instrument of the mouth-organ type is made from a
hollowed out shell with attached reed pipes, while in Borneo
a stringed instrument incorporates a bottle gourd as a
sounding-board. If the entire fruit is dried, the rattling of loose
bean seeds inside the shell makes the instrument known to
devotees of Latin American music as maracas.

Because of their buoyancy, the gourds have also been used as
floats.

Distribution: Qld, N.S.W.

MAKING FIRE

Fire was very important in the life of the Australian Aborigine.
Apart from using it for cooking and providing warmth in cold
weather, he heated resin to make it pliable for cementing his tools
and weapons, and warmed sheets of bark to bend them for
making canoes. With the exception of a few large shells such as
balers, he had no vessels for heating liquids, but overcame this
lack in some areas by heating stones in the fire and putting them
in a wooden vessel with the liquid; this was of value in preparing
some medicinal decoctions. It was important also to have a source
available when he wanted to fire the countryside, a frequent part
of Aboriginal hunting methods.

The Aborigine made fire by friction, using a variety of ways;
the methods seem to have been widespread, the woods used being
different depending on what was available.

The grass tree, *Xanthorrhoea*, was a widely used plant for
fire-making. A dry flower-stalk was taken and the old flowers and
fruits scraped from it into a small heap to serve as tinder; in some
cases dry grass was used instead. The stalk was broken from the
upper end to give a narrower 30-40 cm length; the thicker piece
was split lengthwise and placed, flat side up, on the heap of

tinder. Then the shorter piece was pressed into this and twirled rapidly back and forth between the palms of the hands, the friction finally producing sparks which set fire to the dry flowers. This whole process would be completed in less than three minutes, even in wet weather. However, if the weather was very wet, the fire-makers used dry leaves from under the 'skirt' of the grass tree for tinder instead of the wet flowers. White men attempting to copy the method usually find it very difficult, if not impossible.

In some parts of north Queensland, these sticks for making fire were valued sufficiently to be kept and carried with the men. They often had a special cap to sheathe the end; this was made of *Pandanus* leaf, cemented with beeswax and frequently decorated with seeds of *Abrus precatorius* or *Adenanthera abrosperma*.

This method, with variations and with different woods, was widely used. In parts of Victoria, a woomera of cypress pine was used as the base; a conical hole was made in it and the grass tree stem twirled in this so that the smouldering dust from the friction fell through the hole to make a small heap in which the fire started.

Another widespread method of making fire involved rubbing one piece of wood across another. A description given in 1884 refers to fire-making by Aborigines of the lower Murray-Darling area. Soft dry grass was placed in a crack of a hard sun-dried log, usually red gum or cypress pine, leaving the upper 1 cm unfilled; a piece of dry wood, preferably saltbush, about 35 cm long, 5-7 cm wide, with one side formed to a blunt edge, was rubbed back and forth across the top of the crack, at first slowly, but building up until 'for about the space of half a minute the rubbing is done so rapidly it is almost impossible to distinguish the rubbing stick'. The heat of friction ignited the wood filings produced by the rubbing; they were lifted out folded in the dry grass, which burst into flame when waved gently. P. Beveridge, who wrote the description, said it was so easily carried out that the Aborigines frequently did it for him to light his pipe.

Other observers have described the same method as being used in north-west and south-west Queensland. In Northern Territory, a spearthrower of a hard wood such as mulga was held by two men and rubbed with a sawing motion across the edge of a shield of soft wood, often bat's-wing coral tree, so that the smouldering powder dropped on to dry tinder placed ready.

Amongst other plants used for producing fire by friction were: *Clerodendrum floribundum, C. inerme* (sorcerer's flower,), *Guettarda speciosa, Premna dallachyana* (a good wet season fire-stick), *P. obtusifolia, Sesbania aegyptica, Ventilago viminalis* (vine tree).

FIRE-STICKS

Although the Aborigines, at least in some areas, were very skilful at making fires, when possible they would conserve their fire in sticks as they travelled from place to place. The Tasmanians had not developed the skill of making fire, so conservation of it was essential, and it was customary for them to carry their fire-sticks when walking along. In a number of accounts from the early days of settlement there are descriptions of Aborigines carefully husbanding a burning or smouldering piece of wood as they travelled; as they crossed rivers by canoe, fire would be transported stuck in a lump of clay in the canoe.

Obviously, slow-burning materials were the most suitable fire-sticks. Amongst those recorded as having been used were ironbark wood, mulga bark and dried cones of *Banksia*.

The large dry fruiting-bodies of some fungi have been found suitable for this purpose, in other countries as well as Australia. The herbalist Gerard wrote about puffballs that 'in divers parts of England, where people dwell farre from neighbours, they carry them kindled with fire, which lasteth long'. Hard dry bracket fungi, the sort that project as thick, hoof-shaped shelves from a dead log or a living tree, have this property of holding a fire for a long time. They were used in Tasmania by the Aborigines as a means of carrying fire from one camp to another, it being the task of the women to look after it as they travelled.

CANDLES AND WICKS

Commercially obtained candles are usually made from various waxes and fats such as paraffin, spermaceti and coconut oil, with beeswax used for some special purposes such as church candles.

The wick, which is generally of cotton, enables the candle wax to burn with sufficient air to give a clear flame.

There are several different types of candle that can be prepared wholly or partly using plant material. As described previously (p.40) candles have been made, especially in the Pacific area, by spearing a row of oily nuts such as candle-nut on a skewer; alternatively the nuts may be crushed, mixed with cotton wool, and pressed around the bamboo splint, which acts as a support rather than a wick.

In the early colonial days, bushmen used the barren cones of *Banksia integrifolia*, which are very porous, as a base for candles by impregnating them with fat. These burnt relatively slowly and were used as night-lights. The fat could be tallow or dripping, which was a common fuel for illumination in the past.

Almost any dry porous material can be used as a wick. The rushlights used in bygone days in Europe were simply the pith of peeled rushes soaked in fat, which burnt with a smoky flame. We have prepared such a light with *Scirpus validus*, the river club-rush, but some other sedges and rushes could be used just as well. In peeling the stem it is necessary to leave a narrow strip of green skin on one side to give some firmness to the candle. Similarly peeled rushes and sedges can be used as wicks in oil lamps; *Cyperus haspan* is one which has been used in south-east Asia.

FISH HOOKS

The long slender thongs of the lawyer vine, *Calamus*, are armed with very sharp recurved prickles that make a patch of the vine almost impenetrable. However, these structures were put to good use by the northern Queensland Aborigines who used them as fish hooks.

Another climber of northern rainforests is *Durandea jenkinsii* (formerly *Hugonia jenkinsii*). A woody plant, it has yellow flowers and leathery alternate leaves, but is more easily recognized by its hook-like tendrils curled back sometimes in a coil; these become very hard on ageing, and are recorded by Roth as having been used as fish hooks by the Aborigines of the Tully River.

Distribution: *Calamus* spp — Qld, N.S.W.

             Durandea jenkinsii — Qld

MAKING SOAP

Soap is made by chemically combining a fat or oil with an alkali. The fat may be animal fat such as tallow from beef or mutton suet, or oils from plants such as coconut, olive etc.; seed oils described in chapter 1 can, in general, be used. In the commercial process the alkali used is usually caustic soda which produces a hard soap, or caustic potash which gives a soft product.

Making of soap was not known until a couple of thousand years ago; it is thought to have been discovered by the Gauls who, some time after they were conquered by the Romans, developed the process of boiling goat fat with beechwood ashes to produce a soap. During the centuries that followed different oils and different alkalis were introduced, but soapmaking was a domestic, rather than a commercial, process until the latter half of the nineteenth century.

In the early days of settlement in Australia wood ash was used as the lye, or alkali, for making soap.

Avicennia marina   GREY MANGROVE

Barilla, an alkaline ash used for the making of soap, was obtained in the Australian colonies mainly from the burning of mangroves. Although said to be not the best source for barilla, mangrove was widely used first at Sydney, then in the Port Phillip district and Moreton Bay.

Nancy Bird has given an interesting account of an active industry in the Westernport Bay area of Victoria producing barilla in the 1840s by burning mangroves. The men doing this unpleasant work suffered difficulties including having their prepared ash stolen and having it washed away by rain before it had cooled enough to bag; it seems Victorian weather has not changed much. During 1843-4 30 tons was marketed, but a steep drop in price from £10 to £4 per ton was a death-blow to the industry. This was about the time that chemical conversion of common salt to soda became generally used.

At the Moreton Bay settlement, convicts were detailed for burning the mangrove trees at the mouth of the Brisbane River to produce ash for making soap.

The ash of *Avicennia* has a detergent action and was used in India directly for washing clothes.

Distribution: All mainland States

Casuarina paludosa SCRUB SHE-OAK

A number of different species were burnt to produce the alkaline ash, often known as lye, for soap-making. Amongst these were species of *Casuarina*, the she-oak, a characteristic Australian tree with fine green pendulous stems resembling the needles of a pine. A traveller in New South Wales in 1834 wrote: 'An excellent lye for soap, is made from the "swamp oak", when burnt.' This ash would have been boiled with tallow to make soap. The species referred to was *C. paludosa*, but others have been used in both Australia and the Pacific Islands.

Distribution: Some species in all States

C. *paludosa* — N.S.W., Vic., Tas., S.A.

Salicornia quinqueflora SAMPHIRE, GLASSWORT

Plants which grow in salty situations are generally rich in mineral salts, so give a larger than usual amount of ash. One of these is samphire, which is a low, succulent, purplish red plant with jointed stems found growing on the tidal mudflats behind the mangrove swamps.

There are a number of species of samphire in different parts of the world. They are particularly rich in soda, which can be obtained by burning the plants (a difficult task, as the stems are very fleshy). In a number of European countries this was formerly used as a source of soda for both soap and glass-making, but there seems to be no record of similar use in Australia.

Distribution: All States

NATURAL DETERGENTS

Saponins are naturally occurring detergent substances which produce a lather in water, just as soap does. They are present in varying amounts in a number of plants and these can be tested very simply by shaking crushed plant material with water and observing whether a lasting froth is formed. Where there is a high concentration the plant can be used as a substitute for soap to wash the hands. The red ash, *Alphitonia excelsa*, is well known for this purpose, and its use was recorded by the Queensland Government Botanist in 1909: 'The leaves, with water, rubbed on the hands by school children to remove ink stains.' With the problem of debris that would arise these plants can hardly be used directly in the bathtub or laundry, but an extract can easily be prepared by boiling the plant material with the minimum amount of water to cover it. In the case of red ash, the extracting process also draws out brown colouring matter from the plant, and no one in his right mind would want to wash clothes in the product; we have, however, used it on occasion for washing dishes.

Albizia lophantha

The genus *Albizia* includes a large number of tropical trees and shrubs with twice-pinnate leaves, and generally handsome cream or pink flowers with a mass of showy stamens united in a short tube, the flowers generally being clustered in rounded heads or spikes.

A. lophantha is a tall shrub or tree of the western part of the continent. Several overseas species are well known for their high saponin content, the bark of *A. saponaria* having been used commercially as a soap in Malaysia. Dried roots of *A. lophantha* are reported to contain 10% of saponin, and to have been valuable in silk and wool factories. Other details are not available, but it is known that plant saponin extracts were sometimes preferred when gentle washing action was required for delicate fabrics, rather than using harsher soaps.
Distribution: W.A.

Cayratia saponaria　　　　　　　　　　　　　SOAP STEM

Cayratia belongs to the grape family, and as such can be recognized by bearing tendrils on the side of the stem opposite to the leaves. *C. saponaria* is a tropical climber whose compound leaves have three broad but long-pointed leaflets, five-veined at the base.

This species occurs also in some islands of the Pacific, and in

Fiji has been used as a soap substitute both for washing clothes and as a shampoo effective against vermin. The stem was cut in lengths of 30-45 cm, which were heated on hot stones until soft, when they would produce a lather said to almost equal that of soap.

Distribution: Qld

Entada phaseoloides MATCHBOX BEAN

This tropical climber of the legume family is most easily recognized by its huge pods, up to a metre long, with flattened chocolate-brown seeds.

The bark and stem of *Entada* contain saponin, and were used widely through South-east Asia for shampoo, being marketed in the Philippines as 'gogo'. Lengths of the vine were cut into strips, pounded flat and dried for selling or storing. For use, the strips are soaked in water and rubbed to make a lather; this was said to be 'almost the chief hair-wash throughout Malaysia'. Gogo has been used also as an ingredient of hair tonics. In South Africa it was used as a soap.

Half-ripe seeds were used as a shampoo in parts of Indonesia; being rather poisonous, they were regarded as very effective in cleaning the hair.

Distribution: Qld.

Ganophyllum falcatum

This tropical coastal rainforest tree belongs to the Sapindaceae, which includes *Jagera pseudorhus* and many other saponin-containing species, a fact suggested by the family name.

The bark of *Ganophyllum falcatum* has been used in parts of Java as a soap which has the useful property of killing lice. In the Philippines it has been used in the same way as gogo.

Distribution: Qld.

Jagera pseudorhus FOAM-BARK

The saponin in the bark of *Jagera pseudorhus* was the basis of the Aboriginal use of this species as a fish poison. Saponins have the property of frothing copiously when shaken in water; this character led to a rather different use, an extract of the bark being added to beer and cordials to produce a head. About nine tons of bark were collected in Queensland for use in this way during World War I. Whether or not such a use was wise from the point of view of public health is doubtful since it has been shown that breakdown of blood corpuscles occurs at a concentration of 1 part of bark to 14,000 of water.

Distribution: Qld, N.S.W.

Saponaria officinalis   SOAPWORT

A southern European native of the carnation family, soapwort has been used for many centuries as a washing agent. It is a perennial with a creeping branched root stock, crowded pointed leaves and flat clusters of pale pink five-petalled flowers. It has escaped to become naturalized in many temperate areas of the world, including southern parts of Australia.

Roots and leaves of soapwort contain saponin and can be used to produce a soap-like lather. The leaves can be used directly with water for hand-washing, or an extract can be prepared, such as has been done traditionally in Europe and the Middle East for washing woollen fabrics. In Switzerland the process was formerly moved one step earlier, and sheep were washed with soapwort before being shorn.

Like foam-bark above, the roots have been used in some areas to make a head on beer and ale; as saponins can be poisonous, and the plants are known to be toxic to stock, the practice is not widespread.

Distribution: N.S.W., Vic.

A considerable number of other native plants contain saponins, and a number of them can be used as soap substitutes; we have, for example, found that the leaves of *Pittosporum revolutum* are satisfactory for this purpose. These plant detergents are much milder in their action than the commercial synthetic products, and leave the skin feeling pleasantly soft.

DISHMOPS

Those in the community who still use dishmops should be impressed to hear of one that costs nothing and never becomes smelly. One of the minor bush crafts is to prepare a dishmop from a stick of mulga, *Acacia aneura*. The end of the stick is beaten out to a mop of fibres which the users claim has the big advantage that it never goes sour, as bought dishmops tend to do.

Aborigines may not have had much use for dishmops, but in some areas they prepared mops similar to those from mulga for extracting honey from bees' nests which were too far inside a hollow trunk to be reached. The mops could be made from various stems, including lawyer vine; they would be rinsed out in water to prepare a sweet drink.

STARCHES AND SUGARS

Power alcohol can be produced from any material with a high sugar content by fermenting the sugar and distilling the alcohol so formed. From time to time different native plants and weeds have been proposed as sources of this fuel alternative. They include *Macrozamia communis, Nypa fruticans, Xanthorrhoea* (grass trees), *Opuntia* (prickly pear, shown to have too low a sugar content). At present none of these is an economic proposition in this country.

Macrozamia communis   BURRAWANG PALM

'If anyone should have the desire of viewing the plant in its native habitat, he may do so at the foot of the hill near Bondi on the Old South Head Road. He should turn to the right down a track that leads to Bondi beach, and there numerous plants may be seen occupying an area of about two acres on the bank of a watercourse about one hundred yards from the main road.'

These words were written in 1876 by Dr F. Milford about the burrawang palm which was then a fairly common plant around Sydney. Its main area of occurrence is, however, on the south coast of New South Wales.

Burrawang palm is not a palm at all, in spite of its appearance. It is one of the cycads, comparatively primitive seed-plants which produce large seeds in a cone rather than in a fruit. The leaves, shaped like those of a feather palm, are rigid and durable, and have been popular for decorative purposes such as use in churches for Palm Sunday.

The short, swollen trunk of the burrawang is very rich in

starch. It has been described as one of the two most important natural sources of starch in Australia, the other being the bunya pine, *Araucaria bidwillii.* In the early 1920s a factory to extract starch from the tubers was set up on the Clyde River; the tuberous stems were ground and washed, the fibrous matter sieved out and the starch was allowed to settle. This starch was highly regarded for laundry purposes, being found to be 50-70% stronger than the best rice starch. The starch remaining in the pith after this first extraction was then removed and used to make commercial adhesive paste. In 1934, ten tons per day of this paste was made and sold in New South Wales. The factory operated successfully for some years, but later closed down; one of the difficulties was a slight brown discolouration in the starch grains.

Burrawang seeds are large, about 4 cm long, 2-3 cm broad, and a brilliant red colour when ripe; two seeds are produced on each scale of the cone which is shaped like a pineapple up to 45 cm long. The seeds also are a rich source of starch, which can be extracted in much the same way as from the stems; they are poisonous, but the poison is removed in the extracting process.

Some years ago, detailed investigations were made into the possibility of power alcohol production from burrawang tubers. There was found to be wide variation in production from plants of different areas, the best result being about 80 litres per tonne from large plants growing in the Bateman's Bay area. The age of the specimens used was estimated as up to 120 years; it seems perhaps unnecessary to destroy plants of this age for starch or alcohol production rather than harvesting the seeds which could be used similarly, the trees being left to produce repeated crops. In any case, the project has been shelved.

In older literature, this species is referred to as *Macrozamia spiralis.*
Distribution: Qld, N.S.W.

Macrozamia reidlei

This species from Western Australia is a stout trunked palm-like tree up to about 3 m tall; a single plant may weigh about a tonne. It occurs in large numbers in the south-west of the continent, and was exploited by the early settlers as a source of starch.

Extraction was similar to that for *M. communis,* but not

identical: the stem pith was dried and shredded, then soaked for six hours, shaken and filtered; the sediment was washed several times before drying and powdering for use. It was used as a laundry starch but was not obtained sufficiently pure to be a commercially acceptable product, as it was too difficult to remove the last of the fine fibrous material.

Distribution: W.A.

Nypa fruticans   NIPA

This palm of the mangrove swamps and brackish waters in the tropics is well known as a thatch. In some countries of Asia, especially the Philippines, use has been made of the copious supply of sugar passing to the developing fruits. As is done with several other species of palm, the sugary juice is tapped and allowed to ferment to produce a kind of toddy known in the Philippines as 'tuba'. *Nypa*, however, is more convenient to tap than many other palms as it is a trunkless species and the large globular heads of fruits about 30 cm diameter are produced no more than waist-height from the ground. Some plants yield about a litre a day of tuba over several months.

Tuba has been used as a source of power alcohol, on a large scale in the Philippines, and experimentally elsewhere. The fermenting juice was collected and taken to distilleries where power alcohol was produced. Total costs were very low but this depended on extremely low wages paid to the collectors, and with Australian wages would be uneconomic, even if the plant were available in quantity, which it is not.

Distribution: Qld, N.T.

TOBACCO PIPES

Aborigines chewed pituri and native tobacco, but did not smoke it before the coming of the white man, so there is no long tradition of use of native plant material as pipes. However the shape of some of the larger gum-nuts suggested the bowl of a pipe to at least one manufacturer, and some pipes were prepared using capsules of *Eucalyptus miniata,* the Darwin woollybutt. This is a handsome-flowered species from northern Australia that has become popular in cultivation because of its clusters of large orange flowers and woody barrel-shaped ribbed capsules up to 6 cm long. Gum-nut pipes have not become popular, although they are no more clumsy than the American corn-cob variety.

The pipes were produced by the Australian Calabash Pipe Factory, Pitt Street, Sydney; they placed greater emphasis on the pipes made from the calabash gourd, *Lagenaria siceraria* (p. 230) and made some very fine silver-mounted specimens from the bases of dried gourds; one illustration shows a pipe more or less the shape of a meerschaum. The firm announced that they were willing to buy suitable gourds at £12 per 1000, which a writer in the *Queensland Agricultural Journal* of 1907 considered should be very remunerative.

Eucalyptus   GUM TREE

A number of Australian timbers have been tried for the manufacture of more conventional pipes. It is necessary to have a strong wood without too much essential oil, and one that will not burn readily; good colour, and ability to season well are also important. Highly recommended for the purpose is *Eucalyptus botryoides*, southern mahogany, a handsome tree of the coastal belt in southern New South Wales and Victoria; its wood is reddish brown, strong and durable. Similar woods, which have also been recommended for making pipes, are *E. marginata* (jarrah), *E. diversicolor* (karri), and *E. robusta* (swamp mahogany). Distribution: Some species in all States

Hakea leucoptera   NEEDLEWOOD

Several species of *Hakea* have sharply pointed leaves and this one amply justifies its common name, the cylindrical leaves being drawn out at the apex to a fine needle point. The plants are small trees or shrubs of arid regions.

The root stock was once used for the manufacture of tobacco pipes of high quality and in 1895 the Australian Needlewood Pipe Company was formed to exploit the species. Distribution: All mainland States

AGAR AND ALGINATES

Eucheuma speciosa   JELLY WEED

Eucheuma speciosa is a tough, gristly red seaweed up to about 30 cm high whose branches are densely covered with slender, spiny branches. On boiling, it yields a viscous solution which sets as a jelly on cooling. The setting material is an agar or agar-like substance similar to that described under *Gracilaria*. Early settlers in Western Australia used it for making jellies and named it jelly weed. During World War II when agar supplies from overseas were cut off, a local meat-canning firm used *Eucheuma* collected from drift material along the shore to provide the setting material in some of its canned products.

Distribution: W.A.

Gracilaria verrucosa   SEA NOODLES

Agar is a constituent of the cell wall of some seaweeds known as red algae. This material dissolves in boiling water and on cooling forms a firm gel even at concentrations of about 1%. It is less subject than gelatin to attack by micro-organisms and is therefore used in large quantities in the preparation of culture media for bacteria and fungi. Agar has been used also in confectionery and cosmetics, as a thickening agent in jams and some other foodstuffs, and in meat and fish canning; the jelly-like substance in tinned camp pie is usually agar.

Before World War II, Australia's agar came from Japan but with the opening of hostilities between the two countries, the supply was cut off abruptly, and it was necessary to locate a substitute source. This was found in *Gracilaria verrucosa*, a plant with branched, cylindrical, tapering stems not more than 2 mm wide and often 0.5-2 m long, although exceptionally nearly 4 m long. In colour it varies from pale fawn through olive green to red, purple and purple-black. It is widely distributed in protected waters in Australia but the main beds of commercial size were found along the east coast at places such as Bateman's Bay, Botany Bay, and Moreton Bay. It grows on sandy floors in water usually up to about 7 m deep although in some places at greater depths.

In 1943 it was possible to harvest over 200 tonnes (dry weight), mainly from Botany Bay and Sydney Harbour, by dragging iron hooks through the beds from dinghies. For a few years Australia produced its own agar but when Japanese supplies became available again local production ceased.

In outline, the processing of the harvested weed involves drying and bleaching on grass or racks, boiling the chopped material for several hours (approximately 4% *Gracilaria* in water), filtering, and freezing the liquor. On thawing, water with impurities escapes, leaving the agar in a form like crêpe rubber. Drying completes the process. In commercial processes, some refinements are made to this outline but it is possible to prepare agar in the home by this method from any of the species of *Gracilaria* and use the product to prepare milk or fruit jellies or ice cream. Although the setting qualities will probably be adequate, appearance and flavour may leave the gourmet dissatisfied. Colour is likely to be a dirty grey-brown and the flavour to have more than a hint of the seashore. However, for the enthusiast, repeated boiling, freezing and thawing will lead to improvement in quality.

Gracilaria is by no means the only red alga from which agar may be prepared. *Hypnea* shows considerable resemblance to *Gracilaria* but usually has numerous short lateral branches giving it a softly spiny appearance; it gives an agar usually with less gel strength than that from *Gracilaria*. *Pterocladia capillacea* is another good agar seaweed; it has something of the appearance of small red fern frond, but grows only near low-water mark on wave-beaten rocky shores and is unlikely to be commercially attractive because of difficulty of harvesting.
Distribution; All States

Macrocystis pyrifera   GIANT KELP

Macrocystis pyrifera is a giant among seaweeds, reaching a length of 60 m. From a basket-like attaching organ arise numerous stems along which at close intervals are corrugated, lance-shaped 'leaves', the largest a couple of metres long. At the base of each 'leaf' is a hollow float, which acts as a buoy holding the stems near the surface.

This seaweed, along with some other large brown seaweeds in other countries and *Durvillea* in Australia, is an important source of a group of substances known as alginates. Between 1965 and

1973, Alginates (Australia) Pty Ltd used *Macrocystis* as the raw material for an alginate industry based at Louisville on the east coast of Tasmania. The kelp was harvested by a specially modified vessel with cutting blades at the front; an endless belt behind the blades loaded the cut material into the vessel.

Alginates are used commercially in many products. The alginate most commonly used is sodium alginate which dissolves in water to form a sticky, mucilaginous solution whose viscosity can be increased by the addition of small amounts of acid or calcium salts. Foodstuffs, including ice cream and quick-set puddings, pharmaceutical products and cosmetics are products in which alginates find a use. Here they serve mainly as stabilizing and thickening agents. Some dental impression materials have been based on alginate.

Macrocystis contains considerable quantities of potassium salts and at one time, on the Pacific coast of North America, was an important source of potash. In Europe, other large brown seaweeds served as potash sources for the manufacture of soap and glass, and for fertilizer; the weed was dried and burnt, ash remaining being the kelp, a name now transferred to any large brown seaweed. During World War I small quantities of *Macrocystis* were burnt for potash on Pelican Island, Tasmania, the production being about one tonne per week.

Distribution: Tas.

OTHER USEFUL PLANTS

Acacia pendula   MYALL, WEEPING MYALL

When plants are burnt, the ash remaining represents the mineral content of the plant. Sometimes this ash is of use as fertilizer, although often it is wasted. J. H. Maiden recorded two unusual applications for the ash of weeping myall; it was added by the bushmen to their flour in the preparation of damper, and used by housewives for whitening fireplaces.

Distribution: Qld, N.S.W., Vic.

Aeschynomene indica   KATH SOLA

This widespread shrub of the legume family is found in tropical Africa and Asia, extending to Australia, where it occurs in the north. It is an annual of very wet positions, freely branched and slender-looking with long pinnate leaves bearing numerous leaflets about 5 mm long; the flowers are yellow, and of the pea type.

Aeschynomene indica is closely related to *A. aspera*, the sola pith plant; this is the source of the pith used for pith helmets, or sola topees, which were traditionally worn by white men in the tropics. *A. indica* has pith of inferior quality, but it can be used for much the same purposes as the sola pith where a cheap substitute is required; it has been used for topees, often with a surface dressing of the higher quality sola, and for fishing floats, rafts, and elephant pads in India. There has been no exploitation in Australia. Distribution: Qld, N.T.

**Eichhornia crassipes*   WATER HYACINTH

This South American water plant has been introduced to many countries for the beauty of its lilac-blue flowers, but has become an uncontrollable weed of waterways in warm parts of the world. The plants float and multiply very rapidly, producing a thick mass of branching roots, and choking dams and slow-moving streams.

One redeeming feature of this pest is its high potash content: when dried it burns readily giving an ash which is a good soil fertilizer. It is also an excellent plant for compost. On analysis it was shown that rotted water-hyacinth has about the same level of nitrogen, phosphate and lime as farmyard manure, and a much higher content of potash, although the figures are variable. Distribution: All mainland States

Ficus   FIG

Birdlime is a general term for sticky material of plant origin which is spread over branches to ensnare small birds. The figs yield a clear or milky latex becoming very sticky on drying as anyone who has picked or peeled figs knows. In Australia there are numerous species of native fig and the Aborigines of the Tully district used the latex of one of them, whose identity is not now known, as a birdlime, spreading it on branches and among blossoms where small birds were expected.

W. E. Roth describes the method of preparation as follows: 'After removal of the bark the sticky mass is scraped off from its inner surface with a shell, and collected onto the end of a small stick: the latter is twirled round and round in the process, warmed over a fire and hammered — it is hardly touched with the fingers.'

In India, a latex of the cluster fig, *F. glomerata*, also occurring in Queensland, was used as birdlime.

Some of the native figs have leaves covered with short but robust hairs which give their surface a sandpapery texture. Leaves of this type were used by the Aborigines in the final smoothing of weapons and implements. *Ficus coronata, F. fraseri* and *F. opposita* are species of this type.

It has been reported that Papuan women use fig leaves of this type to remove hairs from their legs.

Distribution: Qld, N.S.W., Vic., N.T.

Lantana camara   LANTANA

This introduced shrubby weed grows so vigorously on cleared rainforest soil both here and overseas that many attempts have been made to use it, while other studies have been directed towards its control. Amongst other uses suggested has been paper-making, but it has been found unsuitable. In China the stems have been used to make toothbrushes; however, looking at a mountain half-covered with lantana two metres tall, one feels that toothbrush manufacture will not use all the material available. The leaves, which have a rough surface due to the presence of silicified hairs, can be used as a fine sandpaper for polishing wood.

There are a number of varieties and probably several species going under the name of *Lantana camara*. All are square-stemmed prickly shrubs with opposite rough leaves and handsome heads of small tubular flowers, the flowers in a head shading outwards from yellow to red or from cream to pink. Most of the varieties are poisonous to stock. There is now a degree of biological control of the weed following introduction of the lantana beetle.

Distribution: Qld, N.S.W.

Livistona australis   CABBAGE PALM

This fan palm is well known in many coastal districts of eastern Australia. The tall trunk has a hard outer shell enclosing a broad

fibrous core. It was an easy matter for the settlers to split the trunk and remove the core to leave useful pig troughs. These did not have the durability of troughs hewn out of eucalypt logs but were a good deal easier to prepare.
Distribution: Qld, N.S.W., Vic.

Mucuna gigantea   VELVET BEAN

Mucuna gigantea is a rainforest climber bearing chandelier-like groups of green pea-flowers on long, pendulous stems. The dark brown pods, containing black seeds something like small match-box beans, have rust-coloured, hair-like bristles lying flat against the surface. These readily penetrate the skin if the pods are handled. In Malaysia these hairs have been used in animal poisoning, and if the irritation the hairs cause to hands is any guide the victims of such action must undergo considerable suffering.
Distribution: Qld, N.S.W., N.T.

*Opuntia   PRICKLY PEAR

Fifty or sixty years ago the worst plant pest to infest Australia was occupying thousands of hectares of agricultural land in the eastern States: this was *Opuntia*, the prickly pear. There were several species, all with flattish jointed stems studded with vicious spines and less visible but more irritating fine bristles. The weed is now under control, thanks to the introduction of the *Cactoblastis* moth which feeds on it, but there are still some specimens about.

One minor use to which the plant was put was to make gramophone needles from the sharp rigid spines. These will not be satisfactory for hi-fi and other modern equipment, but they worked reasonably well on the old hand-cranked 78 rpm machines. The needles have a limited life and a new one was advisable for each playing of a record, but in those days there were plenty more where the first ones came from.
Distribution: Qld, N.S.W., Vic., S.A.

Persoonia laurina   GEEBUNG

Aborigines of southern Queensland used the term geebung for a species of *Persoonia*, *P. media*. Eventually the name was taken for a Brisbane suburb, and is now applied to numerous other species of the genus *Persoonia*.

P. laurina is a small shrub with roughly elliptical leaves 4-10 cm long and small yellow flowers with four apparent petals rolling back strongly as the flower opens. The Aborigines steeped the bark of this shrub in water and used the infusion for soaking bark from which they manufactured fishing lines. The treatment was said to give the lines greater strength but it is possible that its action was simply a preservative one.

Distribution: N.S.W.

Piptoporus   PUNK

Species of *Piptoporus* are bracket fungi with hoof-like fruiting bodies up to 35 cm or more in diameter, some of which appear on eucalypt trunks several metres above the ground; the undersurface is marked with numerous small pores scarcely visible without magnification. One specimen from South Australia weighed just over 4 kg. These fruiting bodies are prone to insect attack and some specimens are found completely riddled. However, if cut open before this attack, the substance of the fungus is a fine pith.

Pieces of fungi of this type have been used for mounting insects in entomological collections, as slowly smouldering tinder, as styptics to stop bleeding, and as razor strops.

Distribution; Qld, N.S.W., Vic., S.A.

Sphagnum   PEAT MOSS, BOG MOSS

Peat is associated with Ireland in most people's minds, yet peat and bogs are by no means restricted to that country. Peat is formed by the partial decay under pressure of various mosses, sometimes a few flowering plants, but mainly of *Sphagnum,* the peat moss. This remarkable moss genus includes a large number of species occurring in most countries of the world, including Australia. It inhabits swamps and bogs, and in cool wet places may cover large areas. Peat is obtained for fuel in the northern hemisphere by draining the bogs, cutting the peat into blocks, and drying it. In Australia the peat bogs are much less extensive and fuel is less difficult to obtain, so peat has not been cut.

Plants of peat moss are pale green to yellow with soft branching stems tangling and matting together; leaves are produced all along the stem, with crowded clusters at the apex. Occasionally the fruiting bodies are found; these are round black spore-cases on short colourless stalks. The moss is semi-aquatic, and will be found either growing in still swamp water or emergent on the mud.

Sphagnum has been used for several purposes. The plants have an unusual structure; in the leaves, and to some extent in the stems, there is a high proportion of empty cells which can act as water reservoirs. Dried plants can soak up fluid at a prodigious rate and it is this attribute which has been exploited. During the two World Wars the moss was used as a substitute for cotton surgical dressings; plants were collected, cleaned and dried, then sometimes treated with an antiseptic. This material was used either loose as surgical cotton or compressed to make bandages which were said to be three times as absorptive as those made of cotton, and more comfortable as well.

In countries were *Sphagnum* is very plentiful, it has other uses. It can be used for stuffing mattresses which are not only soft and comfortable, but absorptive to use for sick people or babies, and disposable where necessary. It is said that American Indian mothers used to place a wad of *Sphagnum* beneath their babies when carrying them on their backs. In Australia and elsewhere the moss has been used as wet packing for orchids and other plants being transported.

Distribution: Some species in all States

Xanthorrhoea   GRASS TREE, BLACK BOY, YACCA

Although the grass tree has been economically important mainly as a resin producer, it had a minor use as makeshift water pipes on some gold diggings. The trunk was split longitudinally, the fibrous core removed, and the troughs of resin-compacted leaf bases linked together to run water from one area to another.

From the centre of the dense crown of slender, arching leaves grass trees produce a distinctive pole-like flowering spike, up to about 3 m long in some species. When dry, the stalk is not particularly strong but it is very light and straight, and made a useful haft for Aboriginal fishing spears. In New South Wales *Xanthorrhoea resinosa* was used in this way and it is likely that other species also were used. Modern Australian children have found these poles to make good toy spears.

Distribution: Some species in all States

EPILOGUE

We could extend the text of this book to include many more entries; but the work would always be incomplete — it is not possible to include all the uses to which Australian plants have been put, such as the local uses of various timbers for fencing, even the valuable if ephemeral use of a leafy twig to brush away flies or to shelter young seedlings in the garden.

Many of the applications we have described have outlived their usefulness in this modern age, but it is surprising how often we find a temporary use for some plant: a strip of fibrous stem for makeshift repairs to the picnic basket, a home-made fishing rod for a junior member of the family, or even just a pleasurable sniff at a crushed leaf.

The breadth of this subject will inevitably mean that readers with special interests will wish to pursue a particular topic. There are various sources of further information; specialist books on crafts such as dyeing and tanning are listed in the references. Those who are interested to obtain some of the more unusual timbers, perhaps for cabinet work or boatbuilding, can generally obtain advice from the Forestry Department of their own State. Weavers' guilds in different States can share knowledge on dyeing. For those with a general interest in the native flora, naturalists' clubs and branches of the Society for Growing Australian Plants are to be found in many centres, bringing together professionals and amateurs with the same enthusiasms.

We conclude with the hope that these chapters will stimulate awareness of native plants, and that readers will share our enjoyment of them.

SELECTED REFERENCES

ANDERSON, R. H. *The Trees of New South Wales.* Government Printer, Sydney, 1968.

ANON. *Tanning Materials of the British Empire.* Hazell, Watson and Viney Ltd, London, 1929.

ASKEW, K. and MITCHELL, A. S. 'The fodder trees and shrubs of the Northern Territory'. *N. Territ. Divis. Primary Ind. Extension Bull.,* no. 16, pp.1-84, 1978.

BAKER, R. T. *Cabinet Timbers of Australia.* Government Printer, Sydney, 1913.

BAKER, R. T. *The Hardwoods of Australia and their Economics.* Government Printer, Sydney, 1919.

BAKER, R. T. and SMITH, H. G. *A Research on the Pines of Australia.* Government Printer, Sydney, 1910.

BAKER, R. T. and SMITH, H. G. *Research on the Eucalypts Especially in Regard to their Essential Oils.* 2nd edn. Government Printer, Sydney, 1920.

BLAKE, S. T. and ROFF, C. *The Honey Flora of Queensland.* Government Printer, Brisbane, 1972.

BOAS, I. H. *The Commercial Timbers of Australia, their Properties and Uses.* Government Printer, Melbourne, 1947.

BREAKWELL, E. *The Grasses and Fodder Plants of New South Wales.* Government Printer, Sydney, 1923.

BROWN, W. H. (ed.) *Minor Products of Philippine Forests.* 3 vols. Bureau of Forestry, Manila, 1920-1.

BURKILL, I. H. *A Dictionary of the Economic Products of the Malay Peninsula.* 2 vols. Ministry of Agriculture and Co-operatives, Kuala Lumpur, 1966.

CARMAN, J. K. *Dyemaking with Eucalypts.* Rigby Ltd, Adelaide, 1978.

CHANDLER, B. V. 'Quality of Australian honeys'. *Food Res. Quart.,* vol. 37, pp.1-9, 1977.

COGHILL, D. 'A survey of the tanning materials of Australia'. *C.S.I.R. Bull.,* no. 32, pp.1-136, 1927.

COLEMAN, R. S. 'Honey flora of Western Australia'. *J. Dept Agric. W. Aust.,* vol. 3 (8), pp.649-64, 1962.

EDWARDS, R. *Aboriginal Bark Canoes of the Murray Valley.* Rigby Ltd, Adelaide, 1972.

EVERIST, S. L. 'Use of fodder trees and shrubs'. *Qld Dept Primary Ind., Div. Pl. Ind. Advis. Leaflet* no 1024, pp.1-44, 1969.

FRANCIS, W. D. *Australian Rain-forest Trees.* Australian Government Publishing Service, Canberra, 1970.

GOODACRE, W. A. *The Honey and Pollen Flora of New South Wales.* Government Printer, Sydney, 1938.

HALE, H. M. and TINDALE, N. B. 'Aborigines of Princess Charlotte Bay, North Queensland'. *Rec. S. Aust. Mus.,* vol 5 (1), pp.63-116, 1933.

HALE, H. M. and TINDALE, N. B. 'Aborigines of Princess Charlotte Bay, North Queensland'. Part II. *Rec. S. Aust. Mus.,* vol. 5 (2), pp.117-72, 1933.

HALL, N., JOHNSTON, R. D. and CHIPPENDALE, G. M. (1970). *Forest Trees of Australia.* Australian Government Publishing Service, Canberra, 1970.

HALL, N. et al. *The Use of Trees and Shrubs in the Dry Country of Australia.* Australian Government Publishing Service, Canberra, 1972.

HAMLYN-HARRIS, R. and SMITH, I. 'On fish poisoning and poisons employed among the Aborigines of Queensland'. *Mem. Qld Mus.*, vol. 5, pp.1-22, 1916.

HEDLEY, C. 'Uses of some Queensland plants'. *Proc. R. Soc. Qld*, vol. 5 (1), pp.10-13, 1889.

HILLIS, W. E. and BROWN, A. G. (eds.) *Eucalypts for Wood Production*. Griffin Press Ltd, Adelaide, 1978.

LEIGH, J. H. and NOBLE J. C. *Plants for Sheep in Australia*. Angus & Robertson Pty Ltd, Sydney, 1972.

McKERN, H. H. G. 'The natural plant products industry of Australia'. *Proc. R. Aust. chem. Inst.*, vol. 27 (7), pp.295-308, 1960.

MAIDEN, J. H. *The Useful Native Plants of Australia, (including Tasmania)*. Treubner and Co., London, 1889.

MAIDEN, J. H. 'Grass-tree gum'. *Agric. Gaz. N.S.W.*, vol. 5, pp.748-58, 1894.

MAIDEN, J. H. 'The gums, resins and other vegetable exudations of Australia'. *J. R. Soc. N.S.W.*, vol. 35, pp.161-212, 1901.

MAIDEN, J. H. *The Forest Flora of New South Wales*. 6 vols. Government Printer, Sydney, 1902-17.

MAIDEN, J. H. *Forestry Handbook. Part II. Some of the Principal Commercial Trees of New South Wales*. Government Printer, Sydney, 1917.

MARTIN, V. et al. *Dyemaking with Australian Flora*. Rigby Ltd, Adelaide, 1974.

MOORE, R. M. (ed.) *Australian Grasslands*. Australian National University Press, Canberra, 1970.

PALMER, E. 'On plants used by the natives of north Queensland, Flinders and Mitchell Rivers, for food, medicine, etc., etc.' *J. Proc. R. Soc. N.S.W.*, vol. 17, pp.93-113, 1884.

PENFOLD, A. R. 'Grass tree resin'. *Bull. technol. Mus., Sydney*, no. 16, pp.1-20, 1931.

PENFOLD, A. R. and WILLIS, J. L. *The Eucalypts*. Leonard Hill [Books] Ltd, London, 1961.

PURDIE, D. J. 'Honey and pollen flora of South Australia'. *J. Agric. S. Aust.*, vol. 71 (6), pp.207-216, 1968.

ROTH, W. E. *Ethnological Studies among the North-west – Central Queensland Aborigines*. Government Printer, Brisbane, 1897.

ROTH, W. E. 'String and other forms of strand: basketry-, woven bag-, and net-work'. *N. Qld Ethnogr.*, no. 1, pp.1-15, 1901.

ROTH, W. E. 'Domestic implements, arts, and manufactures'. *N. Qld Ethnogr.*, no. 7, pp.1-34, 1904.

ROTH, W. E. 'North Queensland ethnography. No. 16. Huts and shelters'. *Rec. Aust. Mus.*, vol. 8 (1), pp.55-66, 1910.

ROTH, W. E. 'North Queensland ethnography. No. 14. Transport and trade'. *Rec. Aust. Mus.*, vol. 8, pp.1-19, 1913.

SPECHT, R. L. 'An introduction to the ethno-botany of Arnhem Land'. *Rec. Amer.-Aust. Scient. Exped. Arnhem Land*, vol. 3 (15), pp.479-503, 1958.

SWAIN, E. H. F. *The Timbers and Forest Products of Queensland*. Government Printer, Brisbane, 1928.

The Wealth of India. Raw Materials. 11 vols. Publications and Information Directorate, C.S.I.R., New Delhi, 1948-76.

TURNER, F. *The Forage Plants of Australia*. Government Printer, Sydney, 1891.

TURNER, F. *Australian Grasses and Pasture Plants*. Whitcombe and Toombs Ltd, Melbourne, 1921.

VIVIAN, J. *Home Tanners' Handbook*. A.H. and A.W. Reed Ltd, Wellington, 1976.

WALLIS, N. K. *Australian Timber Handbook*. Angus and Robertson, Sydney, 1969.

WILSON, D. 'Minor forest produce in Australia'. *Aust. For.*, vol. 24 (2), pp.90-98, 1960.

GLOSSARY

Alga: a seaweed or related freshwater plant

Alkaloids: bitter-tasting chemicals occurring in some plants and having a marked effect on animals including man

Alternate leaves: those borne singly at different levels on the stem

Anther: the swollen uppermost part of the stamen containing the pollen

Axillary: occurring in, or produced from, the angle between the leaf and the stem

Bipinnate: with the leaflets of the leaf arranged along each side of axes which are themselves arranged along a main axis

Bract: a modified leaf, sometimes scale-like, sometimes large and coloured, commonly at the base of a flower stalk

Calyx: the outermost group of appendages (sepals) of a flower

Capsule: a fruit which is dry at maturity and opens by slits or pores

Compound: descriptive of a leaf whose margin is indented so that it is divided into two or more separate, often stalked, segments or leaflets

Coppice: regrowth from the base of a cut stem

Entire: with a leaf margin not indented

Generic: descriptive of the genus, the smallest grouping of species (genera are grouped into families)

Gill: one of the numerous plate-like structures radiating on the undersurface of the cap of a mushroom or similar fungus

Habit: the general appearance or form of a plant

Heartwood: the older part of the wood, in the centre and usually making the bulk of the trunk; commonly darker, harder and more durable than sapwood

Indigenous: occurring naturally in a country; native to a country

Latex: milky sap

Leaf axil: the upper angle made by the leaf stalk with the stem

Leaf axis: the central, elongate structure to which other parts of a pinnate or bipinnate leaf are attached

Leaflet: one of the two or more segments making up a compound leaf

Legume family: the family Leguminosae, characteristically bearing pods, e.g. peas, beans

Nectar: the sugary solution produced by glands usually in the lower part of the flower

Oil-dotted (leaves): having oil-glands occurring in the leaf tissues, visible as translucent spots when the leaf is held up against the light

Opposite leaves: those born in pairs, on opposite sides of the stem

Ovate: with an outline similar to that of a hen's egg (broader below than above the mid point)

Phyllode: a structure formed from a compound leaf by suppression of the leaflets and commonly resembling a simple leaf; characteristic of most Australian species of wattle

Pinnate: with the leaflets of the leaf arranged along each side of an axis

Pinnatifid: the indenting of the margin of a simple leaf to resemble a pinnate leaf but with the indentations not reaching to the midrib

Puffball: a fungus in which the spores are produced inside a closed fruiting-body, and released at maturity as a powdery mass

Rachis: the leaf axis or central elongate structure to which other parts of a pinnate or bipinnate leaf are attached

Root stock: underground stem, often semi-tuberous or woody

Saponin: a glucoside with a detergent action which produces a froth on shaking with water; poisonous to animals

Sapwood: the youngest part of the wood, just beneath the bark

Sedge: member of the family Cyperaceae; grass-like plants with usually three-angled stems, mostly found in swamps and poorly drained areas

Sepal: a member of the outermost group of appendages (calyx) of a flower

Simple: descriptive of a leaf not divided into leaflets to become compound

Spike: a group of stalkless flowers arranged along an axis

Subcoastal: an imprecisely defined term for that part of the country between the coastal strip and inland Australia

Style: the usually slender structure arising from the top of the ovary of a flower

Trifoliate: a compound leaf consisting of three leaflets arising at the one point

Valve: the parts of a dry fruit which become separated by splits which develop on opening

Whorl: three or more leaves or flowers at the one level on a stem

Index